IMAGES
of America

CANYON COUNTRY

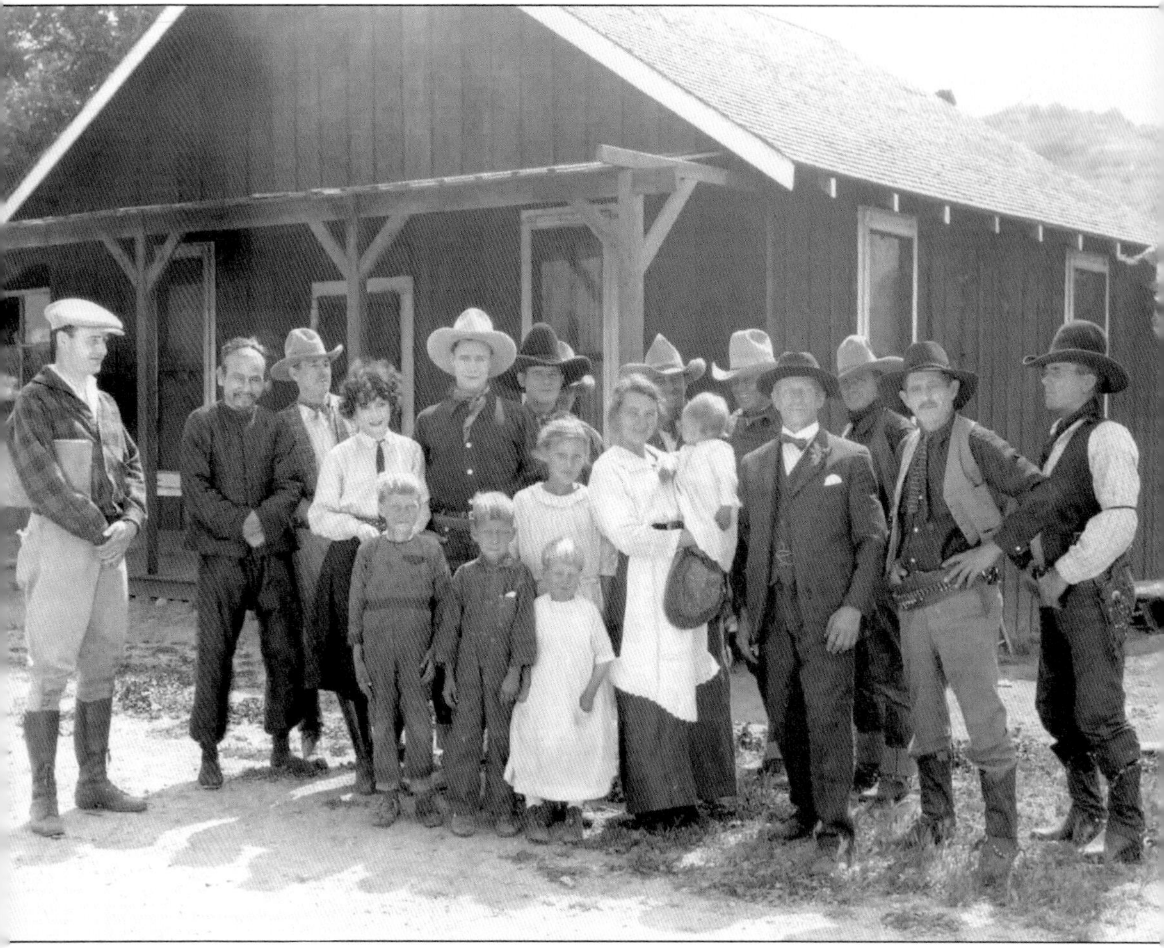

The Warmuth family poses in front of their Canyon Country home with actors and filmmakers during the filming of the 1927 serial *Hawk of the Hills*. The production also filmed at Sulphur Springs School, paying the students $5 per day plus lunch. Minnie Warmuth (center) holds her daughter Mary Warmuth (Sathre), and to the right of them is Minnie's husband, Joseph. To the left of Minnie is her oldest daughter, Josephine Warmuth (Ramey), and in front of Josephine are her younger siblings—from left to right, Joseph J. Warmuth, Henry, and Madeline (Davis). Not pictured is their oldest brother, Frank Warmuth. The family had another child who died at the age of five in the flu pandemic of 1918. (Courtesy of Mary Warmuth Sathre.)

On the Cover: In 1842, six years before the official date of California's first gold discovery at Sutter's Mill, Francisco Lopez discovered gold in Placerita Canyon (in the vicinity of present-day Canyon Country). The discovery of precious metals in the area launched a decades-long rush of miners who populated the eastern side of the Santa Clarita Valley. These men stand in the Red Rover Mine after being stopped from further progress by a large granite block in their path. The Red Rover Mine was owned by Henry T. Gage, who was elected governor of California in 1898. (Courtesy of Santa Clarita Valley Historical Society.)

IMAGES
of America

CANYON COUNTRY

Martha Sharrer Michael

ARCADIA
PUBLISHING

Copyright © 2013 by Martha Sharrer Michael
ISBN 978-1-4671-2997-8

Published by Arcadia Publishing
Charleston, South Carolina

Printed in the United States of America

Library of Congress Control Number: 2013938246

For all general information, please contact Arcadia Publishing:
Telephone 843-853-2070
Fax 843-853-0044
E-mail sales@arcadiapublishing.com
For customer service and orders:
Toll-Free 1-888-313-2665

Visit us on the Internet at www.arcadiapublishing.com

To those who have seen the value in recording history and generously share it so the rest of us can learn.

Contents

Acknowledgments

History is enjoyed most when it is shared. In researching and acquiring photographs for this book, I saw, time and again, the eyes of an octogenarian brighten as he or she relayed stories of a Canyon Country childhood. There were so many more residents I could have met and interviewed, but as anecdotes and images even now continue to be unveiled, it is clear that I ran out of pages before including every significant event, leaving copious characters' tales yet untold. I could have stayed in the research phase forever.

I owe a debt of gratitude to Ed Marg, who championed my book and gathered all the necessary paperwork to bring it to fruition. I also want to thank Alan Pollack for reading the book to verify the historical facts, and I appreciate the time that Pat Saletore gave to my research as we looked through countless computer files.

I also want to thank the following people: Carole Morton, of the San Fernando Valley Historical Society, for swiftly and eagerly sharing resources for the book; Vivian Sathre Sumner, for digging up Warmuth family photographs and soliciting help from Mary Warmuth Sathre; Diane Southwell, who connected me with Mike Moreno of the Sierra Pelona Rock Club, and Ron Kraus, who had treasured photographs to share; Kathy and Bob Kellar, who made my project a priority, digging up images for the book; Cathy Cox Kraeger, for access to Cox family photographs and help with captions; Karilyn Crolius, who encouraged me to keep looking for Cliffie Stone, and to Steve Stone, who helped me find him; John and Faye Therrien, my go-to couple for legal licensing questions, at least where Hollywood was concerned; Rich Escalante, for introducing me to his family, including Frank and Rosie; Steve Minor, for sharing his father's Depression-era talent behind the camera's lens; Gary and Celeste Thornhill, for sharing their professional photography with me; Janice Dosh, for help with my research; and Becky Bataille, for her work on Ace Cain.

I would also like to thank the following individuals who shared their photographs so liberally: Jim Backer, Gail Ortiz, Dena Maloney, Alan Ferdman, Larry Westin, Bob and Gwen Kofnovec, Angie Bilson, Joshua Randall, Maggi Perkins, and George and Gayle Starbuck.

Thank you to my personal photographic and computer experts, R. Scott Goodspeed and Skip Sharrer, and thank you to Sara Miller for her editing assistance.

I am grateful for my parents, Dr. Norman E. and JoAnn Sharrer, who gave me the belief that any goal was within my grasp. And I am thankful for Aunt Frances Aronson and Mary and Bill Hurley, who fostered an intrigue for looking at the past (and for the use of the T.O. Chateau, complete with chef, as a writer's cabin).

I want to thank my friend and business partner, Jeannie Sutton, for holding down the fort at our shop and for her amazing expertise. She deserves my thanks for being profoundly flexible.

I am also grateful for the selfless service of my sister, Sally Sharrer Kinder, for covering my shifts time and again and for proofreading my pages.

I owe a debt of gratitude to my children for their patience with my lack of attention for a year (which became two years) and to my husband, Keith, who never stifles my passions with his own hopes for more family time or a less cluttered life.

Unless otherwise noted, all images appear courtesy of the Santa Clarita Valley Historical Society.

INTRODUCTION

As a community that has possessed multiple monikers, including Solemint, Saugus, Soledad, and Lang, Canyon Country has proven to be flexible when it comes to establishing an identity. The name became official in 1968, when the Canyon Country Post Office opened near Solemint Junction (at the intersection of Soledad Canyon Road and Sierra Highway). This borough in the eastern part of the Santa Clarita Valley has repeatedly played the role of a hub or crossroads for entities such as the Southern Pacific Railroad, the borax mining company, and the US Route 6 interstate highway.

Canyon Country's earliest history as an important corridor was for the Tataviam Indians, believed to have lived in the Santa Clarita Valley starting around 500 AD. Centuries later, the tribe's artifacts, found throughout the area, have been photographed to share the tribe's existence with later generations. Like subsequent settlers who contributed to Canyon Country's evolving image, the Tataviam passed through the eastern part of the valley. Mapmakers have documented their whereabouts, identifying several Tataviam villages in the area.

Canyon Country's first white settler was Thomas Mitchell, who arrived in 1860 to establish a cattle ranch among the grizzlies and Native Americans. The impact of Mitchell and his wife, Martha, is still apparent today as elementary school students fill the seats of Sulphur Springs Community School, which the couple established in 1872. The Sulphur Springs School District, which began in the Mitchells' adobe home with the help of John Lang, is the second-oldest school district in Los Angeles.

Thanks to the Santa Clarita Valley Historical Society, images have been preserved to mark the early days of Canyon Country's existence. The photographs in this book, most of which appear courtesy of the historical society, bring to life the earliest residents and history-making people and places from the 19th, 20th, and 21st centuries. There is visual representation of the Borax mining operation and the creation of mining towns Ravenna and Lang. In 1876, it was at Lang Station that Southern Pacific Railroad president Charles Crocker drove the golden spike that connected northern and southern California.

The story continues with images of the families that staked land in Canyon Country—the Reynier and Warmuth families in Sand Canyon and borax freighter Remi Nadeau, whose 1,800 acres were turned into the 6-S Ranch Airpark by Helm and Earle Schmidt and later became Canyon Country's first housing development.

A map of US Route 6 winding through Canyon Country literally put the town on the map as part of 1937's "longest U.S. route in the country," according to the US Department of Transportation. Old photographs of The Halfway House and Backwoods Inn, two restaurants that still serve customers on Sierra Highway, underscore the importance of an earlier era for Canyon Country. Retrospective images of local merchants, restaurants, and stores tell the story of the town's changing economic landscape. A photograph of The Honey House, which still stands today, tells of its owners, the Dyer and Warmuth families, and Canyon Country's successful beekeeping industry. Recent photographs of the Zagat-rated Le Chêne French Cuisine restaurant on Sierra Highway appear in curious contrast to images of the same building in the 1920s, when it was an automobile garage and had a walk-up window that was used for food service.

Just as education was one of the first issues of importance for the settlers of Canyon Country, schools continued to open to meet the needs of growing neighborhoods. Central to a pictorial history of the Sulphur Springs School District is an acquaintance with the Cox family, whose photographs document a century of residency in Canyon Country. Images of Sulphur Springs School from the 19th century appear alongside the story of Leona Cox, who became a district leader. The ground-breaking ceremony for the Leona Cox School was held in 1963.

Some of the most colorful characters in Canyon Country were members of the entertainment industry, which significantly shaped the town's personality. Hollywood's impact on the area is shown through photographs of the actors, stuntmen, and canine film stars who lived in Canyon Country. Among the celebrities who have called Canyon Country home is actress Linda Gray, who moved to Sand Canyon in the 1970s, rearing her children there and remaining for several decades, including the time when she played her famous role on the television show *Dallas*. Numerous stunt actors lived and continue to live in Canyon Country. Even in its earliest years, the town was settled by performers. Sam J. Garrett, a trick roper turned actor and stuntman, and his wife, Ruby, established the Circle G Ranch in the area around 1940.

Through the centuries, all residents of Canyon Country and its neighboring communities have been subjected to whatever Mother Nature had in store. Professional photographs of the 1994 earthquake share a chapter with images featuring wildfires and snow; all of this evidence offers a full portrait of life in the Soledad Canyon.

The story of Canyon Country becomes complete with a bridge to the future featured in the final chapter. Readers will become acquainted with the growth and change of the last few decades and with development that is pending in the present day. Aerial and ground photographs of the College of the Canyons' Canyon Country campus offer glimpses into why COC is widely considered one of the top community colleges in the state of California. Change is apparent in the 1970s images of California State Route 14 (aka the Antelope Valley Freeway) under construction and the arrival of Robinson Ranch Golf Club in 2000. An artist's rendering of developer Jim Backer's proposed development lifts the curtain on a project that aims to make a big commercial impact by creating a "downtown" for Canyon Country.

While there are pages of milestones, twists, and ever-changing faces, Canyon Country and the communities surrounding the town maintain an identity as a place of connection. Its unchanging commitment to progressive transit and advances in education keep residents mindful of the region's history as a significant hub for railroads, miners, ranchers, and schooling. The aptly named Canyon Country remains rural in spirit, defined by the drama of canyons and valleys, making it both a separate entity and a part of the wider community of the Santa Clarita Valley.

One

FIRST ON THE SCENE

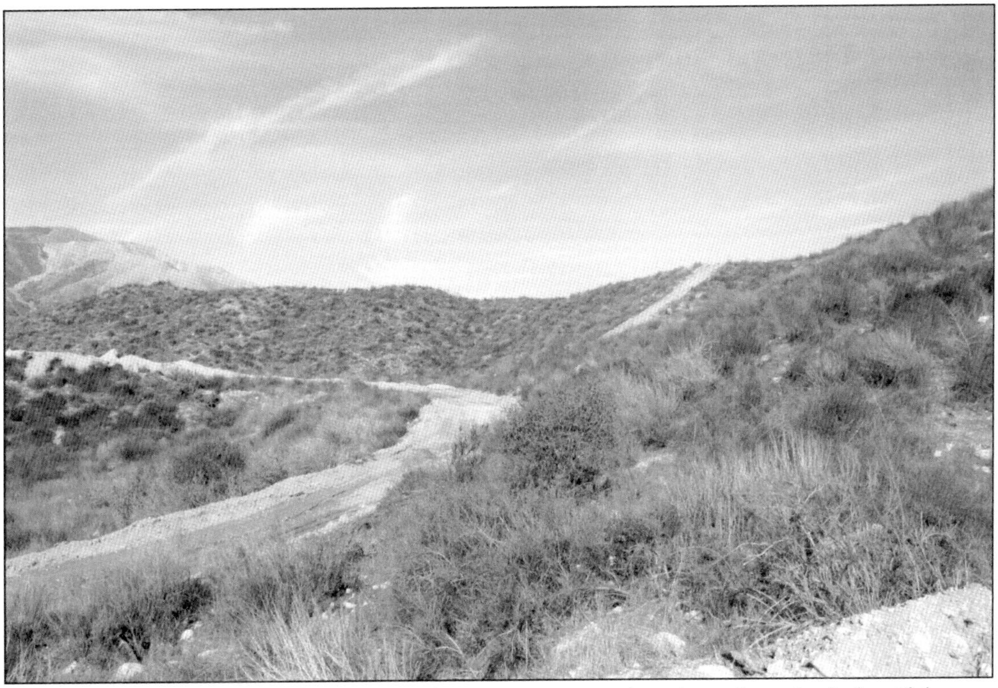

While Canyon Country and its surrounding environs are thought to have had plentiful water tens of thousands of years ago, by the time humans established homes in the area around 500 AD, the landscape looked much like the one pictured here. Whether its label was Soledad, Ravenna, Saugus, Honby, Acton, Agua Dulce, Mint Canyon, or Canyon Country, the region's residents all endured hot, dry summers and mild winters while living in canyons and valleys with some similarity of experience. (Courtesy of George and Gayle Starbuck.)

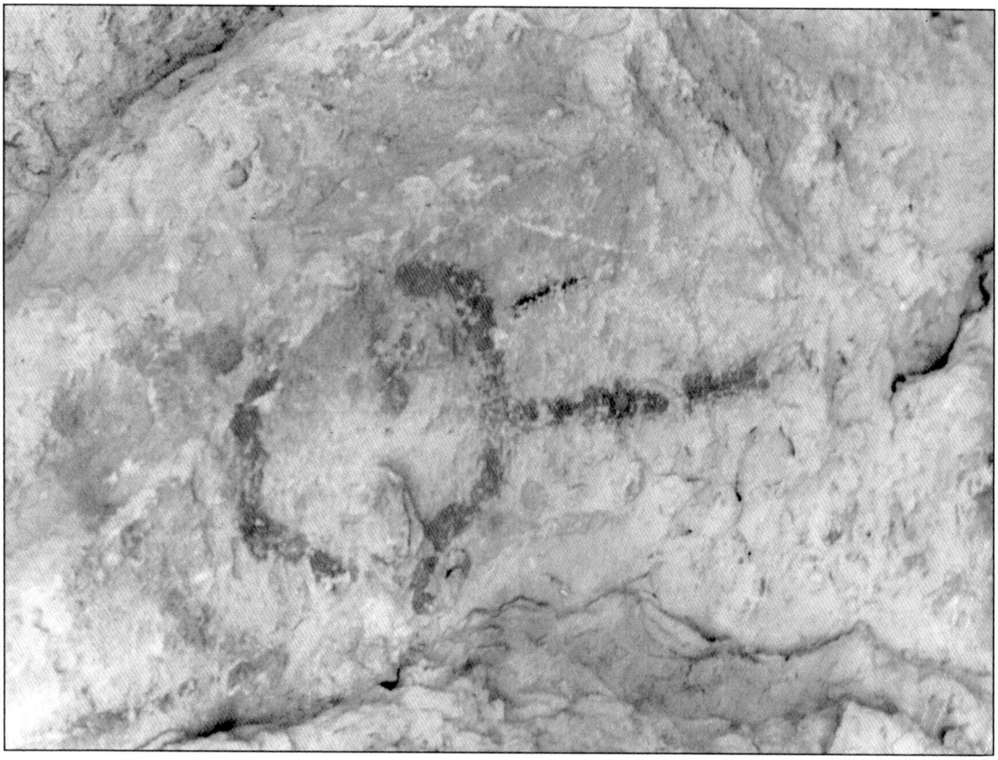

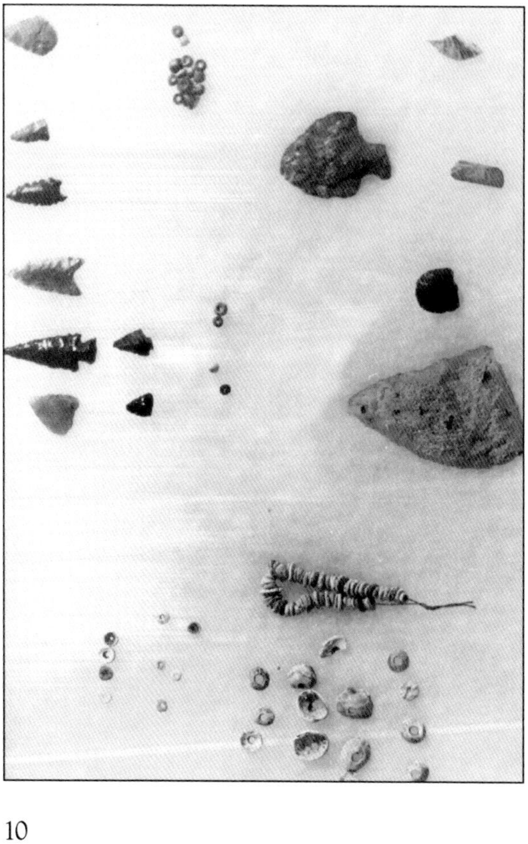

The earliest human settlers in the Santa Clarita Valley were likely bands of hunter-gatherers who arrived several thousand years ago. There is little evidence of these earliest groups, but there are records for the Tataviam Indians, who lived and passed through the area around 500 AD or earlier. Full-blooded Tataviam lived in the Santa Clarita Valley as recently as the early 1900s. Examples of their artwork, as pictured above, have been discovered on rocks in the eastern valley.

Physical evidence of the lives of the Tataviam exists through shards from tools and beads like those at left, which were found at Vasquez Rocks. Samples of Tataviam baskets, jewelry, and other artifacts from the Santa Clarita Valley are housed in the Peabody Museum of Archaeology and Ethnology at Harvard University. With the discovery in Agua Dulce of items such as a grooved ax, which is native to Arizona, and clay objects that are not likely to be of Tataviam origin, it is assumed that the area was a center of significant trade.

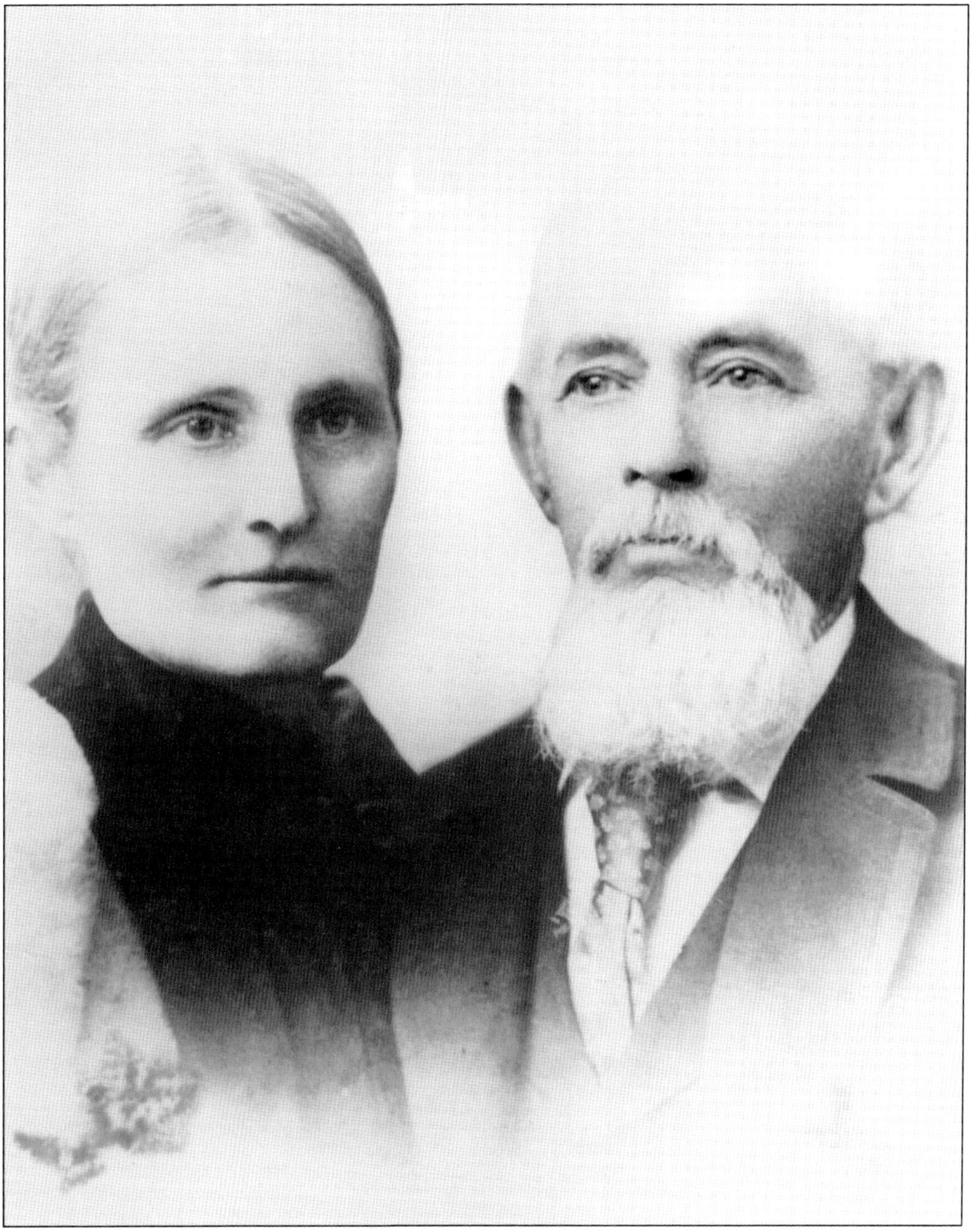

Col. Thomas Finley Mitchell, pictured here with his wife, Martha, was the first American to arrive in the area known as Soledad, which means "solitude" in Spanish. Born in 1827, Mitchell left Virginia to serve in the Mexican-American War with the Texas Mounted Volunteers, Company C. He arrived in California in 1860 and established a cattle ranch at the Santa Clara creek bed. After a few years of sharing the natural environment with grizzly bears, coyotes, and native peoples, Mitchell met and married Martha C. Taylor, who was living in San Gabriel after moving west from Arkansas. The family's ranch at Lost Canyon and Sand Canyon Road eventually grew to encompass nearly 1,000 acres. (Courtesy of Joshua Randall.)

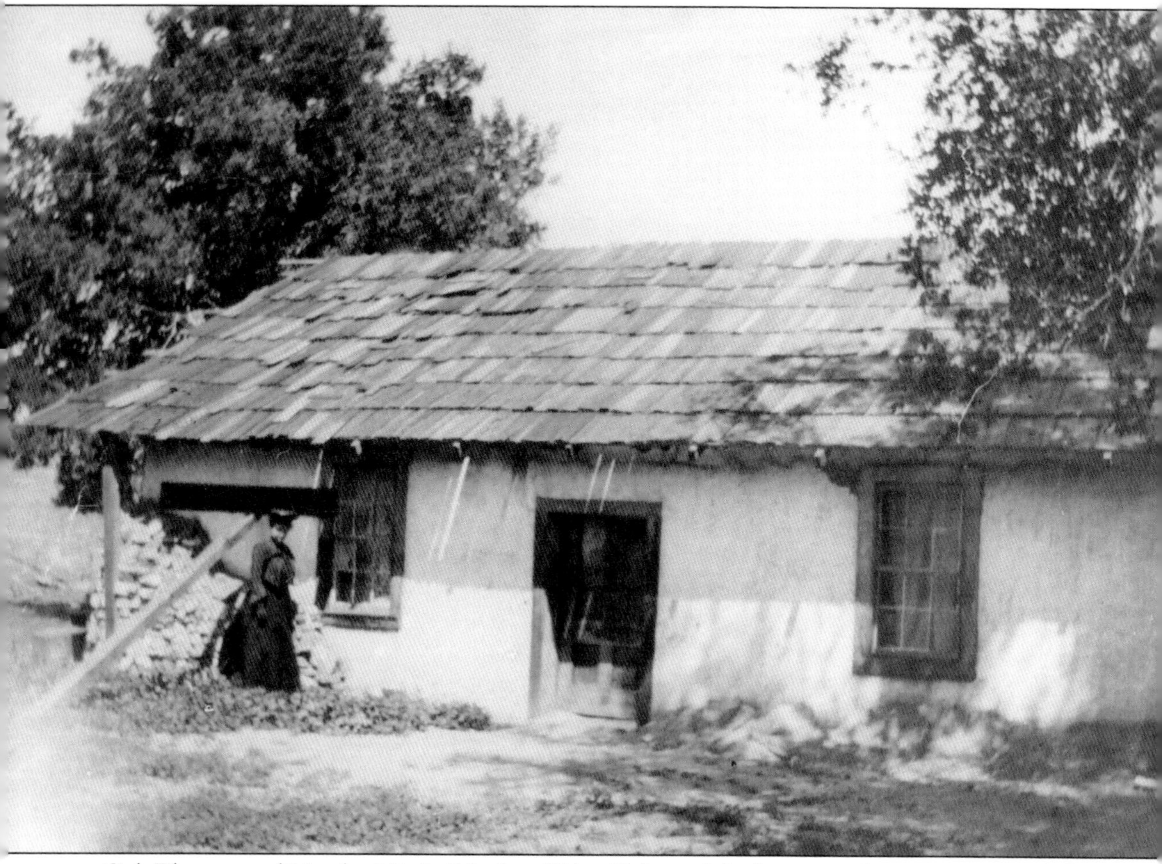

Col. Thomas and Martha Mitchell built a 60-by-45-foot adobe house on their property, and the family grew to include six children. Martha, seen here standing outside the home, might not have realized the historical significance of the little house until she found herself teaching a group of children in its kitchen beginning in 1872. The adobe house eventually became the first school in the area and the center of the second school district in all of Los Angeles County. (Courtesy of Joshua Randall.)

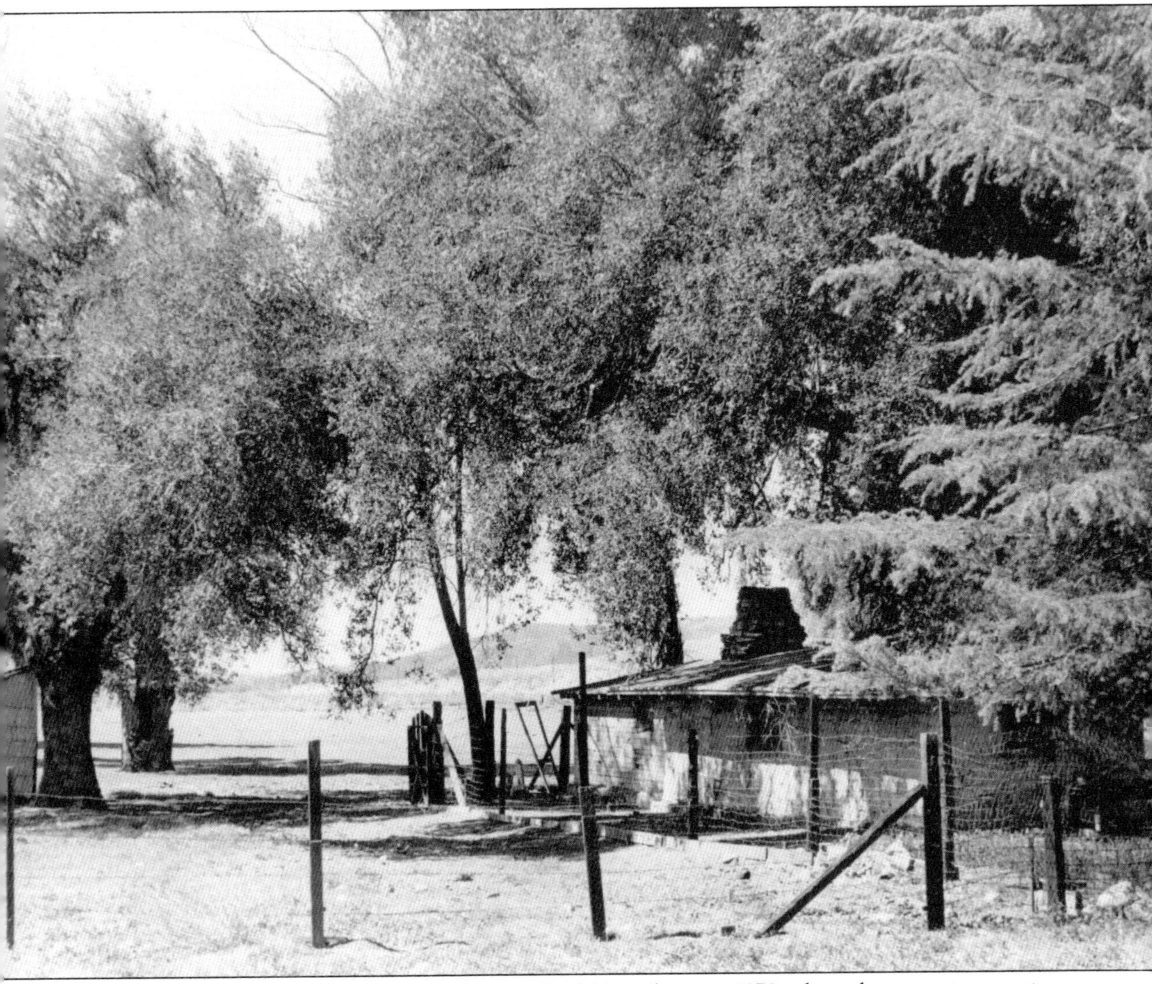

The "Mitchell Adobe," as it came to be known, had 10 students in 1879, when classroom instruction was moved to the nearby Lang Hotel. Long after the little adobe was abandoned, it again made headlines when it was slated for demolition in 1986. The Santa Clarita Valley Historical Society moved three walls of the adobe to Heritage Junction in Newhall, where they became a part of the museum complex. (Courtesy of Joshua Randall.)

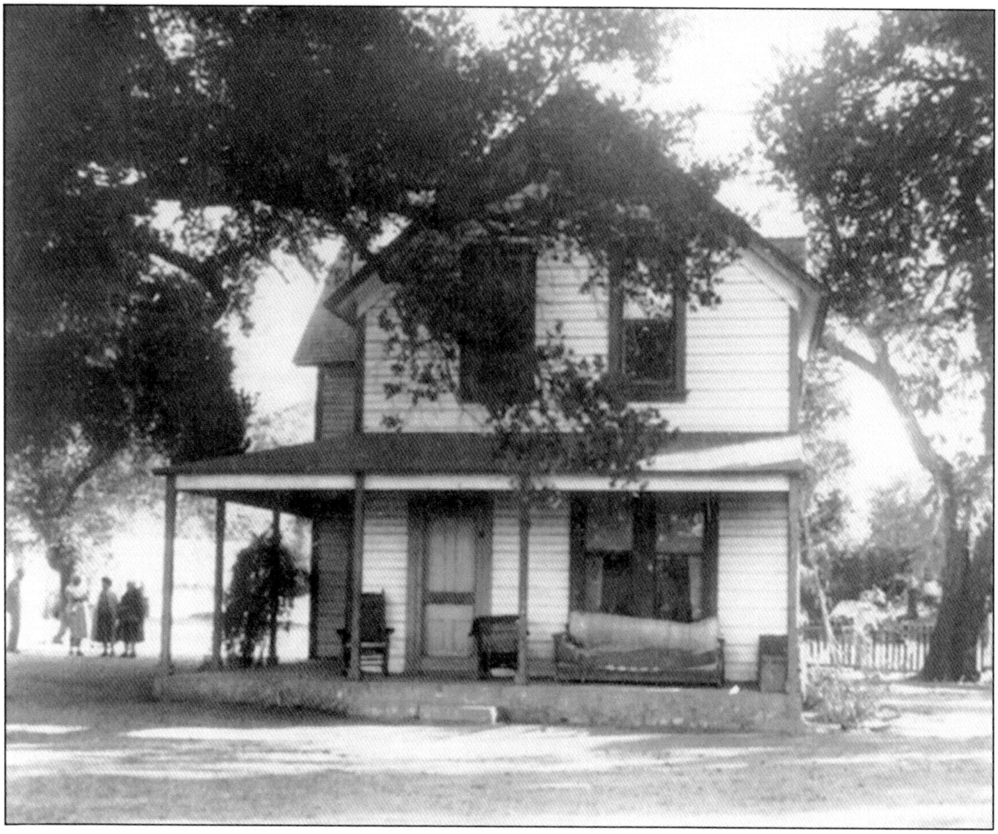

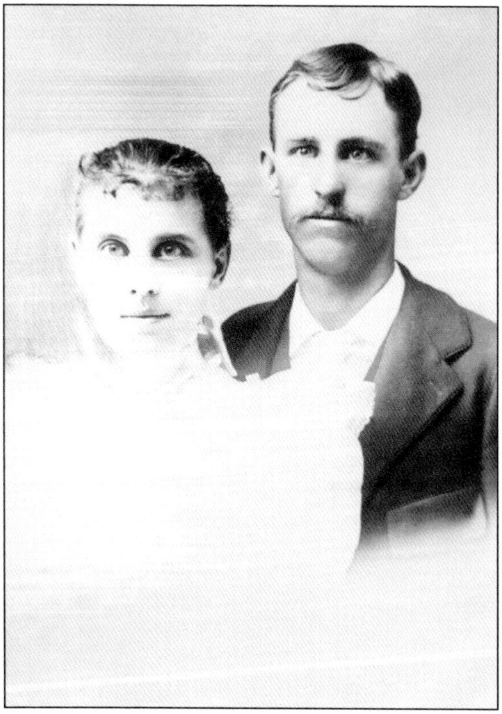

In 1888, Col. Thomas Mitchell built a bigger, two-story house (above) on the family's property near Sand Canyon and Lost Canyon Road, not far from the family's first adobe home. By this time, Mitchell and pioneer John Lang had established the Sulphur Springs School District, and the larger home would accommodate its growth. This building later served as a honey house for Colonel Mitchell's beekeeping business, which reportedly grew to produce 40 tons of honey in a season. Thomas and Martha Mitchell's fifth child, John Wesley, married into another notable family of settlers, the Dyers. John and Iva Angeline Dyer Mitchell (pictured at left) were married in 1902 and settled in Canyon Country (then called Saugus). The couple had four sons, three of whom stayed in the Santa Clarita Valley. (Above, courtesy of Joshua Randall.)

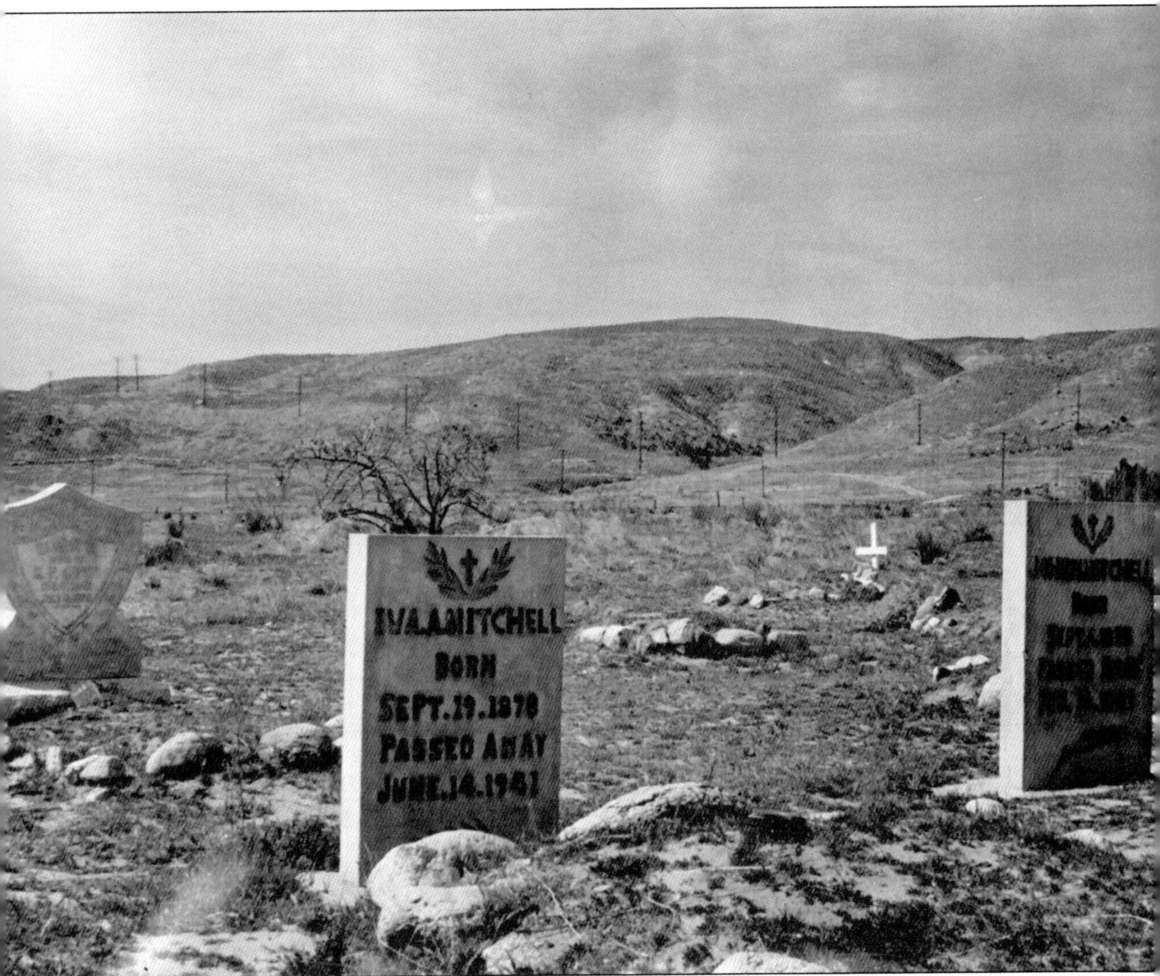

Canyon Country's earliest settlers, Thomas and Martha Mitchell, raised six children, beginning with Mary Elizabeth in December 1865 and Thomas in 1868; neither of these first two children lived to adulthood. The children were buried, along with many from the Mitchell and other settler families, in the Mitchell-Dyer Cemetery shown here. The cemetery was located on the Mitchells' original ranch property. The couple welcomed four more children, including Frank; a daughter, Frances, who was called "Fannie"; John Wesley, who was born on September 6, 1875; and Minnie Ivy, the youngest child. Though the cemetery belonged to the Mitchell family, a few others from outside the family were buried there as well. Blacksmith and artisan Joseph Youngblood, a clerk for the Sulphur Springs School District School Board, was buried there around 1930. This cemetery has sometimes been referred to as the Mitchell-Dyer Cemetery, as some members of the Dyer family are buried there. James Thomas Dyer of Agua Dulce, co-owner of the Dyer Honey House, was laid to rest there in 1960 next to his wife, Mary, who died in 1945.

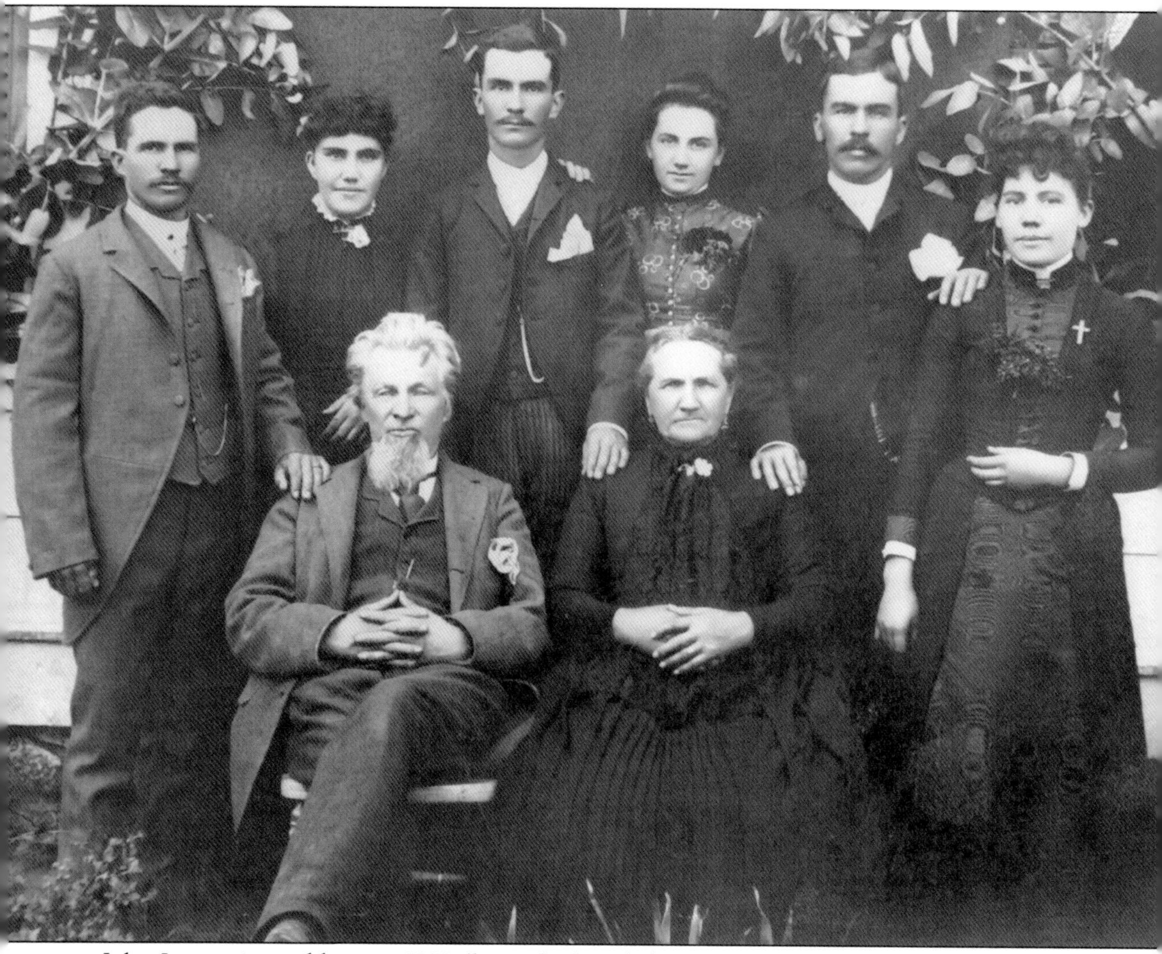

John Lang, pictured here in 1880 (he is the bearded man seated in front), arrived in Canyon Country in 1870, when the area was called Soledad Canyon. Lang bought 160 acres, then planted an orchard and built a two-story resort, the Lang Hotel, where guests could stay, dine, hunt, and enjoy the "healthful qualities" of the area's natural sulfur springs. Lang and his neighbor, Col. Thomas Mitchell, were responsible for establishing the Sulphur Springs School District. Lang is believed to have made the first cheese vats in California, and he was reputed to have tracked and killed a 2,300-pound grizzly bear in 1873.

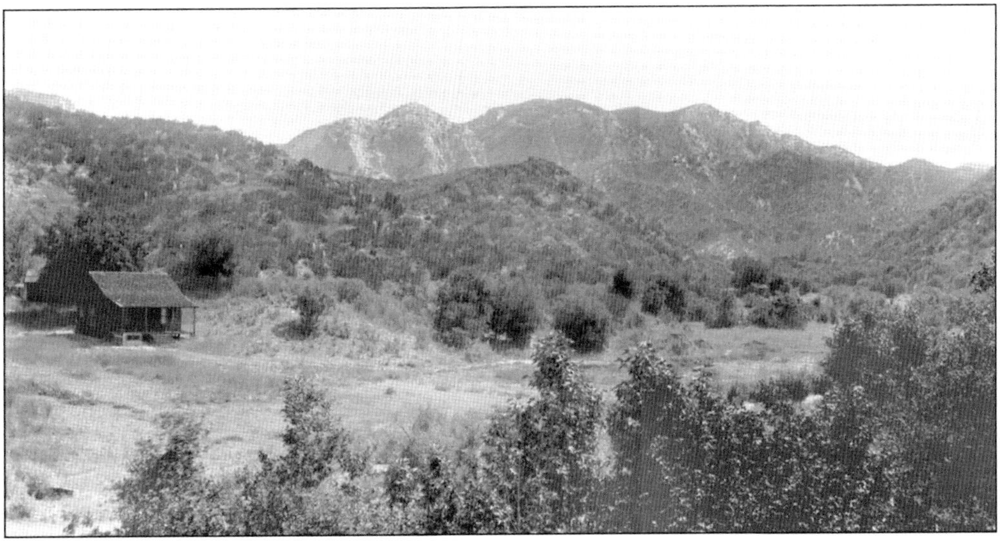

In the Placerita Canyon/Sand Canyon area, grazing was not limited to cattle. Josephine and Jean Joseph Reynier raised sheep on their 600 acres of property, some of which is visible in these two photographs. Jean Joseph homesteaded in Sand Canyon when he arrived in 1868, and he later married Swiss immigrant Josephine Sambien. The Reyniers built a Victorian house in which to raise their three children, all of whom attended the newly established Sulphur Springs School. In addition to raising sheep, the Reyniers were able to grow fruit trees—as well as grapes for wine—due to the year-round streams on their property. (Both courtesy of George and Gayle Starbuck.)

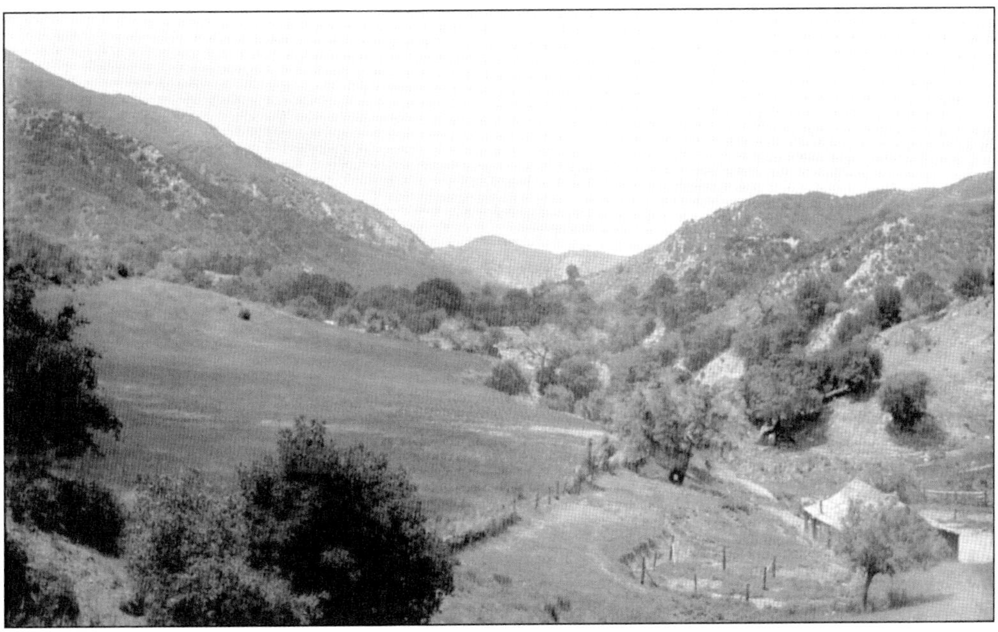

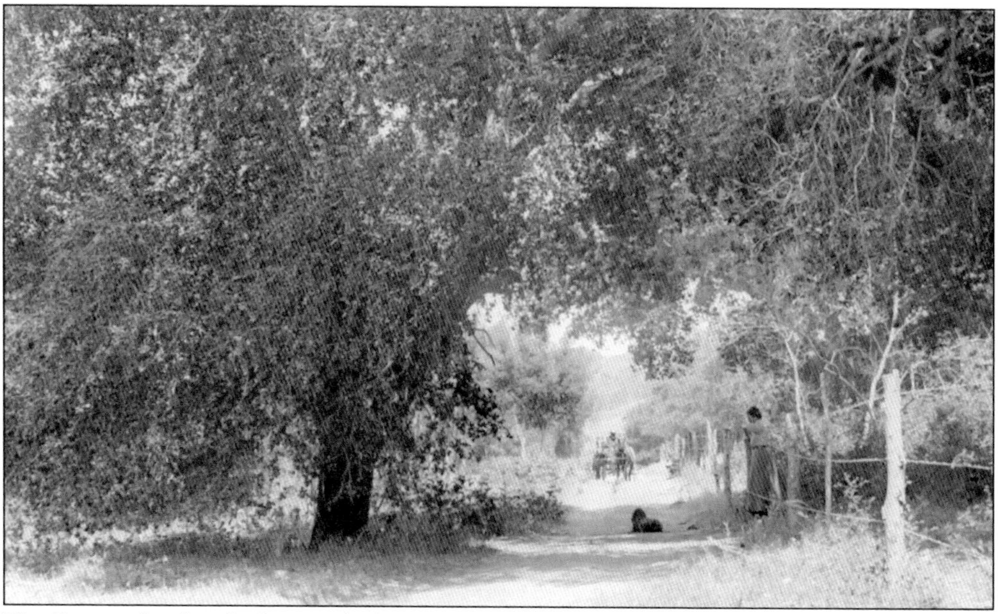

The Reynier family, which started when Jean Joseph and Josephine Reynier wed, grew to include three children—Joseph P., Josephine Emma, and Hortense Victoria. Jean Joseph left his native France in 1864 with his brother, Jean Mathieu, bound for America. They lived in San Francisco for a few years, then purchased a herd of sheep and drove it to Southern California. In 1868, Joseph settled in the eastern Placerita Canyon area. After Josephine's death in 1896, the Reynier children lived with Joseph, who continued ranching. In 1901, he married Della, who gave birth to two daughters: Eugenia, who lived to the age of 17, and a daughter who died in infancy. Both were buried under an olive tree on the family's Canyon Country property. Hortense Reynier married Frank Evans Walker, and the two remained in Placerita Canyon, where they reared 12 children; the couple built a cabin there that was preserved and made a part of the nonprofit Placerita Nature Center. (Both courtesy of George and Gayle Starbuck.)

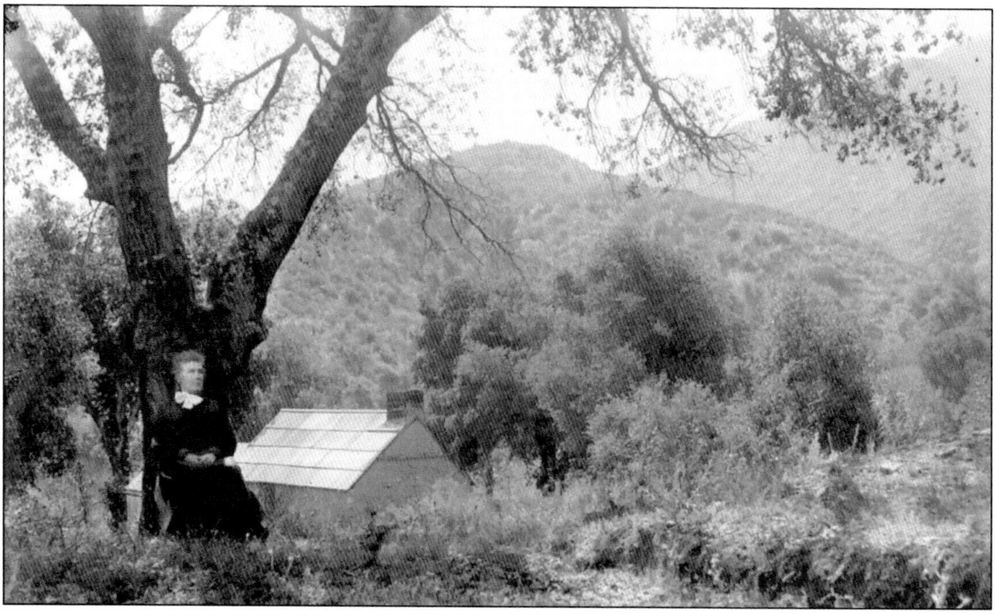

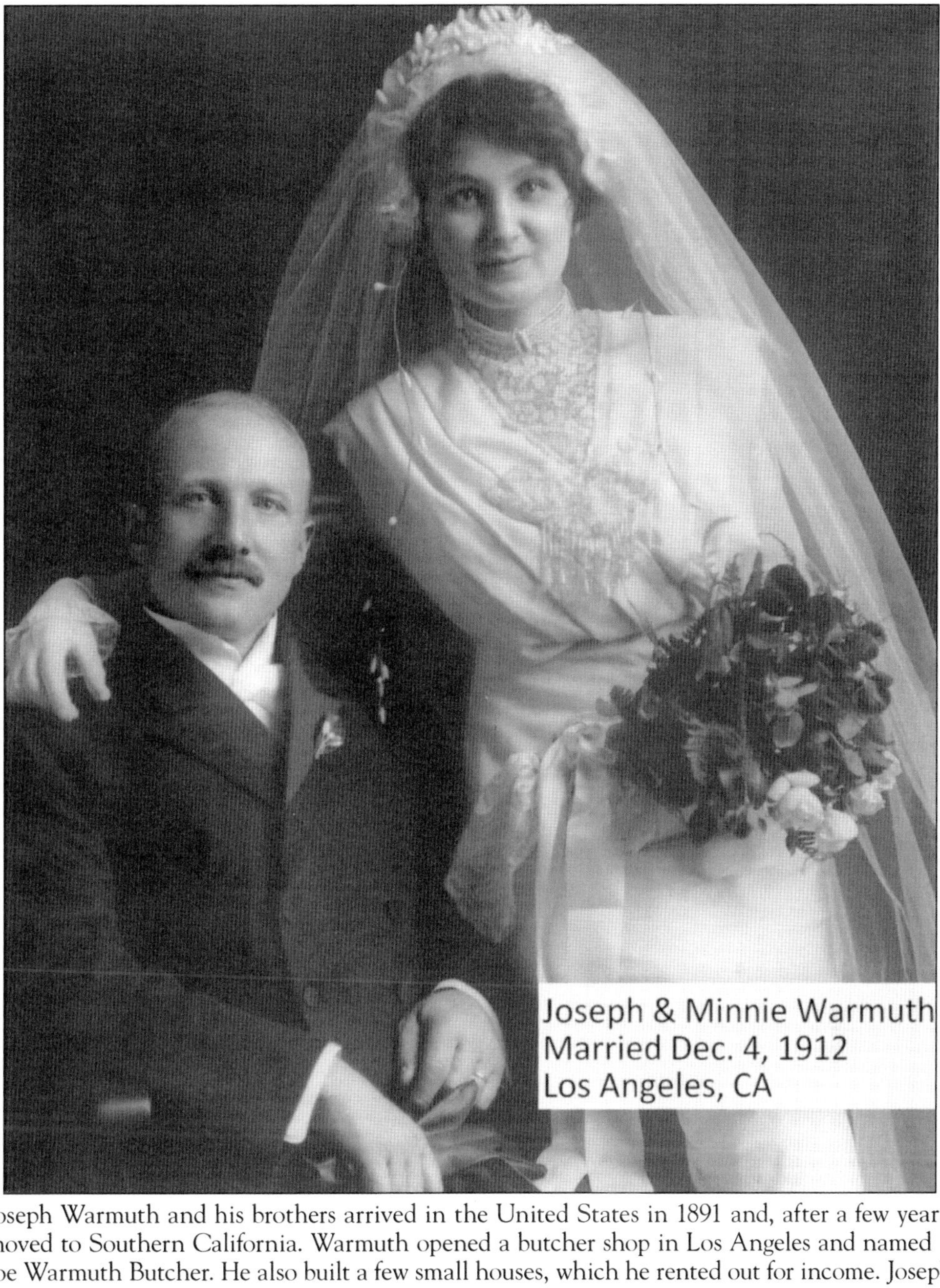

Joseph Warmuth and his brothers arrived in the United States in 1891 and, after a few years, moved to Southern California. Warmuth opened a butcher shop in Los Angeles and named it Joe Warmuth Butcher. He also built a few small houses, which he rented out for income. Joseph and Minnie Warmuth are pictured here on their wedding day, December 4, 1912. Three years later, they purchased 120 acres in Sand Canyon, where they settled in 1920. Joseph had been a butcher in New York, where they lived before moving back to California. Joseph's brother, Kasper, a wood-shop teacher, bought 80 acres of property in Sand Canyon to the west of his brother's land. Joseph and Minnie's children attended Sulphur Springs School, where Florence Mitchell, daughter-in-law of Thomas and Martha Mitchell, taught them from first through eighth grades, all in one room. The Warmuth children walked two miles to grammar school but had to ride the bus 22 miles each way to attend San Fernando High School. (Courtesy of Mary Warmuth Sathre.)

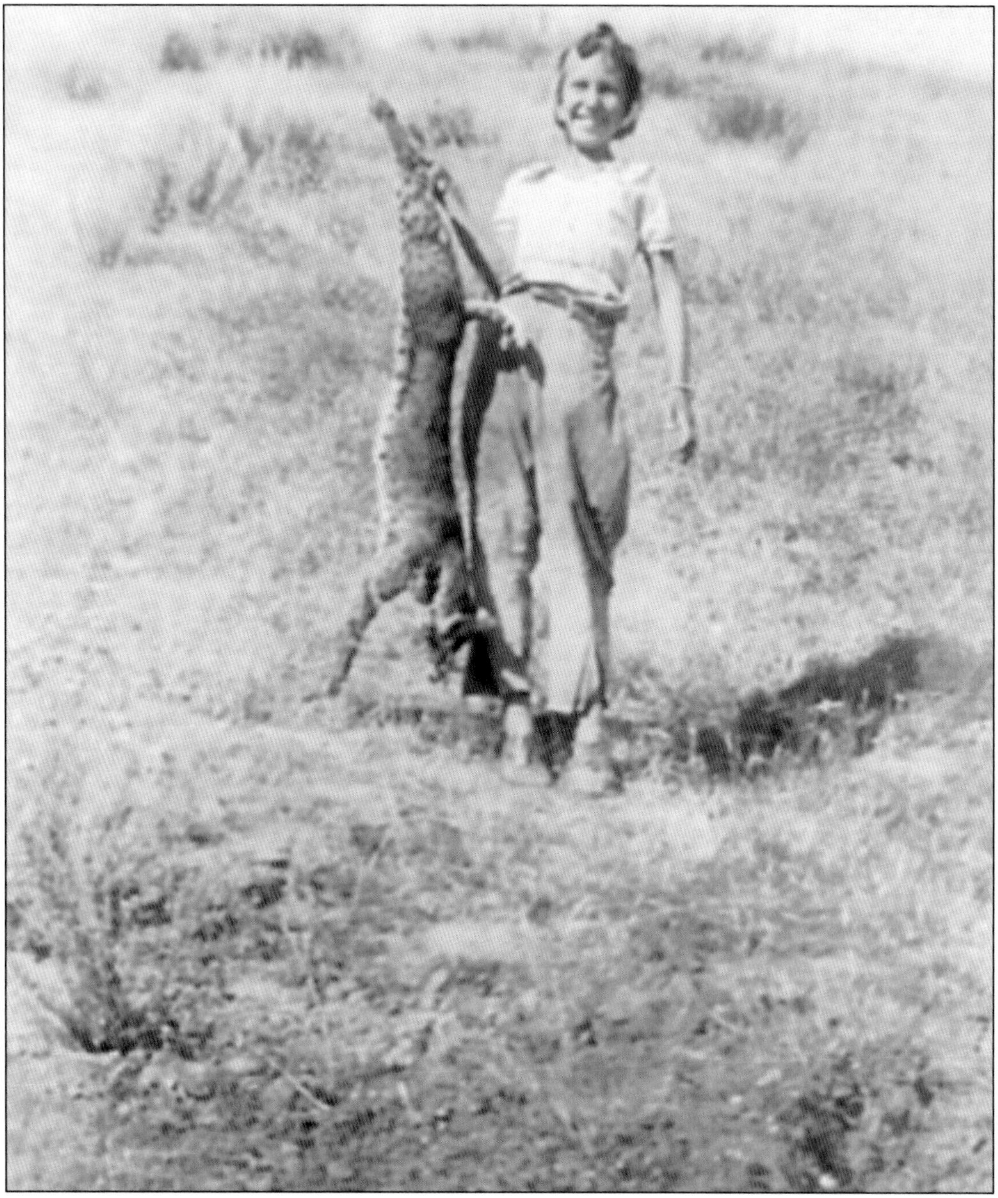

In this August 1934 photograph, eight-year-old Mary Warmuth (Sathre) shows off a bobcat that she caught in a rabbit trap near her family's ranch in Sand Canyon. The Warmuth family, like other families in Soledad Canyon, ate jackrabbits and other local game, except when the jackrabbits had blisters from disease caused by hot weather. Mary graduated from high school at age 16 and worked as a timekeeper at Howard Hughes Aircraft in Culver City along with her sister Madeline, who worked there as a welder. Madeline was featured in the *Los Angeles Times* while taking a welding class at San Fernando High School. Mary lived in Canyon Country until adulthood, when she met Raymond Sathre, who was a chief petty officer in the Navy during World War II. They married and moved to Carmichael, California, where they opened a small watch repair shop on April 1, 1947. When Raymond passed away in February 1989, Mary ran the store until April 1 of that year, meaning that it was in business for exactly 42 years. (Courtesy of Mary Warmuth Sathre.)

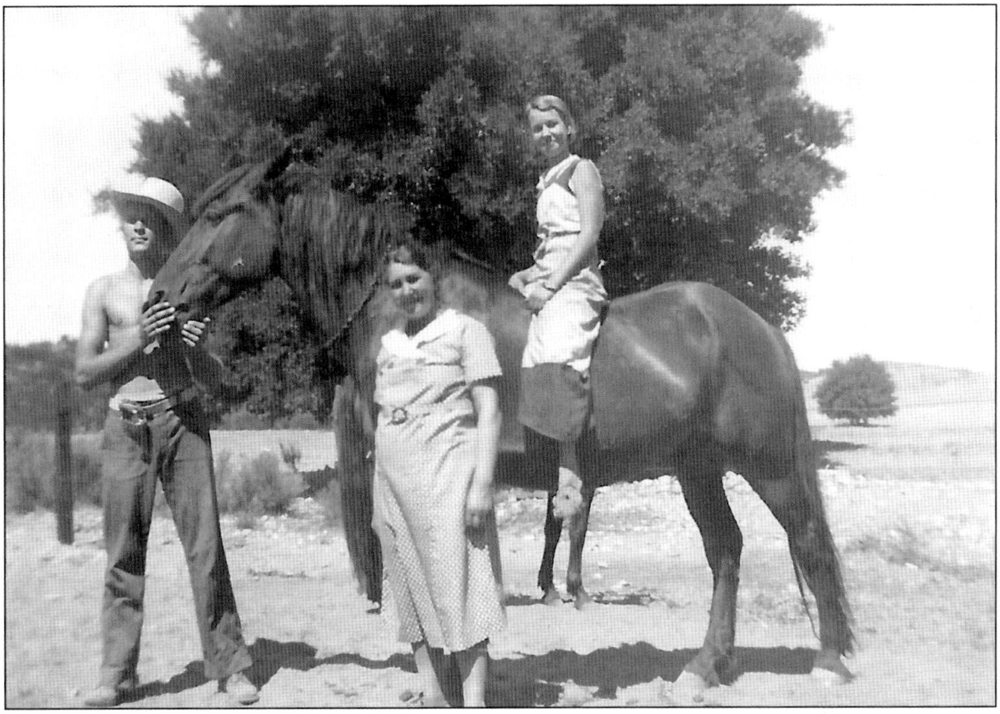

Times were tough for the Warmuth family despite the fact they owned rental property in Los Angeles. Tenants did not always pay, so there were times when the Warmuths had no food. Also, the rural setting meant that the family used kerosene lamps and scrubbed clothes on a washboard. If the wind refused to blow, the windmill would not turn and the family would not have water. In the above photograph, Mary Warmuth sits atop the family's favorite horse, Chief, in 1937; her brother Frank and her mother, Minnie, are also pictured. Chief was used to pull the family's one-horse plow, and the Warmuth boys would connect him to the two-wheeled cart that had a flat, wooden bed on which the children could ride to school. In the 1944 image at right, Mary (right) poses with her mother and one of her other brothers, Henry. Henry was a corporal in the US Air Force during World War II, while his brother Joe served in the US Army. (Both courtesy of Mary Warmuth Sathre.)

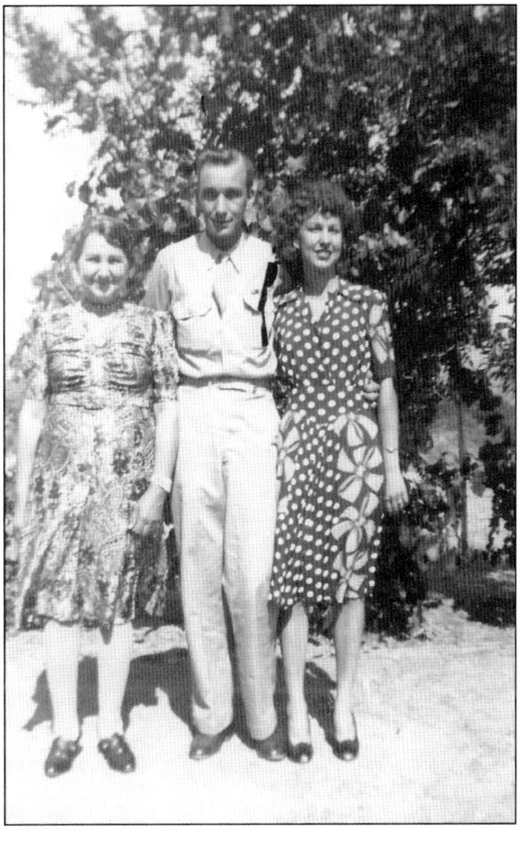

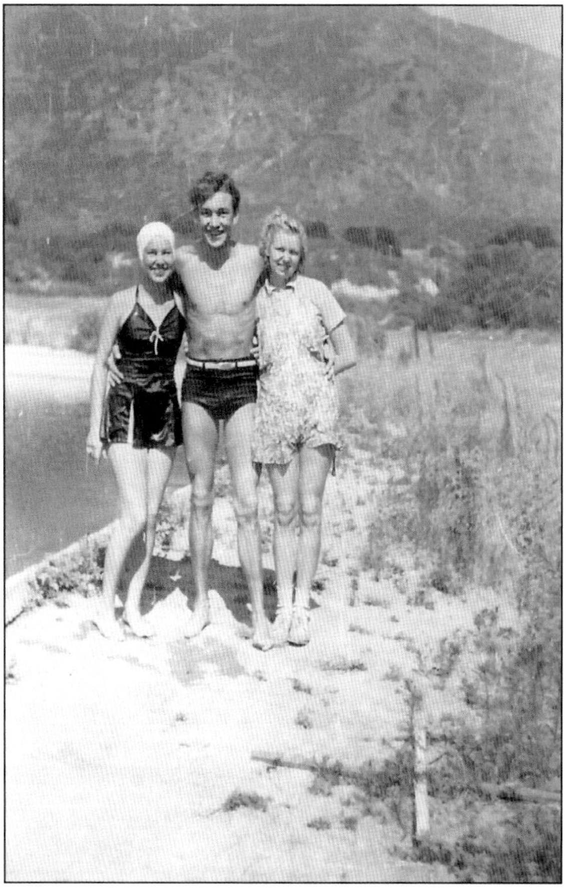

Spending time in local watering holes was one way that Mary Warmuth and her brothers and sisters endured the hot Canyon Country summers. These photographs were taken in 1941, when the family went swimming in a reservoir on the property of their neighbors, the Bellos. The reservoir was constructed in the 1930s for farm irrigation, and it was filled with well water. The Civilian Conservation Corps was located on the Warmuths' Sand Canyon property, which was just north of Iron Canyon Road. Three of the Warmuths—Mary (left), Henry, and Madeline—are pictured at left at the Bellos' reservoir. In the image below, Henry stands nearby as Mary dries her hair. (Both courtesy of Mary Warmuth Sathre.)

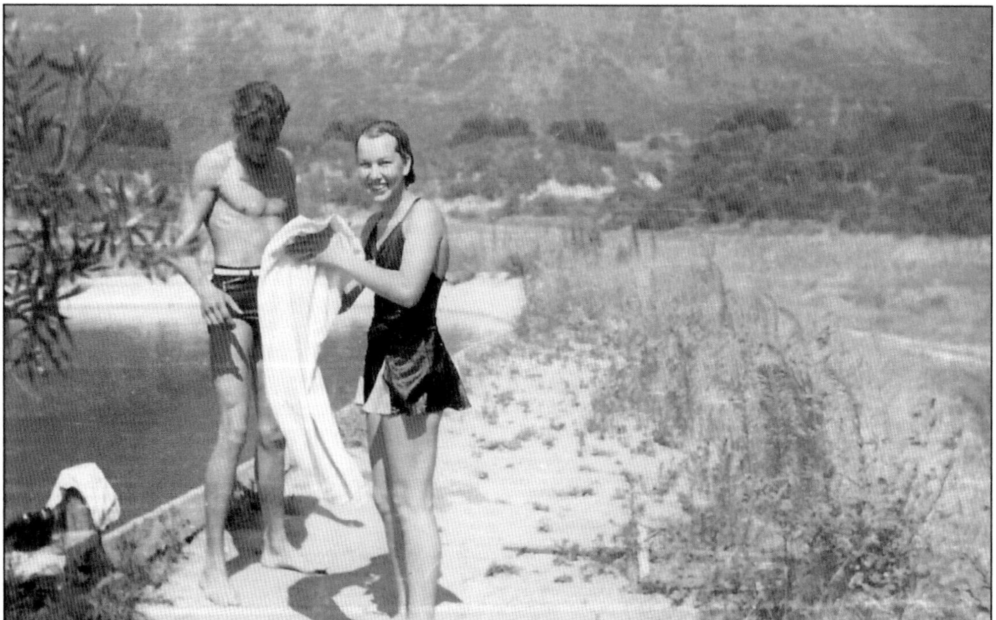

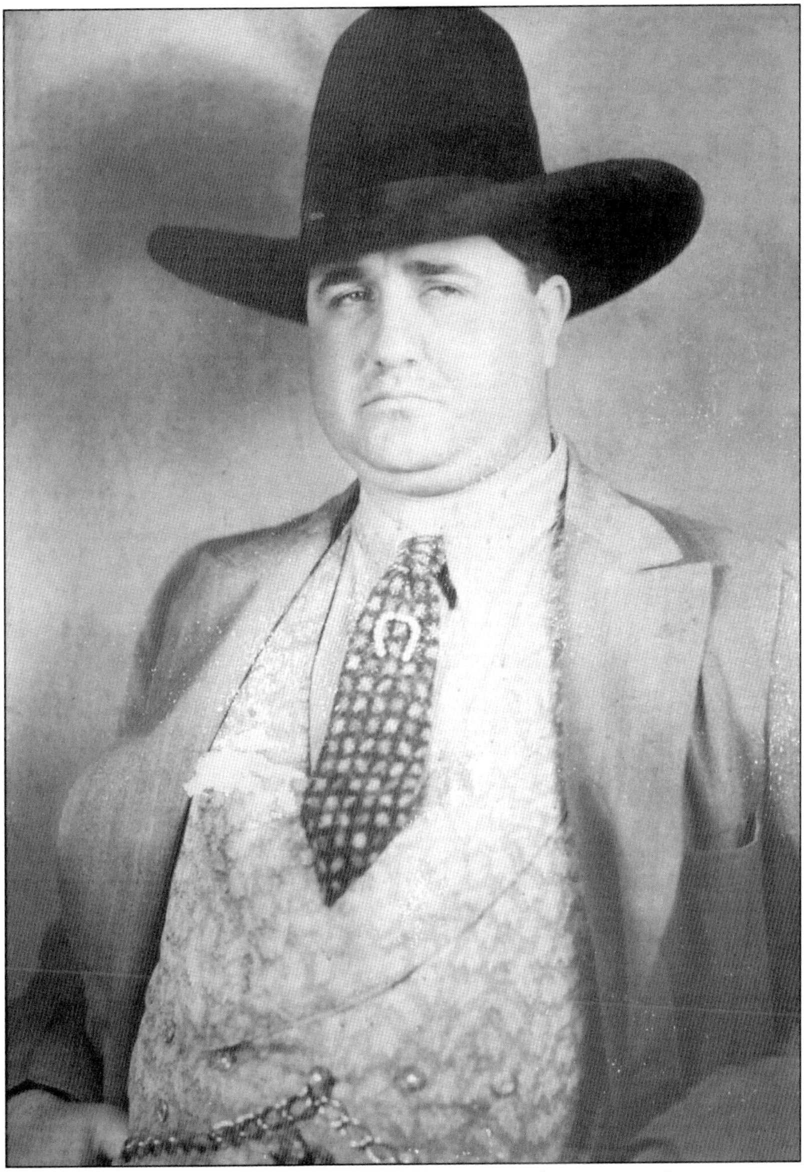

Horace Truman Cain, known as "Ace Cain," was an actor who appeared in numerous Western movies, including *Shotgun Pass* in 1931 and both *Rio Rattler* and *The Texas Rambler* in 1935. Before moving to Sand Canyon in Canyon Country, Cain owned and operated Ace Cain's Café on Western Avenue, near Sunset Boulevard in Hollywood, across the street from the 20th Century Fox studios. Standing 6 feet and 5 inches tall, he landed villain roles in several "poverty row Westerns." He later owned the Uncle Ace Liquor Store and Uncle Ace Motel on Western Avenue near Santa Monica Boulevard. Cain lived on Sultus Street in Sand Canyon until his death in 1973. The Wichita Falls, Texas, native served in the US Army in the 1920s and was known to be a skilled gambler and bootlegger during Prohibition. After owning businesses in Hollywood and appearing in dozens of Westerns, Cain purchased the Rocky Springs Country Club on Sand Canyon Road in what was then called Saugus. At the country club, he employed ex-models and showgirls who were known to be "very friendly," and the establishment was quite popular with residents despite the raising of some local eyebrows.

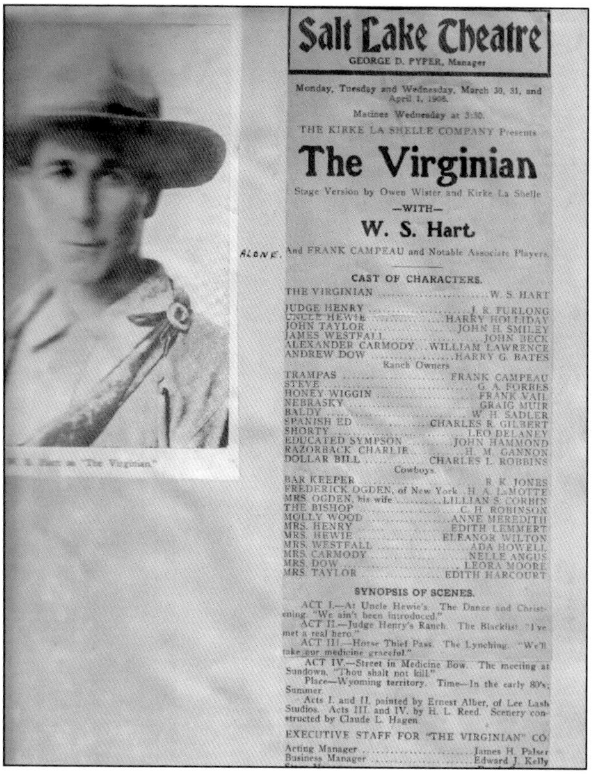

In the Placerita Canyon/Sand Canyon area, ranching was not limited to raising cattle, as the Mitchells did, or sheepherding, as done by Joseph Reynier and his family. One couple arrived in Canyon Country to work on a hog farm in the early 1940s and established residency for generations. A request by actor William S. Hart, shown in the photograph at left, brought Trinidad and Victoria Escalante (below) to the Santa Clarita Valley. Trinidad worked on a ranch outside of Tucson, Arizona, and, assigned to deliver an order of horses to Hart, traveled by boxcar with the livestock. On the trip, Trinidad discovered Art Agajanian's hog farm in Canyon Country; he then returned to Arizona to pack up his family before moving. (Left, courtesy of Kathy Keysor Kellar; below, courtesy of the Escalante family.)

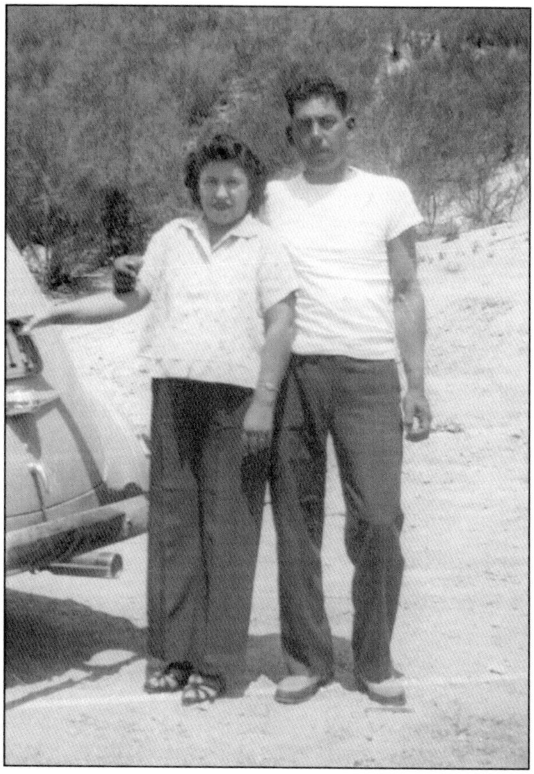

Frank Escalante, pictured in the 1940s photograph at right, was a toddler when his parents, Trinidad and Victoria, moved the family to Canyon Country. On the hog farm, which was situated in the Lost Canyon area next to Thomas Mitchell's ranch, employees lived rent-free in prefabricated houses with cardboard walls and outdoor bathrooms. Approximately 10 families lived at the farm. In many cases, marriages were formed between members of this neighborhood group. Trinidad and Victoria had six children: Trinidad, Mercy, Charlie, Mary "Sukie," Annie, and Frank. The children attended Sulphur Springs School with some of the Mitchell children while it was still a one-room schoolhouse, and later went to William S. Hart High School in Newhall, riding a bus that picked them up on the corner of Lost Canyon and Soledad Canyon Roads. (Courtesy of the Escalante family.)

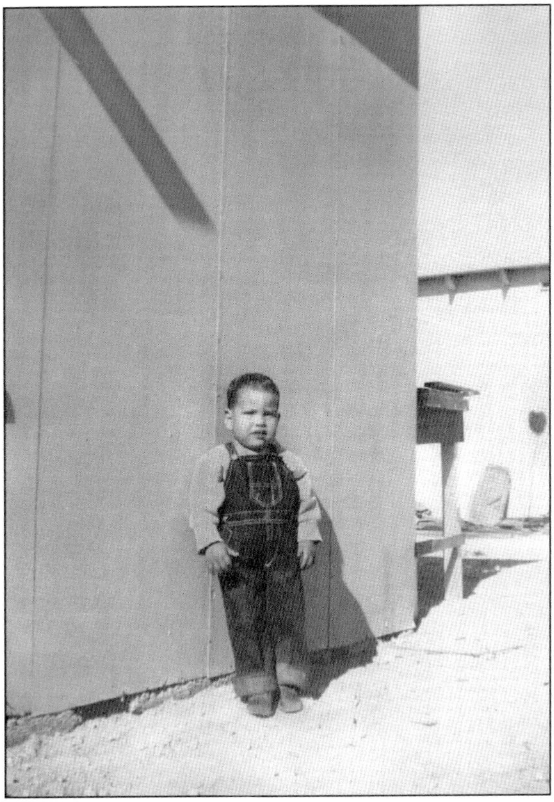

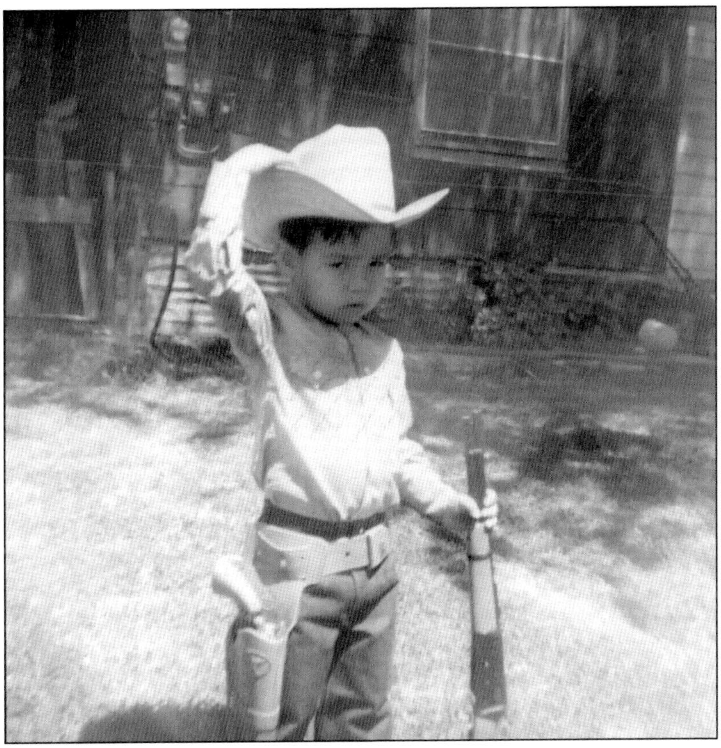

The youngest Escalante, Frank, married Rosie, who also lived at the hog and cattle ranch, and they established a home in Canyon Country. Their son, Richard, pictured in the 1970s image at left, and his siblings—Freddie, Lorraine, Victoria, and Frances—attended Mint Canyon Community School, Sierra Vista Junior High School, and Canyon High School. (Courtesy of the Escalante family.)

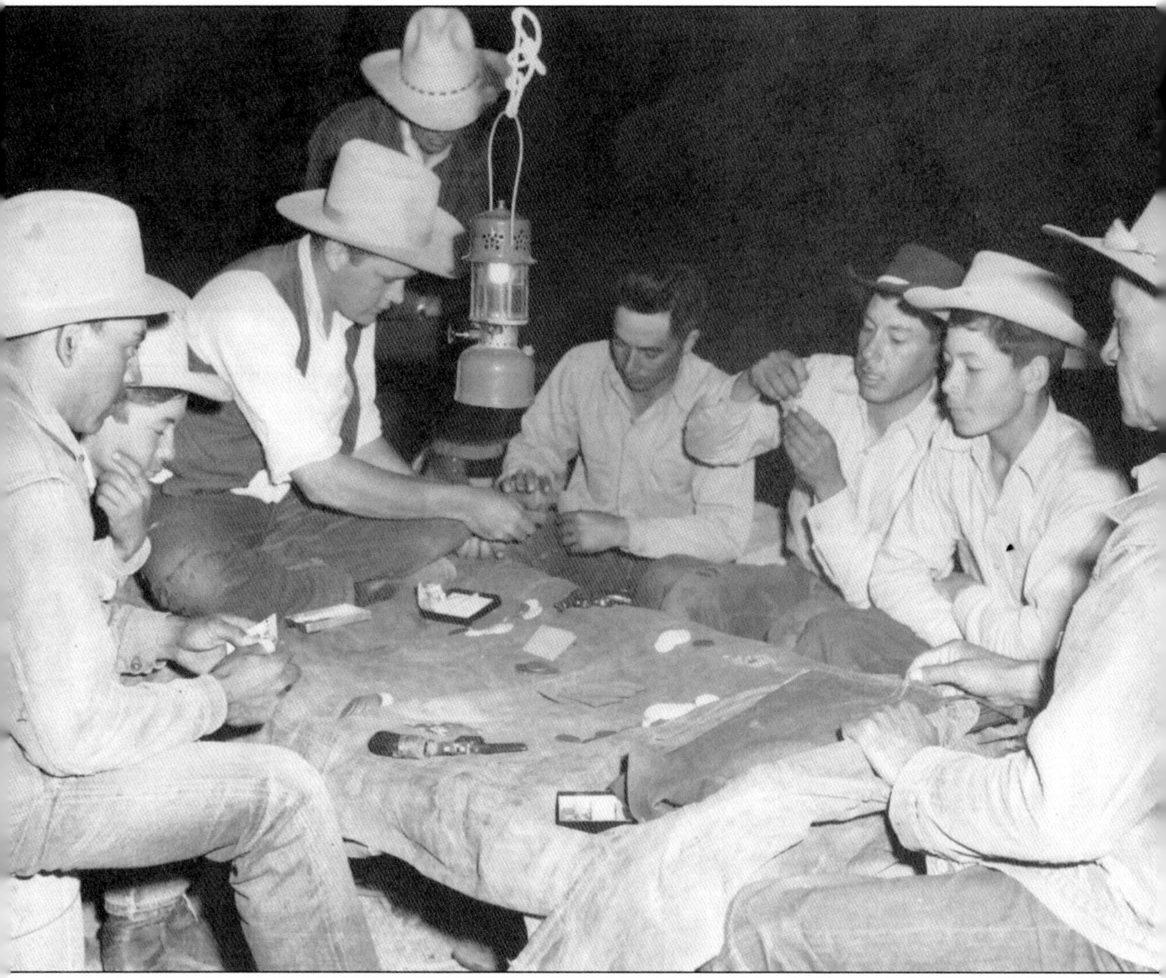

This was a typical night for ranch workers after a day of toil. Trinidad (second from right) and his brother Joe (third from right) are gathered here with friends, such as the dealer, Chris Lopez (third from left), who worked in olive orchards in nearby Sylmar. (Courtesy of the Escalante family.)

Two

Going for Gold and Bringing Back Borax

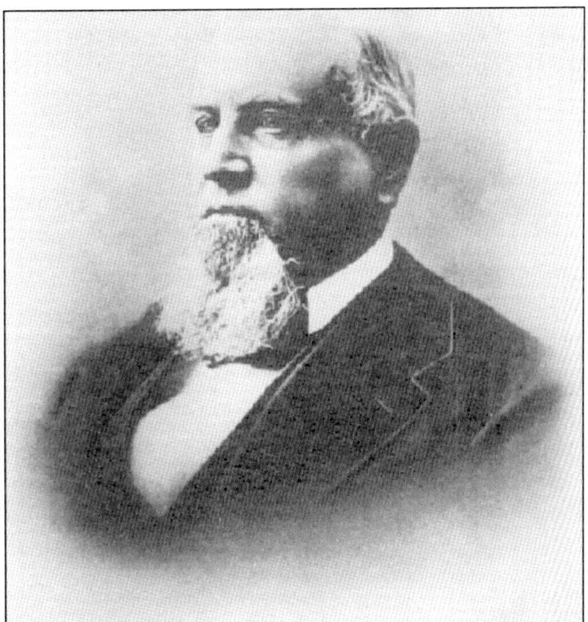

Southern Pacific Railroad president Charles Crocker played a pivotal role in a historic moment. The completion of the San Joaquin Valley Line connected northern and southern California by rail and provided Los Angeles with a direct line to the transcontinental United States. At Lang Station in Canyon Country on September 5, 1876, Crocker struck a silver hammer onto a gold spike in front of a crowd that came to witness the joining of the final tracks. By noon, the ceremony and fanfare of the day included a decorated Engine No. 25 covered with fruit branches, flowers, and American flags. One hour later, the train arrived from San Francisco filled with dignitaries and snaked behind Engine No. 38, also draped with flags.

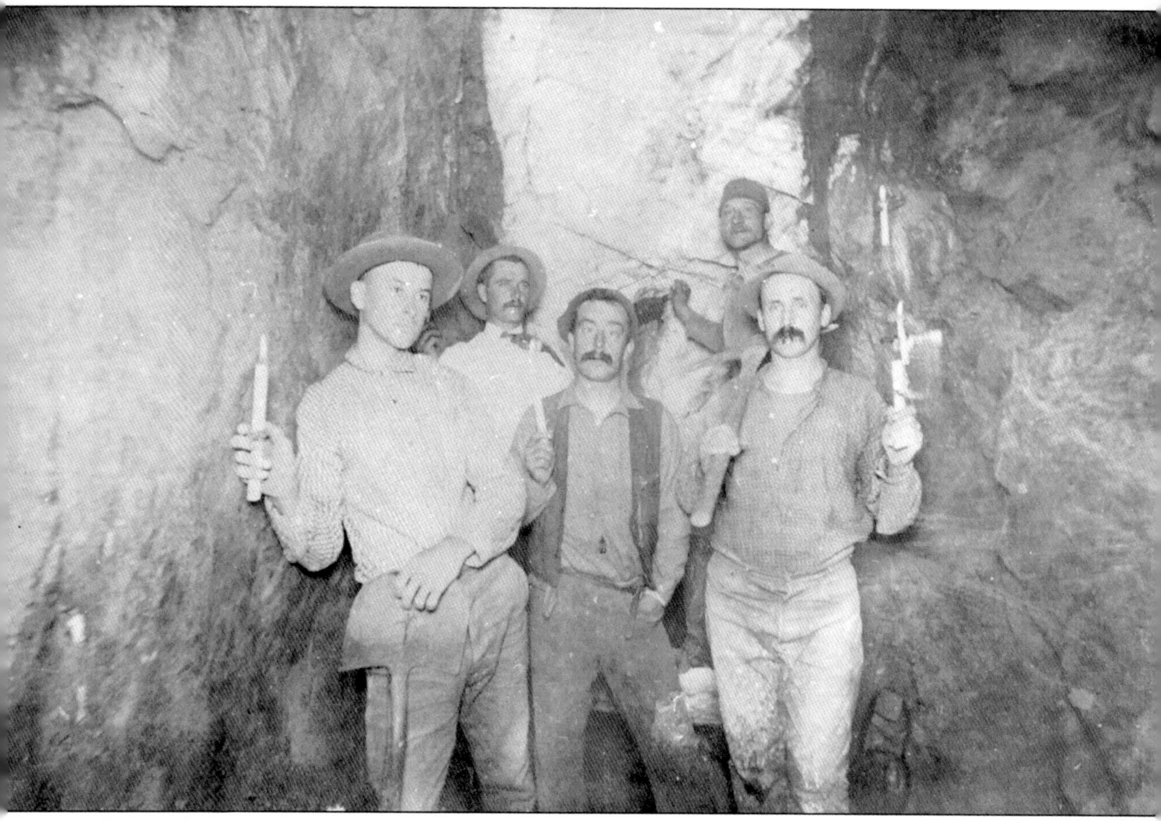

Just as Canyon Country and the surrounding areas were defined by their physical canyons and formations, the community's identity was largely formed by the precious metals underground. The miners in this photograph are typical of those who populated the area during the boom of the late 19th and early 20th centuries. These men standing in the Red Rover Mine are stalled from further entry by a large granite block in their path. The Red Rover Mine, located in the Agua Dulce/Acton area, was a successful operation owned by Henry T. Gage, who was elected governor of California in 1898—he named the mine after his dog.

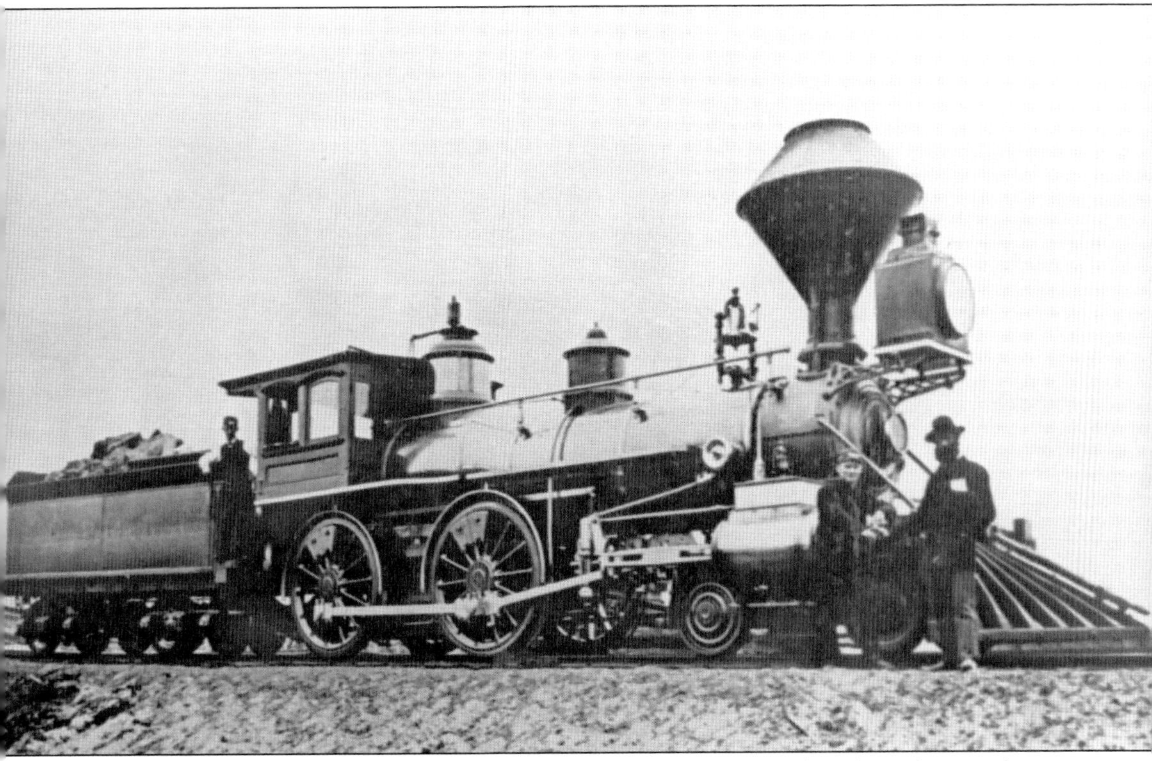

No photographs exist of the golden spike being driven into the railroad tracks at the completion of the Southern Pacific rail line. However, this photograph taken on September 5, 1876, captures the look of a key player—Engine No. 25. In addition to arriving at Lang Station (in present-day Canyon Country) to await the arrival of Engine No. 38, this train carried 335 prominent Los Angeles citizens to the golden spike ceremony.

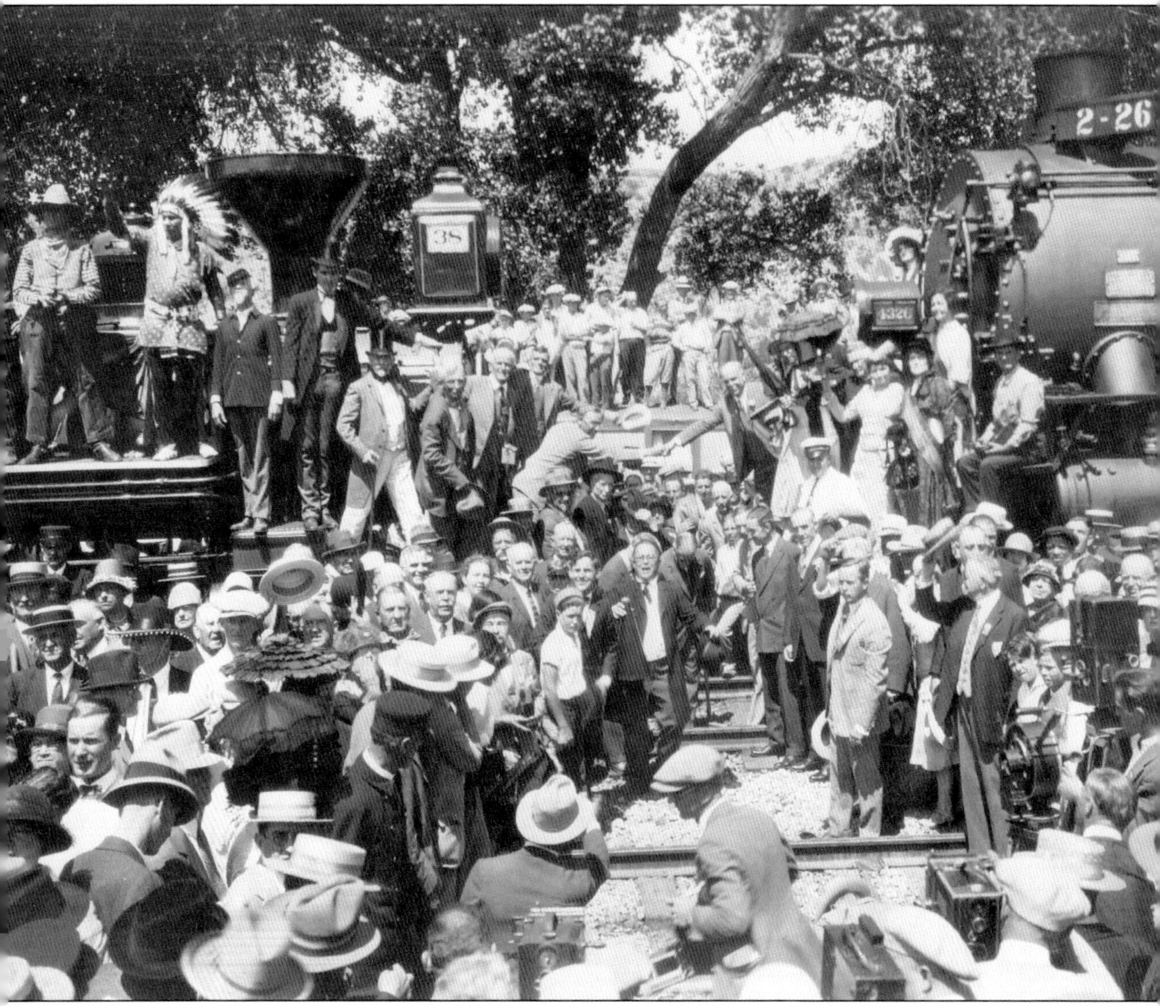

This photograph shows the celebration held at Lang Station on September 5, 1926, to commemorate the 50th anniversary of the completion of the rail line linking Los Angeles to San Francisco. As part of the celebration, a Southern Pacific Railroad engine with an old smokestack marked "No. 38" met a large group to commemorate the golden anniversary of the golden spike ceremony. Just as some of the attendees pictured here are dressed as cowboys or Native Americans, people again donned costumes to mark 100 years since the community's historic day when a Southern Pacific centennial engine arrived for the occasion on September 5, 1976, at the former site of Lang Station.

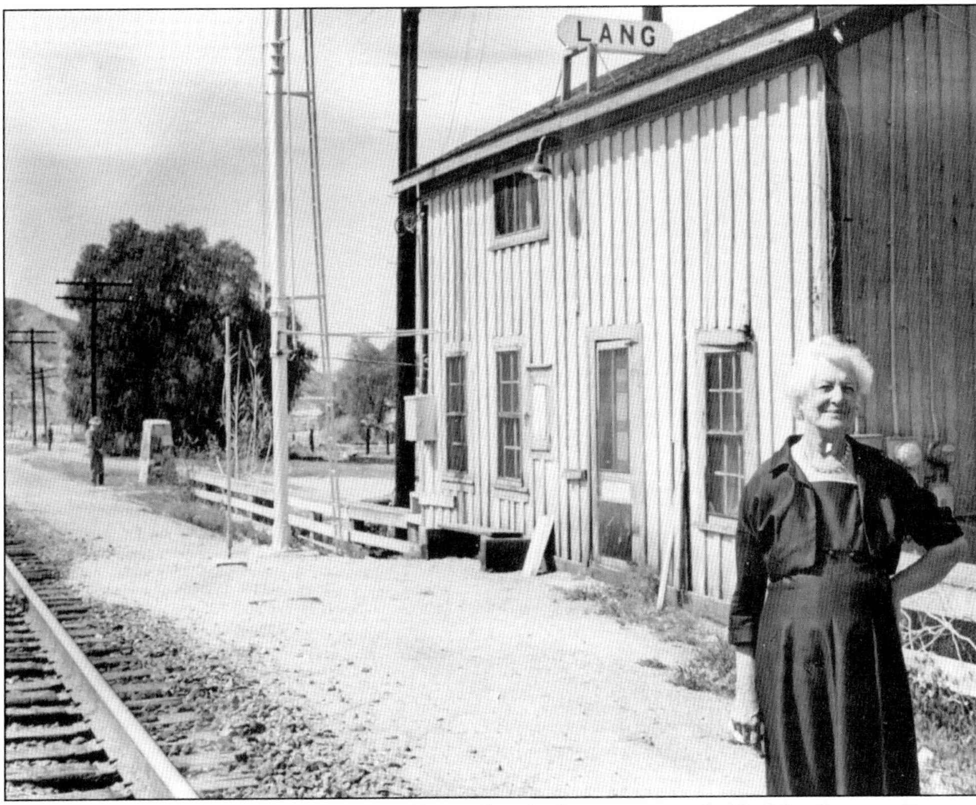

In the above photograph, Minnie Mitchell Murphy, the last surviving child of the Canyon Country founding family of Col. Thomas F. and Martha Mitchell, stands at Lang Station. Minnie's husband, Walter Murphy, is visible in the background at the spot where the "golden spike" was hammered to finish the San Joaquin Valley line. In June 1957, Lang Station became state historic landmark no. 590, and a plaque (visible at left in the image below) was placed at the site by the California Park Commission in cooperation with the Historical Society of Southern California. It reads: "LANG SOUTHERN PACIFIC STATION/On September 5, 1876, Charles Crocker, President of the Southern Pacific Railroad drove a gold spike to complete his company's San Joaquin Valley line. First rail connection of Los Angeles with San Francisco and transcontinental lines."

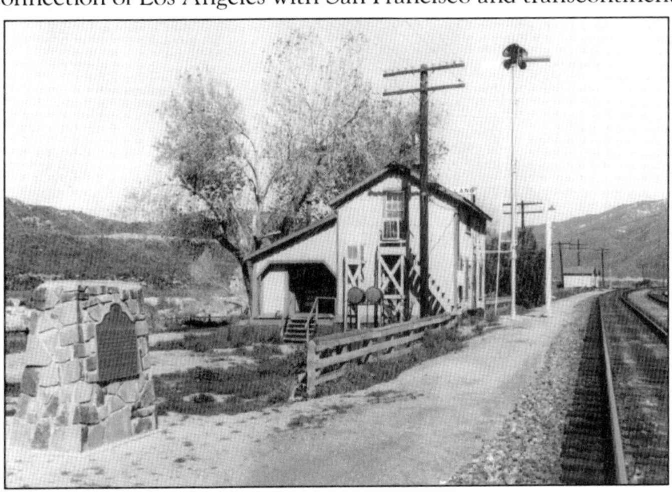

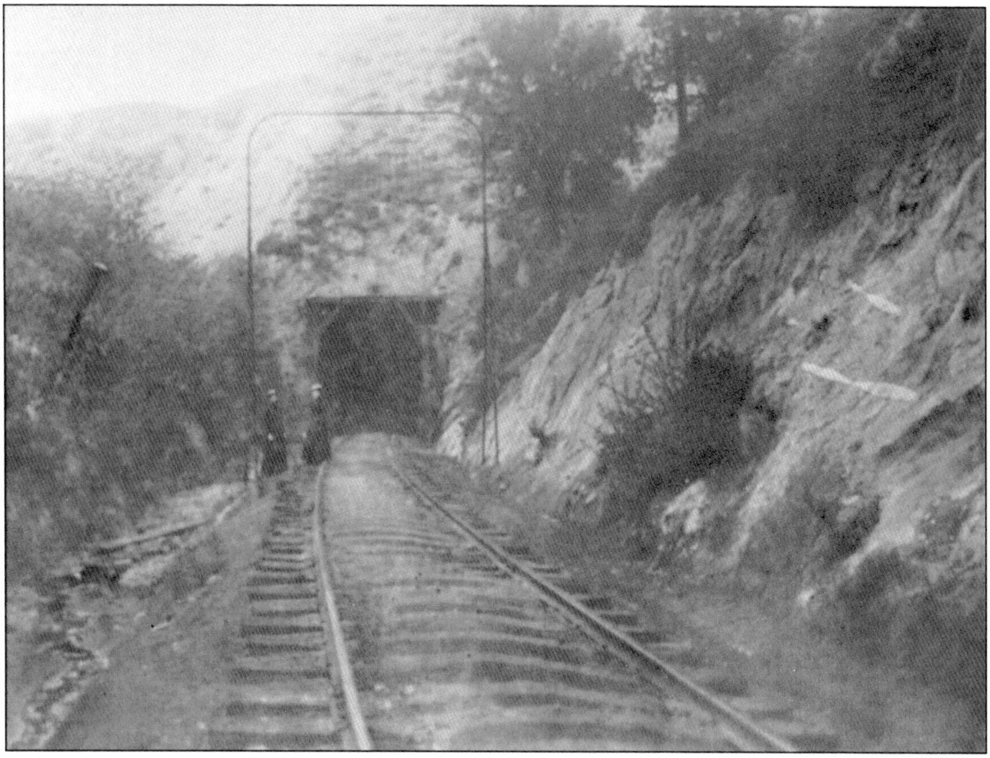

Before the railroads could become connected and thus become an integral part of Canyon Country's importance as a crossroads, other parts of the rail line had to be completed. The San Fernando Tunnel, completed in 1876 and shown in these two photographs, linked the Santa Clarita Valley with the San Fernando Valley. Prior to the project, those traveling by wagon had to go over the steep San Gabriel Mountains. (Courtesy of San Fernando Valley Historical Society.)

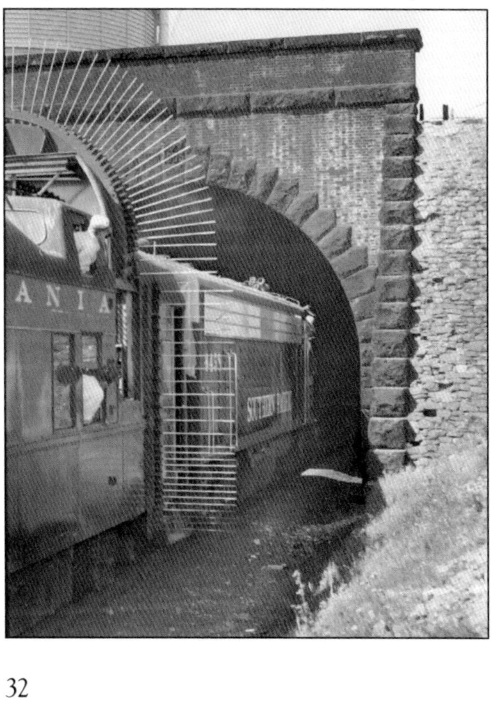

The San Fernando Tunnel, at 6,940 feet in length, was the third-longest tunnel in the nation and the fourth-longest tunnel in the world at the time of its construction. The opening measured 22 feet high and 16 feet wide. Using picks, shovels, drills, and explosives, two crews of laborers worked on either side of the hill, eventually meeting in the middle. When the crews met, their tunnels were only off by half an inch. The workers dug shafts to provide air and to transport debris. The tunnel caved in on a number of occasions during construction, killing or injuring a number of workers. Approximately 1,000 Chinese laborers worked on the tunnel. (Courtesy of San Fernando Valley Historical Society.)

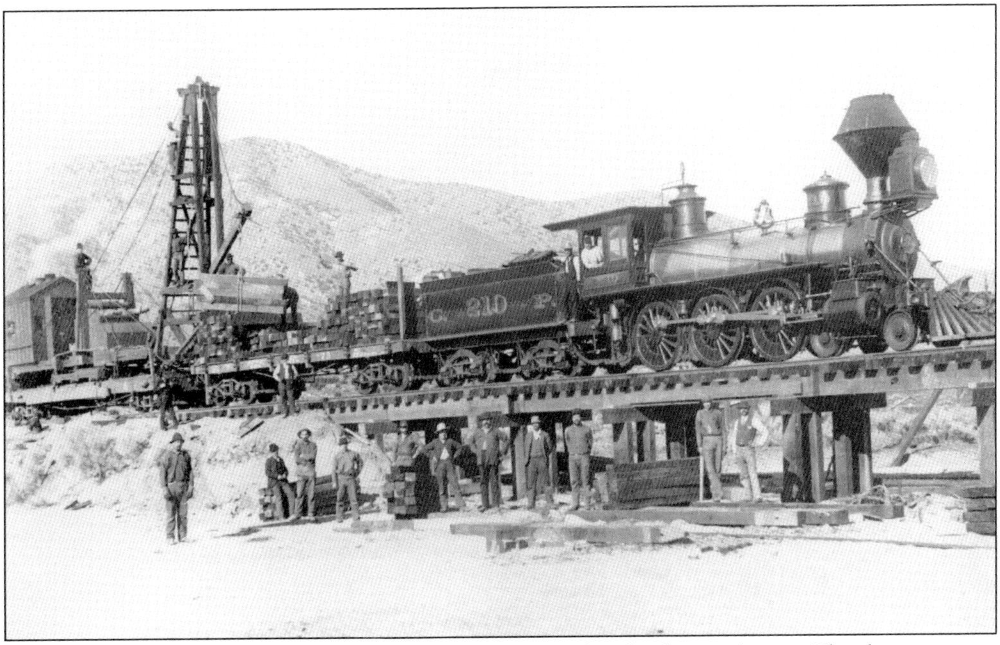

In the image above, engine No. 210 has pulled onto a low bridge in Acton. This location was useful in the hauling of products from the mines to San Pedro, a port in southern Los Angeles. The presence of locomotives in the Canyon Country area and eastward was a boon to the mining effort and helped to define the towns. The photograph below shows John and Gilla Kennedy and their family in front of their home in Ravenna in 1926. John Kennedy, who was originally from Kansas, was the railroad foreman at the Ravenna Station, a small but key venue used in transporting mining products.

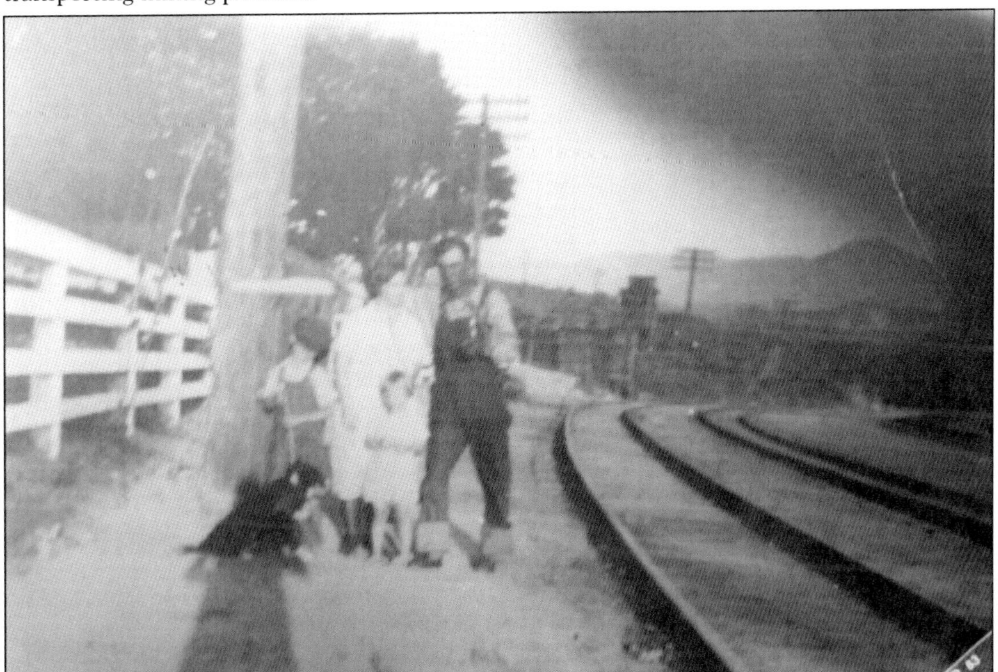

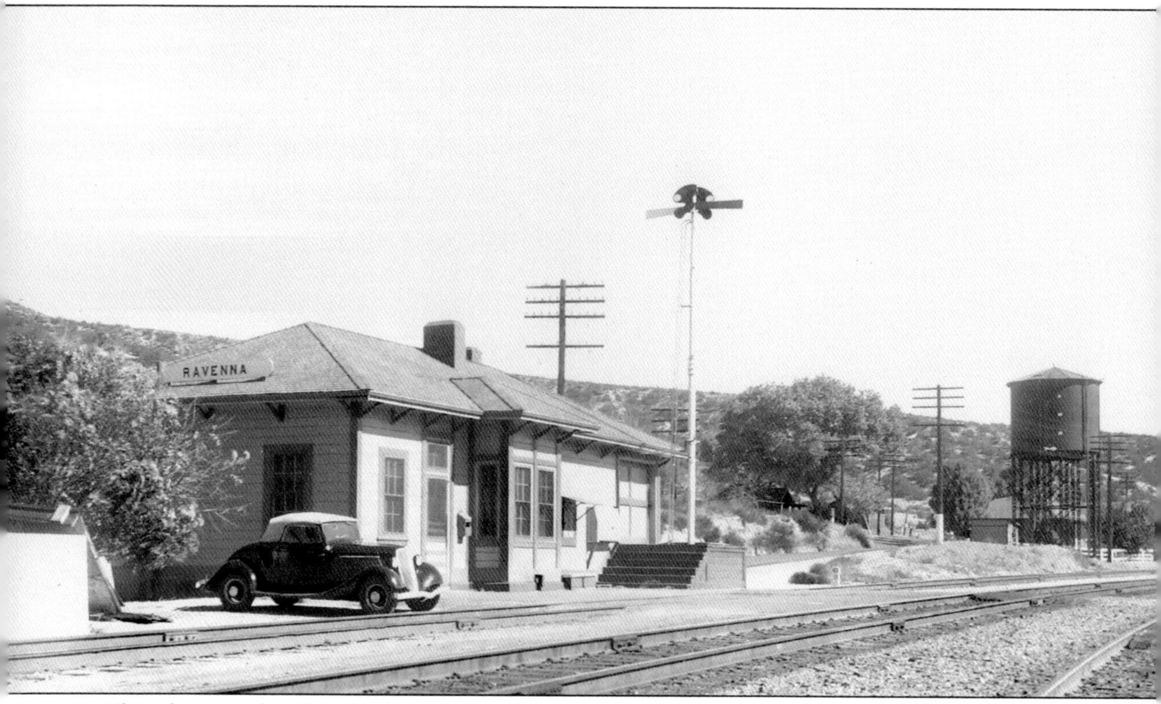

This photograph, taken in the vicinity of present-day Acton, shows the train station in Ravenna. The facility was fairly elaborate, considering there were probably fewer than 30 residents in the town. Located a few miles southwest of Acton in Soledad Canyon, Ravenna was originally called Soledad City. The small town was a collection of miners' cabins and tents, and it changed its location with every boom. When a post office was established there, authorities wanted to avoid confusion with the town of Soledad in Monterey County, so grocery store owner James O'Reilly suggested the tent city be named for the local saloonkeeper, Manuel Ravenna. The town officially became Ravenna on June 12, 1868. (Courtesy of Stephen Hayes.)

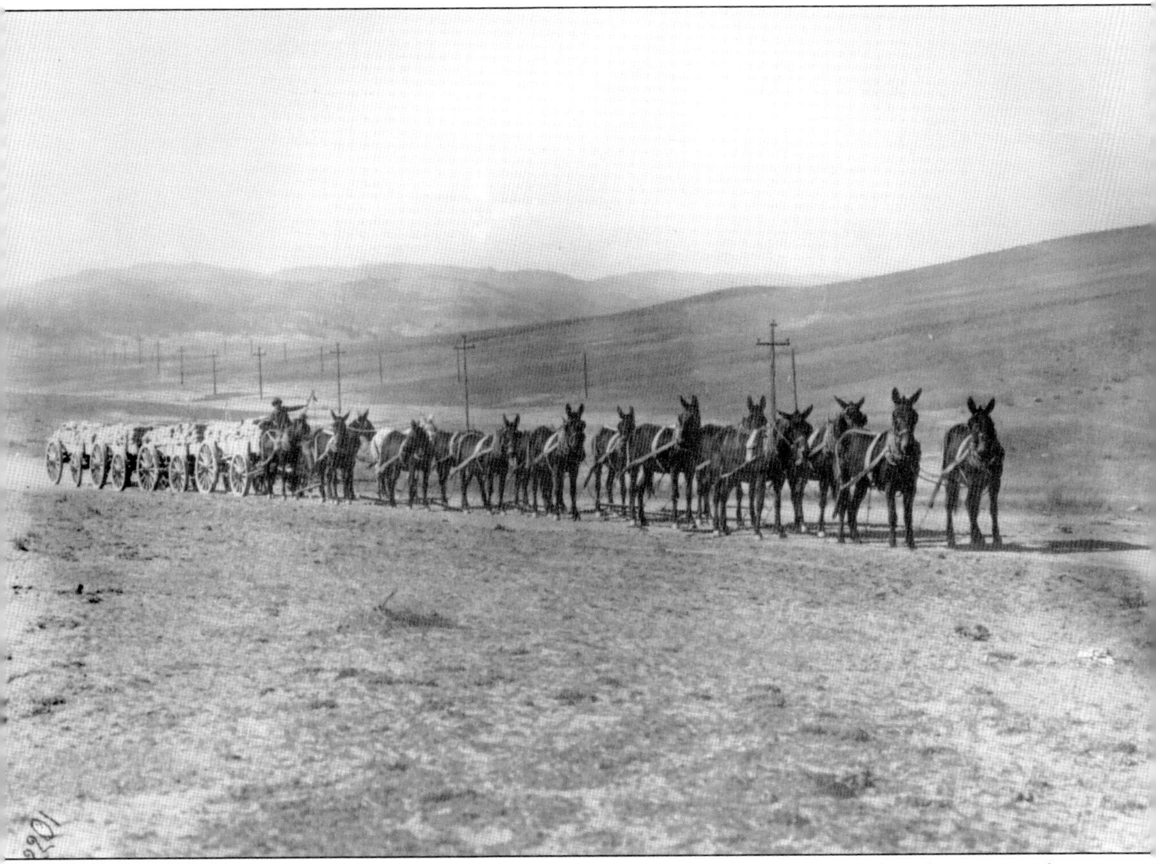

Soledad Canyon was the most direct route for transporting mining supplies and hauling minerals to market. The first large-scale freighting operation belonged to Remi Nadeau, who ran mule teams that served mines of the Cerro Gordo and Owens Valley, as well as Soledad mines. In 1870, Nadeau was employing more than 100 workers and running 80 teams with 14 mules to a team when he opened a new route to the Mojave Desert area from north of Ravenna. It was supposed to connect with a new Soledad Canyon road, but the project was never completed. Stagecoaches transported passengers via the San Francisquito Canyon route, where way stations with meals and overnight accommodations were available. This photograph, taken in Soledad Canyon in 1894, shows one of Nadeau's 14-mule teams demonstrating the length and strength needed to pull the freight. In the early 20th century, Nadeau's teams hauled freight for the construction of William Mulholland's Los Angeles Aqueduct.

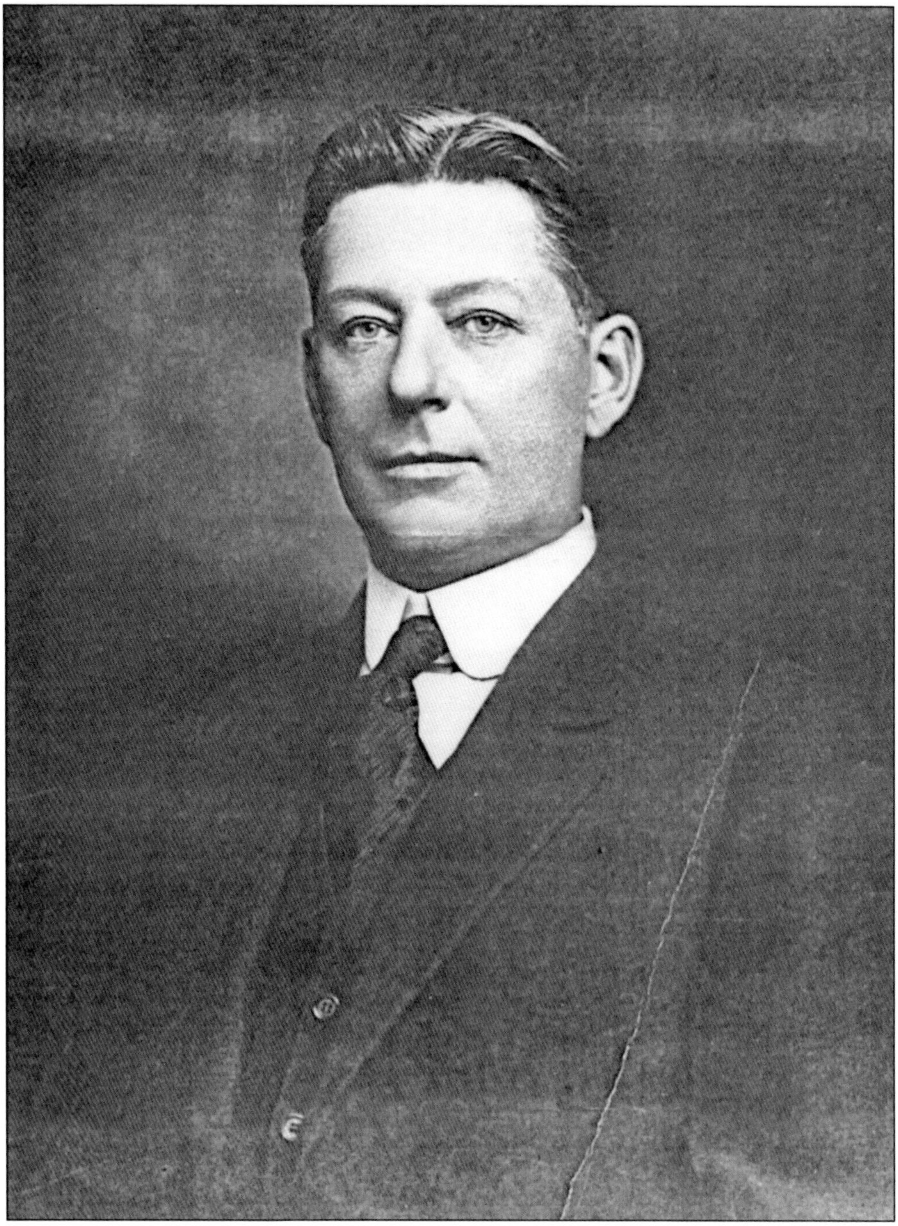

The Sterling Borax Mine, sometimes referred to as the Lang Mine, was located in Tick Canyon between Sierra Highway and Agua Dulce Canyon Road. In 1906, when gold prospectors Henry Shepherd and Louis Ebbenger found that the product in Tick Canyon was largely high-grade borate, they sold the mine to Thomas Thorkildsen (above), who had a borax mine on Frazier Mountain. He formed the Sterling Borax Company and replaced the mule teams, such as those used by Remi Nadeau, with a private, six-mile, standard-gauge railroad spur running from the mine to the Lang siding of the Southern Pacific Railroad. A dinkey hauled approximately 20,000 tons of ore to the Lang Station depot. The ore was then shipped to eastern Sterling Borax refineries for conversion to commercial borax. In 1921, Sterling Borax sold its nearly depleted mining operation to Pacific Coast Borax Company, which launched a scavenging operation to extract the remaining colemanite. It closed in 1922, and the plant was dismantled in 1926.

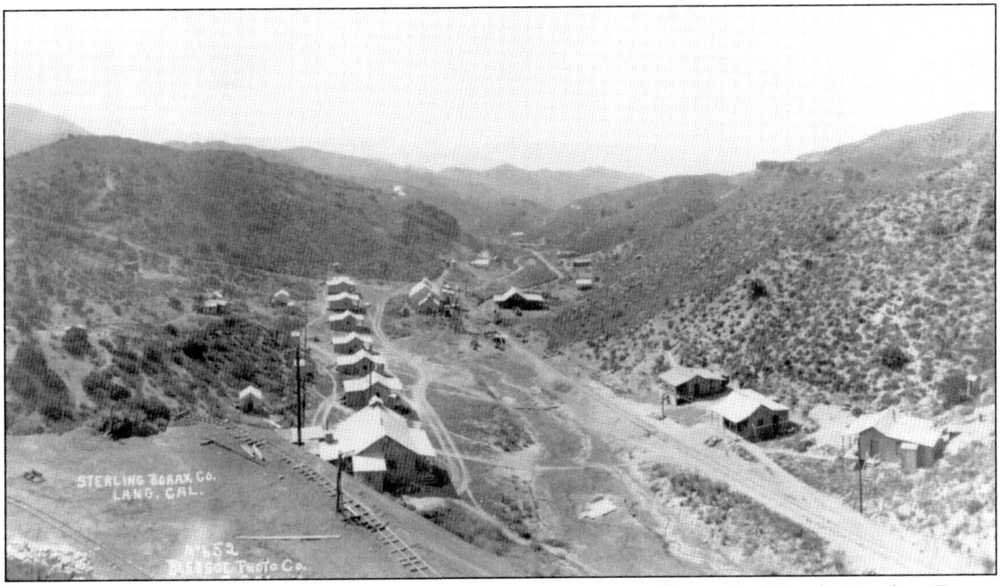

These images show the housing facilities and offices for miners who worked for the Sterling Borax Company in Lang. Mining in Tick Canyon began with gold prospecting, but the area was found to be rich in borate materials. At the Sterling Borax Mine, which was active from 1908 to 1918, colemanite was mined through two vertical shafts that were each 350 feet deep. Thorkildsen's Sterling Borax Company was a consolidation of borax interests, including Stauffer Chemical Company's Frazier Borate Mining Company, American Borax Company, the Brighton Chemical Company, and Thomas Thorkildsen & Company.

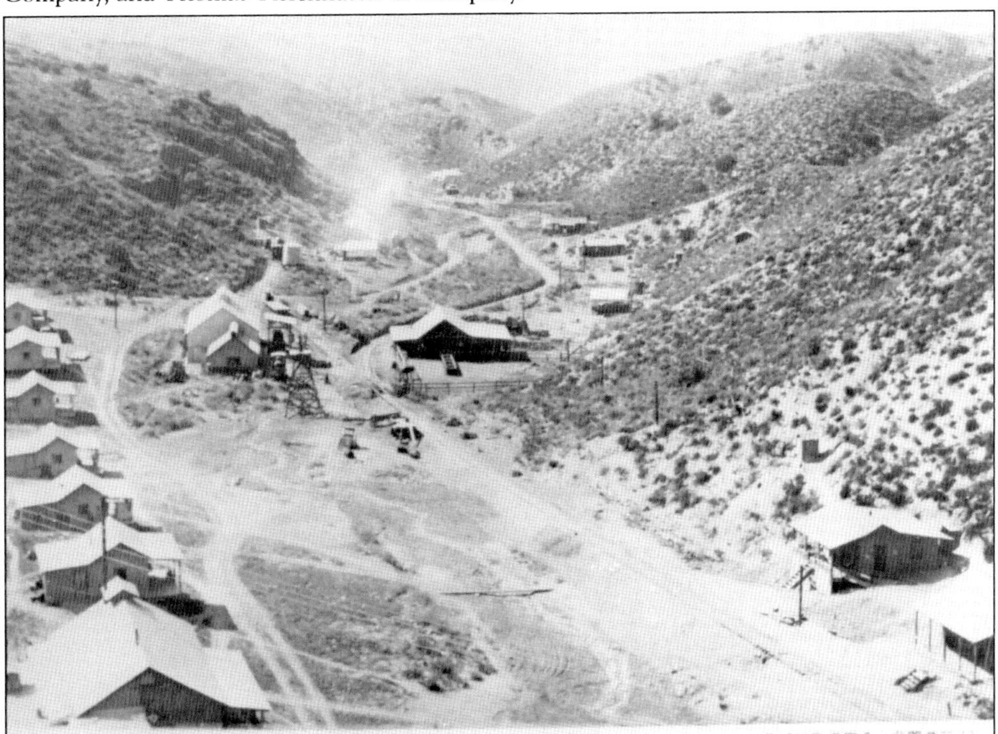

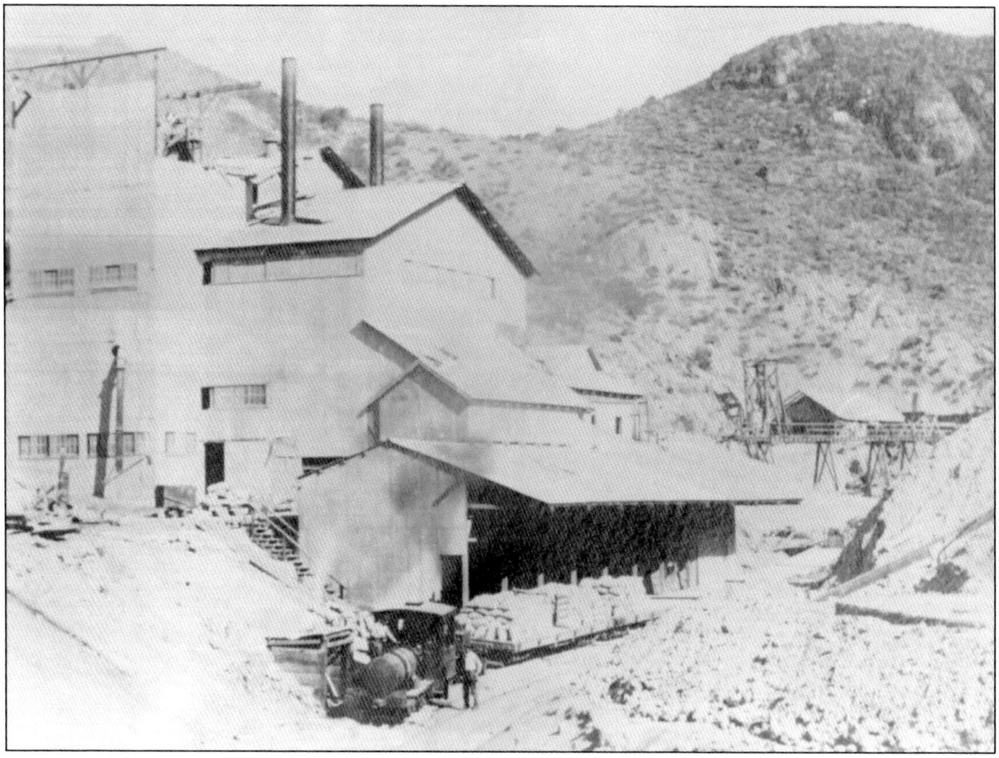

The mines in operation in the Canyon Country area were first established as the Soledad Mining District in 1861, when copper veins were found in the canyon; the district was gone by 1873. The Cedar Mining District—which once included 300 mines—was established in the Acton area by 1880 and produced gold, silver, and mercury.

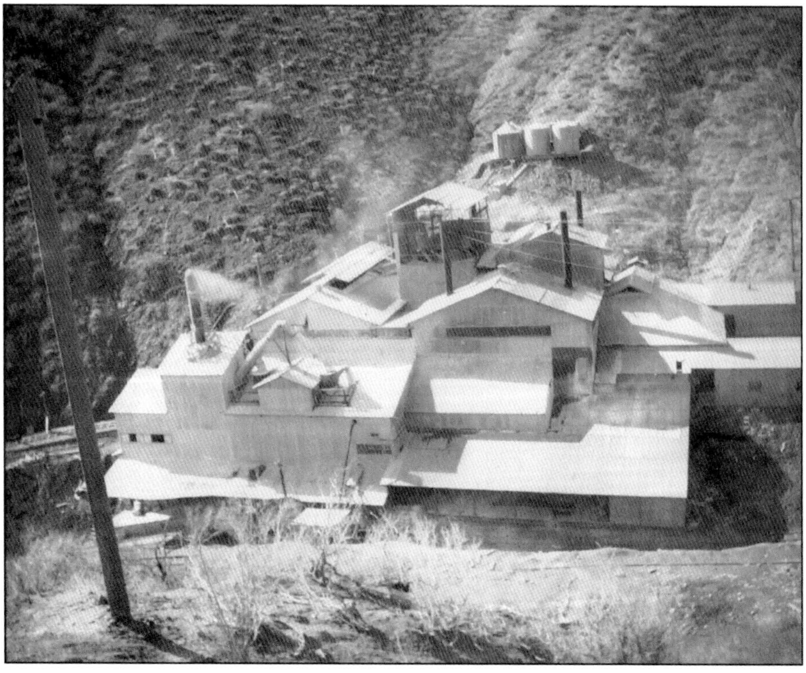

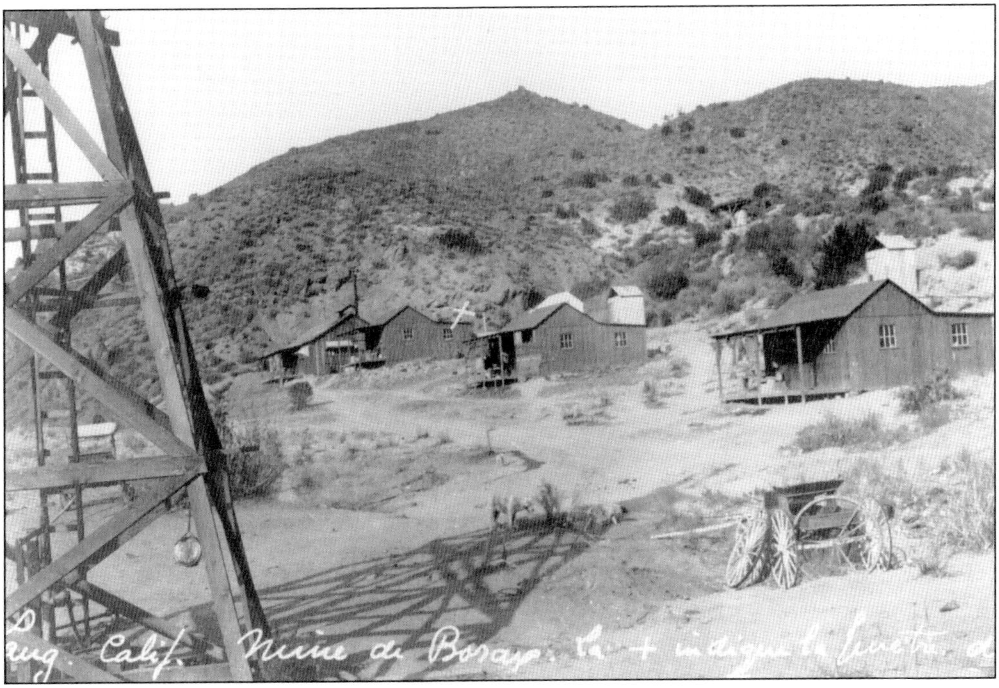

These two photographs depict the Sterling Borax Company operation. Below, Lillie B. and Henry Headley (facing the camera) are shown at the Borax mine; the mining area where they lived was first known as Soledad City and then Ravenna.

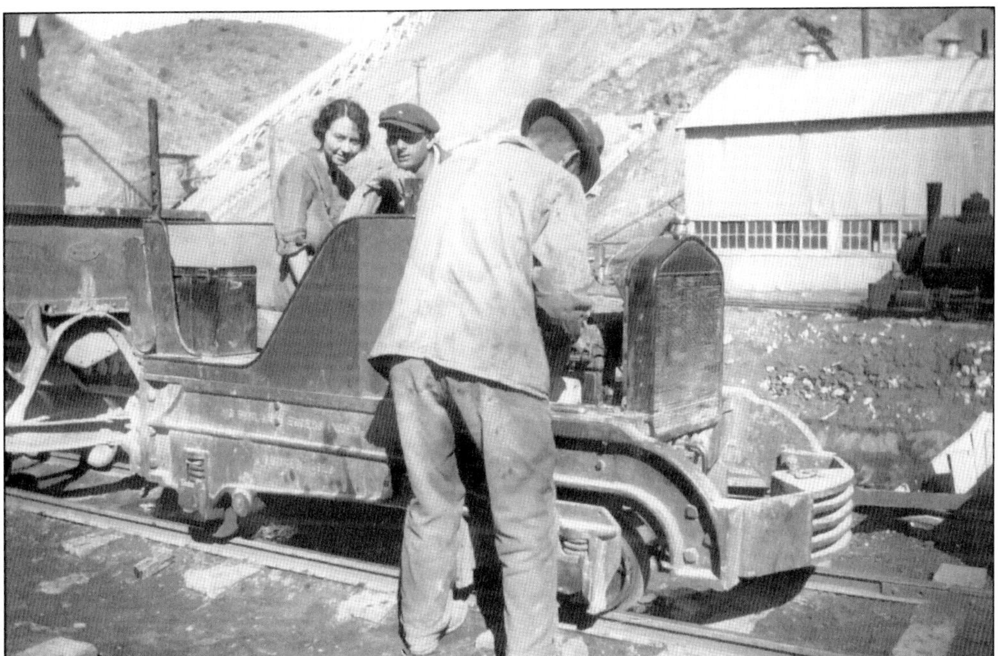

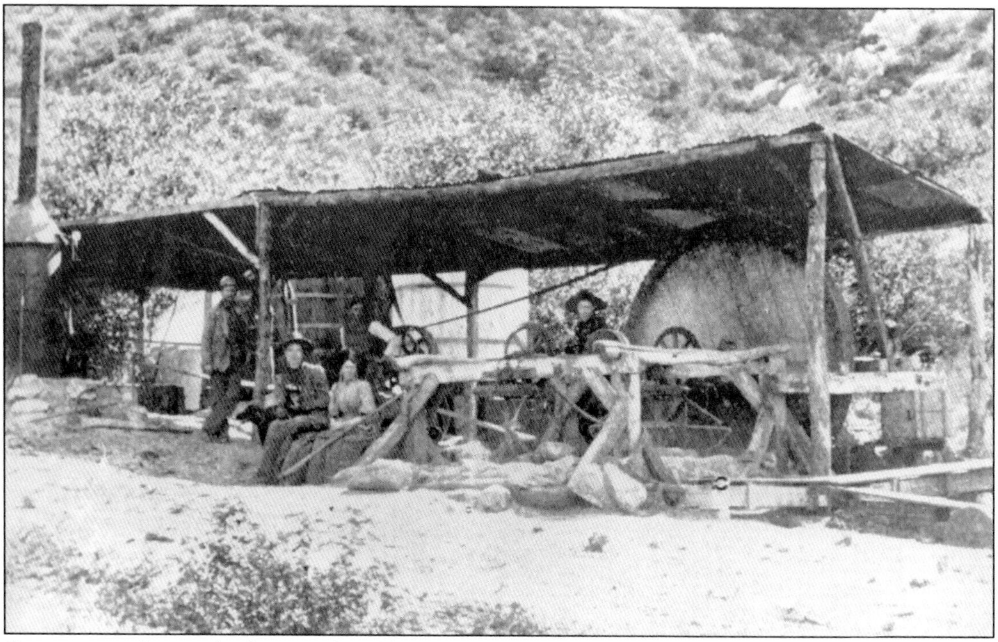

Once mineral veins had stopped yielding enough to stay in business, mines were abandoned by mining companies. Some of those venues were then occupied by men who would garner what was left from the mine. These men would erect arrastras (as pictured above), which contained large boulders that were dragged around in a stone trench by a mule or water wheel. Ore was pulverized and then panned for the gold, a process that required hard work and did not yield the quantity the earlier miners succeeded in finding. The men also found gold in the quartz from the Acton area and established a number of arrastras. The original miners would return during boomlets and set up steam-powered stamp mills (like the one pictured below) to extract the last of the ore.

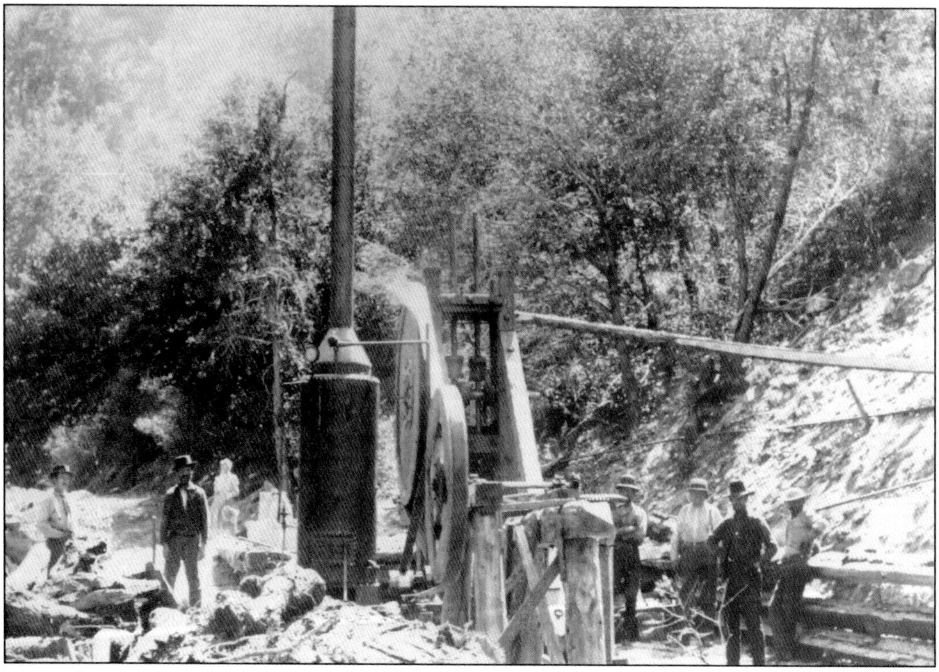

Three

Canyon Country Means Business

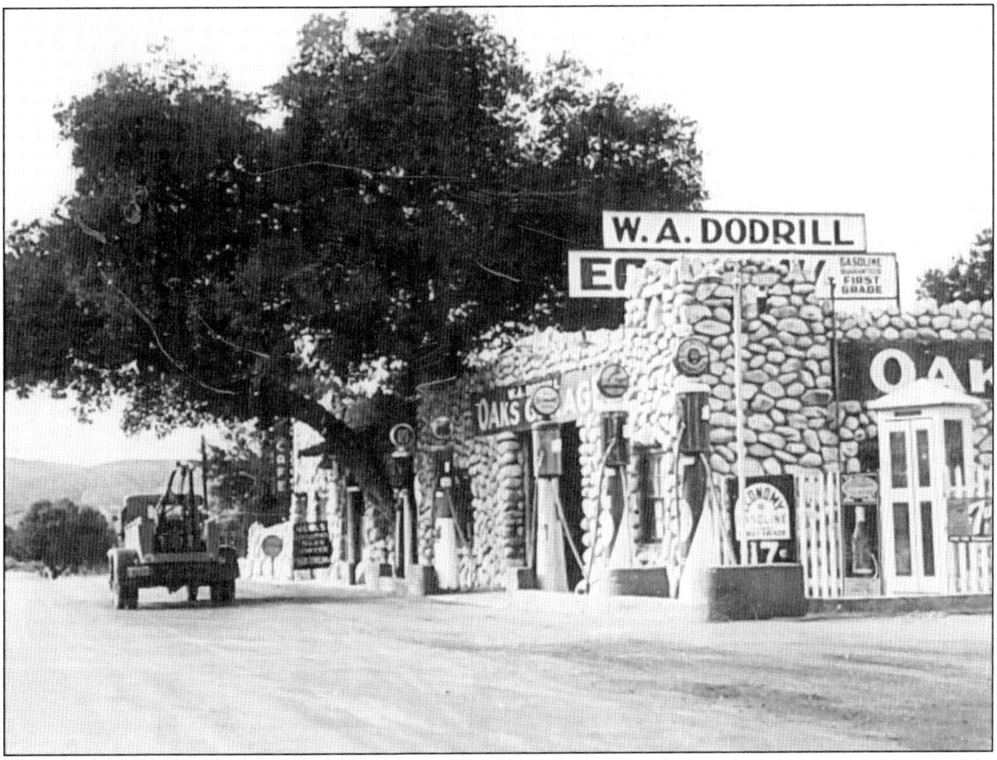

Mint Canyon saw the arrival of the William Arch Dodrill family around 1916. The Dodrills moved onto a piece of property on Sierra Highway, on the border of Agua Dulce and Canyon Country. They erected a tent-covered home in the back and, in 1917, opened the Oaks Garage service station in the front. Originally from England, the Dodrills first operated from a wooden structure that grew to include a snack bar. In 1923, the snack bar was upgraded to a diner when the owners brought in boulders from a quarry in Quartz Hill and added a café to the building, creating a structure that locals called the "rock house," which is pictured here in the 1930s. (Courtesy of Juan Alonso.)

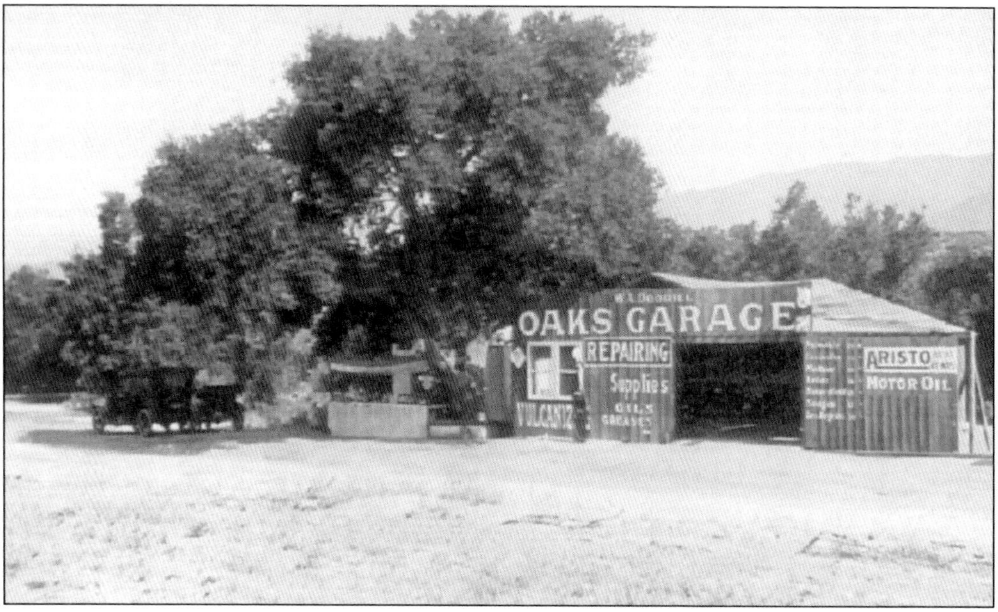

Before remodeling turned W.A. Dodrill's Oaks Garage into the rock house, it was the wooden structure pictured in the c. 1916 image above. Oaks Garage expanded within its first decade, as the c. 1923 image below reveals. By the 1930s, the unique building had acquired several monikers, including "Castle Oaks Garage and Café." In the 1960s, the diner at Oaks Garage was again expanded to include a counter/bar and tables inside. The building was featured in the 1971 movie *Duel*, one of Steven Spielberg's first directorial efforts; for the movie, the film's crew placed a sign over the door that read "Chuck's Café." (Both courtesy of Juan Alonso.)

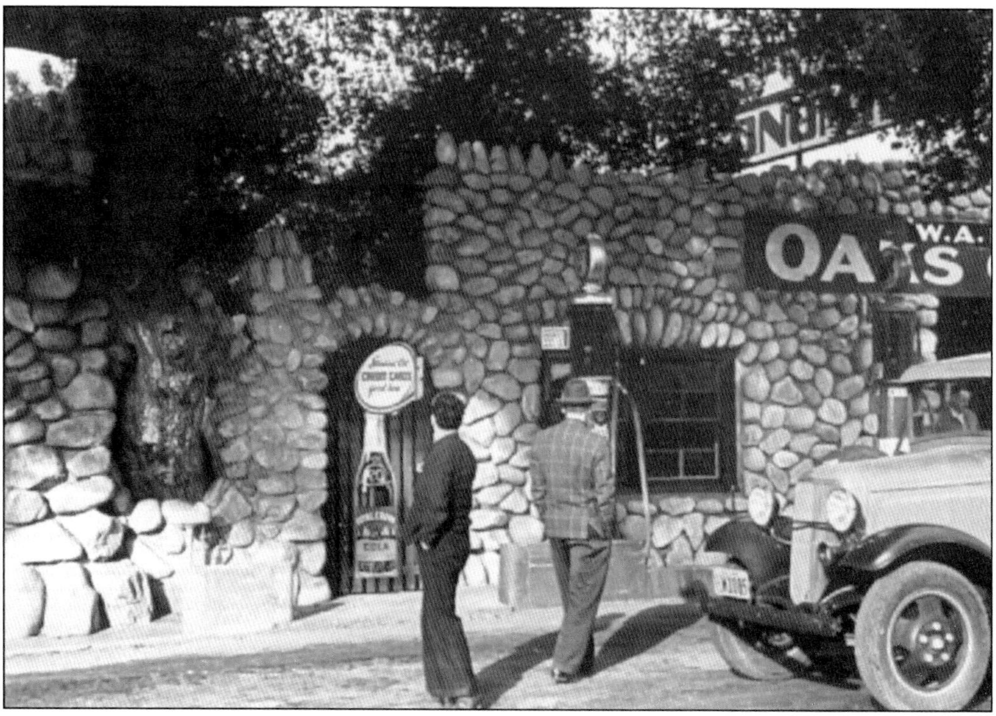

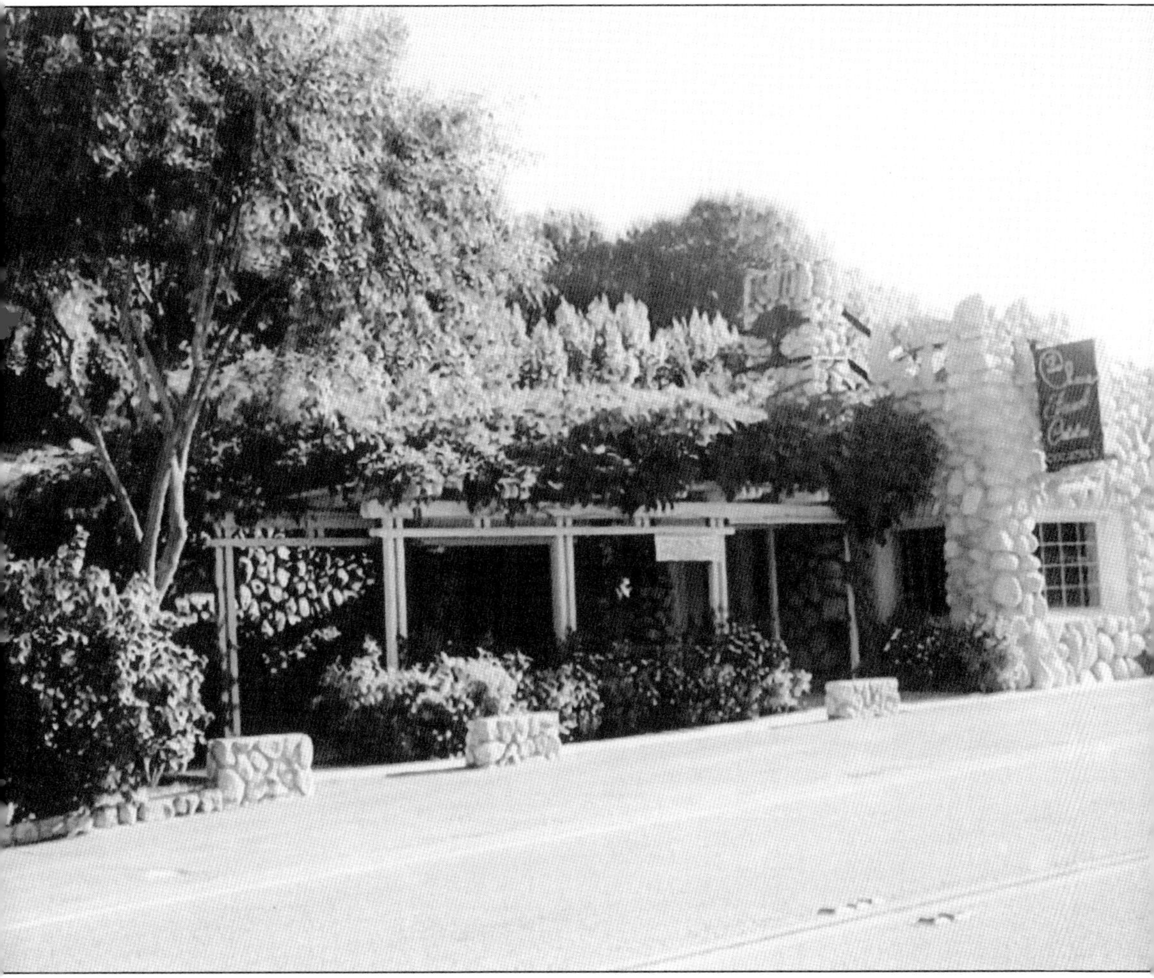

In 1980, restaurateur Juan Alonso leased the Oaks Garage building and grounds, then purchased them one year later. In September 1980, the building reopened as a French restaurant called Le Chêne French Cuisine, drawing patrons from all over Los Angeles who came for its large wine list and exotic dishes such as bison, ostrich, and antelope. Alonso also owned other properties, including vineyards and the Sierra Pelona Motel just north of the "rock house" building. (Courtesy of Juan Alonso.)

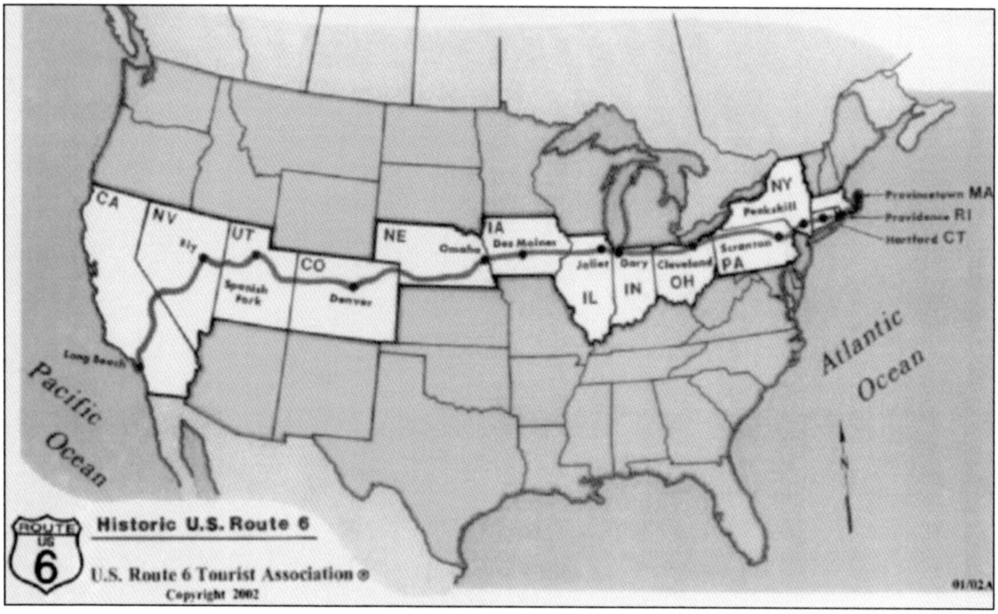

As more businesses opened on Mint Canyon Road (later Sierra Highway), it became more than just a center of town for Canyon Country. It was a stretch of US Route 6, an interstate highway that spanned the longest distance in the United States, at 3,652 miles, between Provincetown, Massachusetts, and Long Beach, California. Route 6, first conceived by the Joint Board on Interstate Highways, became a transcontinental highway when it extended to Long Beach in 1937. It was shortened in 1965 when the route was cut off at Bishop, California. In July 2007, the State of California approved California State Resolution ACR 26, which designated the route as having "served as the main street for many California cities and towns," and calling for signage to acknowledge the route's "state and local historical significance." The sign shown below was placed in the mid-20th century, when the name "Grand Army of the Republic Highway" was adopted for Route 6, and in 1953, a formal dedication took place in Long Beach, California. (Both courtesy of US Route 6 Tourist Association.)

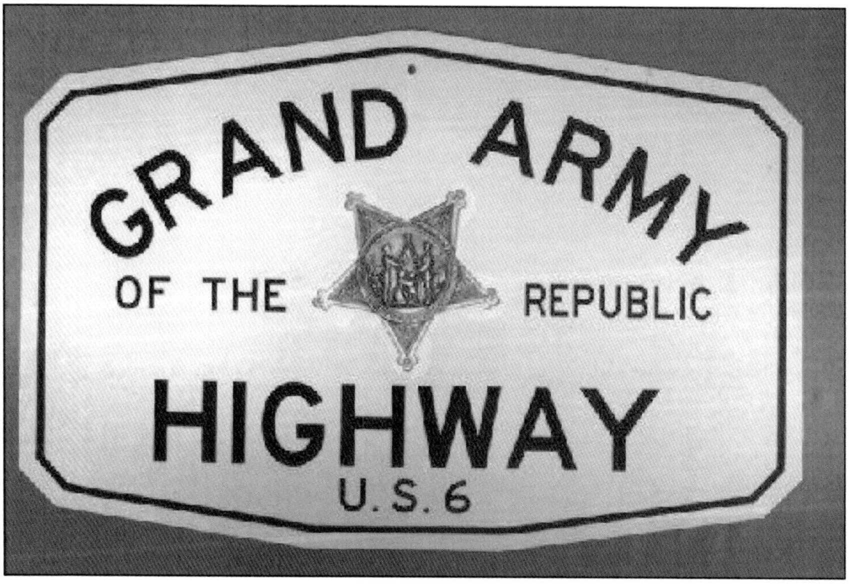

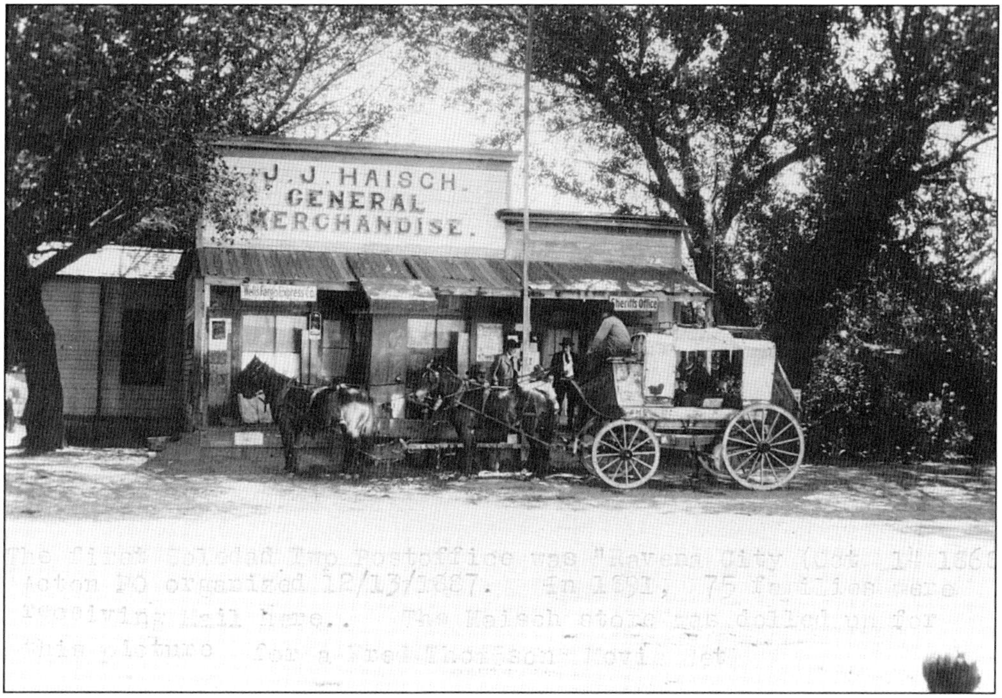

The first "Soledad Township" post office was established on October 14, 1868, and the "Acton" post office was organized on December 18, 1887. In 1891, there were 75 families receiving mail at the J.J. Haisch Store. In the c. 1926 photograph above, taken in front of the J.J. Haisch Store in the early days of Canyon Country, the scene is set for filming a movie starring silent-movie star Fred Thomson. The image below was obtained from a scrapbook of a Depression-era member of the Civilian Conservation Corps, Lee Minor, who wrote below the photo: "Haisch's General Store/One of the three or so stores in Acton, California—A favorite hangout." (Below, courtesy of Steve Minor; photograph by Lee Minor.)

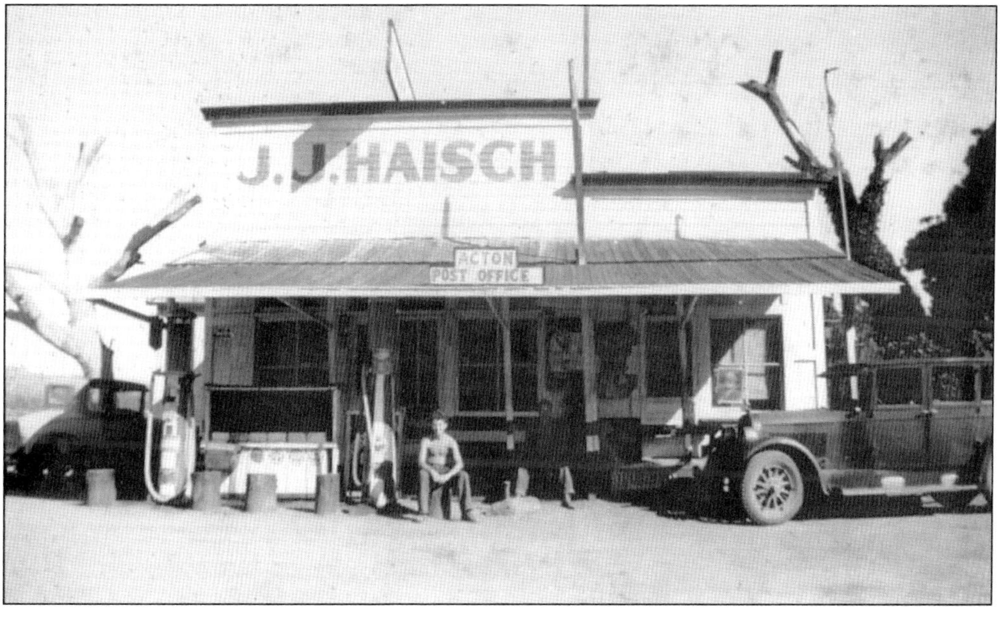

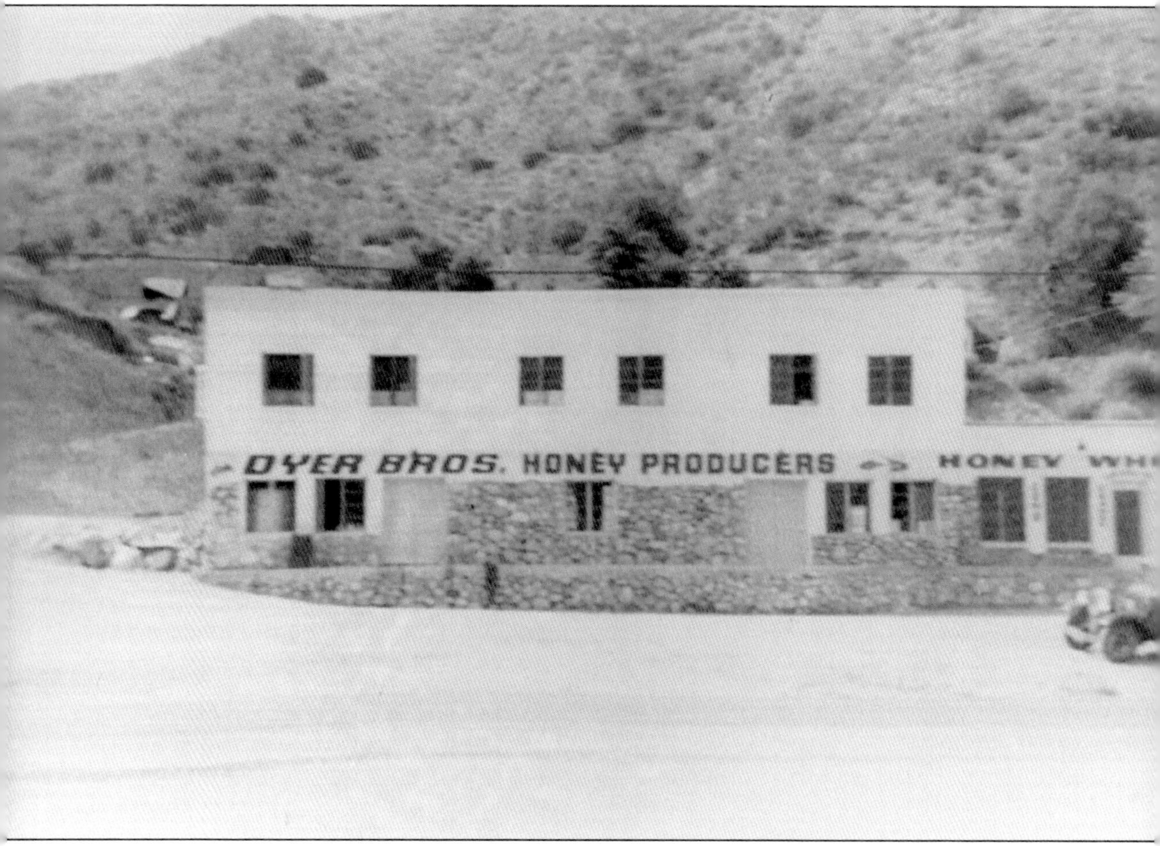

Further south on Sierra Highway stood the Honey House, pictured above sometime before 1968. In 1889, Commodore Perry Dyer moved his family from Missouri to California to run a ranch and keep bees. He started the Dyer family's honey business in Escondido Canyon, and his son, James T. Dyer Sr., continued the business. In 1943, James's sons, Jim and Willis, decided to expand the business and began construction on the concrete building on Sierra Highway (US Route 6). They opened the honey house in 1954, and the Dyers' business produced, sold, and distributed tons of honey.

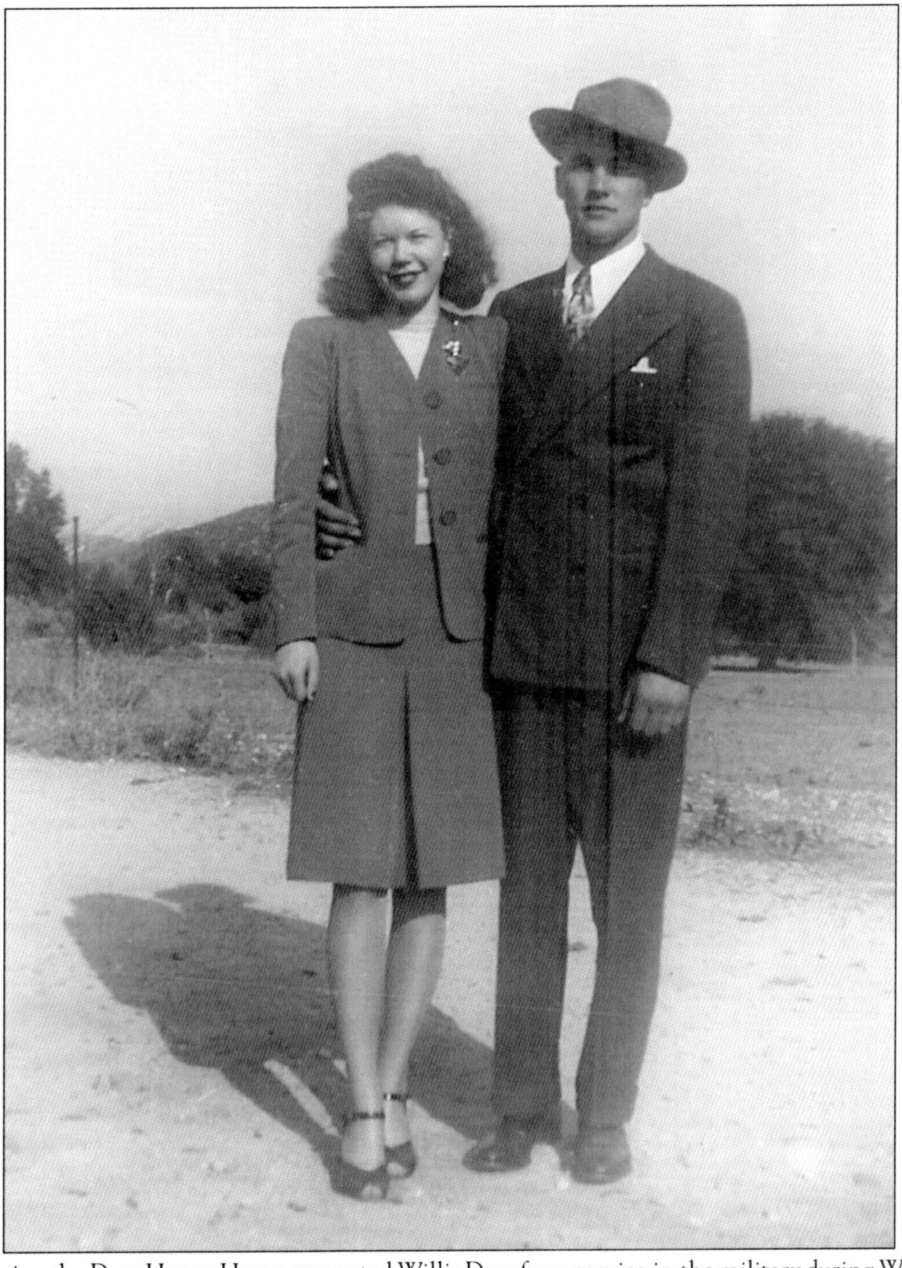

Running the Dyer Honey House exempted Willis Dyer from service in the military during World War II, as honey was considered very important to the war effort. Willis and his brother Jim later split the business, with Jim taking over the operation in Escondido Canyon and Willis keeping the Honey House on Sierra Highway. In 1968, Willis sold the honey business to Margaret and Joe Warmuth, pictured here around 1941. The Warmuth family had a 3,000-colony bee pasture in Sand Canyon and had been beekeeping in Sylmar since 1953. The Warmuths renamed the business Warmuth Honey House and used the location to process the honey and operate a retail store. After Joe died in 1985, Margaret and her daughter, Margleen, ran the store, expanding it to include a saddle and tack shop. Twenty years later, the Warmuths sold the property to College of the Canyons for its new Canyon Country campus. (Courtesy of Mary Warmuth Sathre.)

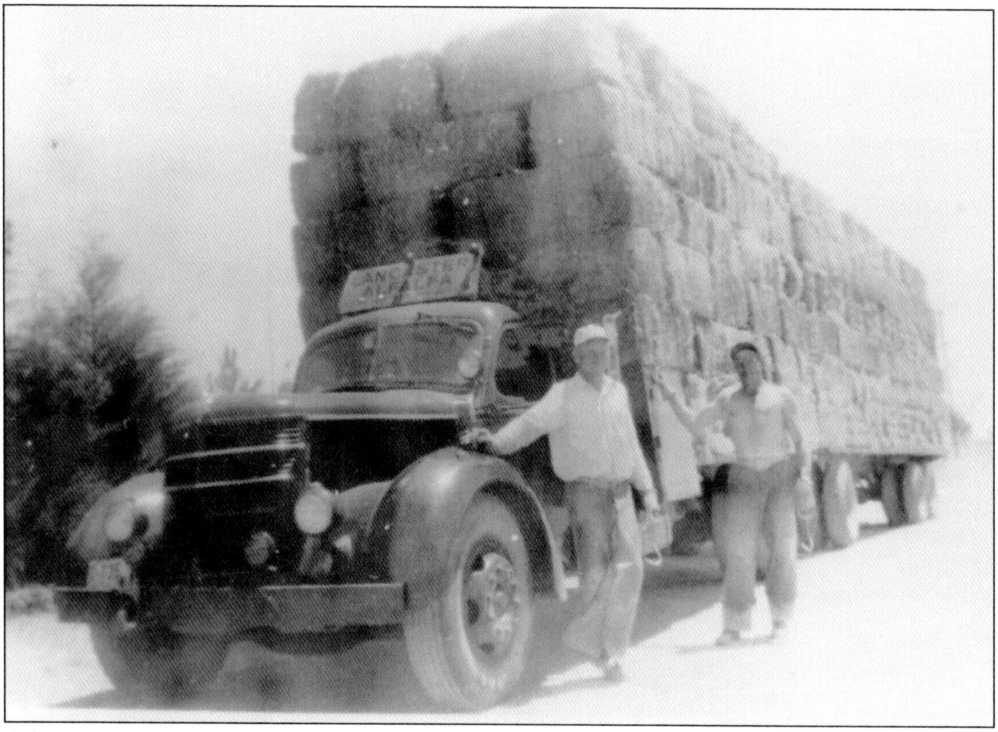

Odie Fox, founder of Fox Feed in Canyon Country, was born in Oklahoma in 1915 and went west during the Depression to work in the hay fields of the Imperial Valley. In the 1940s image above, Fox (left) stands with an unidentified friend next to one of the hay trucks, which he drove throughout California on his delivery route. At times over the years, Fox purchased more modern hay trucks, including the one pictured below that had a personalized cab door. Odie and his son Jerry Fox worked together in the 1960s and 1970s, delivering hay to dairies and opening a storefront on Sierra Highway in Canyon Country in 1976. (Both courtesy of Fox Feed.)

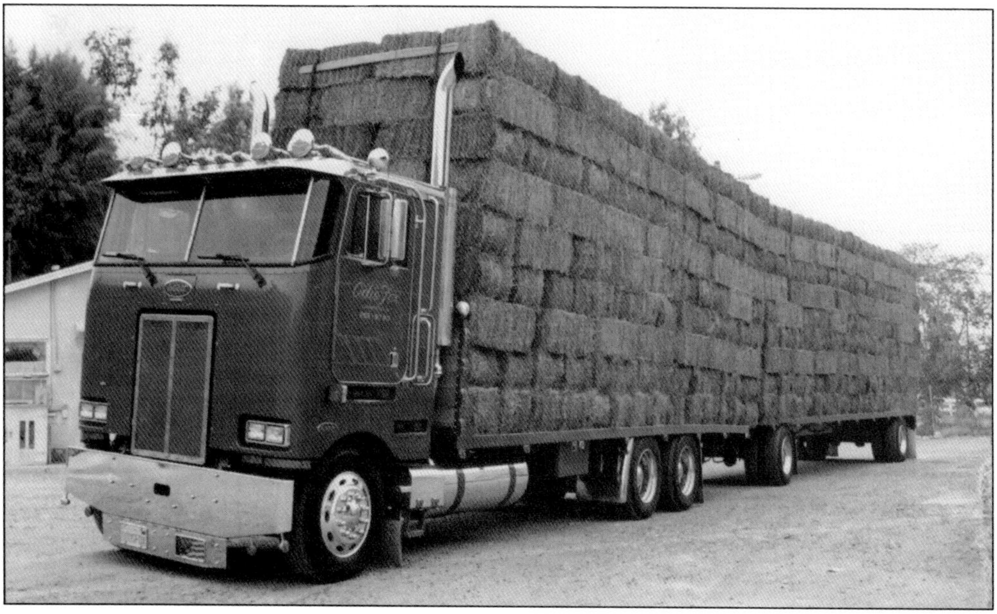

In the 1977 photograph at right, Odie Fox stands in the doorway of his first Fox Feed store on Sierra Highway in Canyon Country. The store was remodeled in 1988 and expanded to include a range of pet foods, horse tack, livestock products, and clothing. (Courtesy of Fox Feed.)

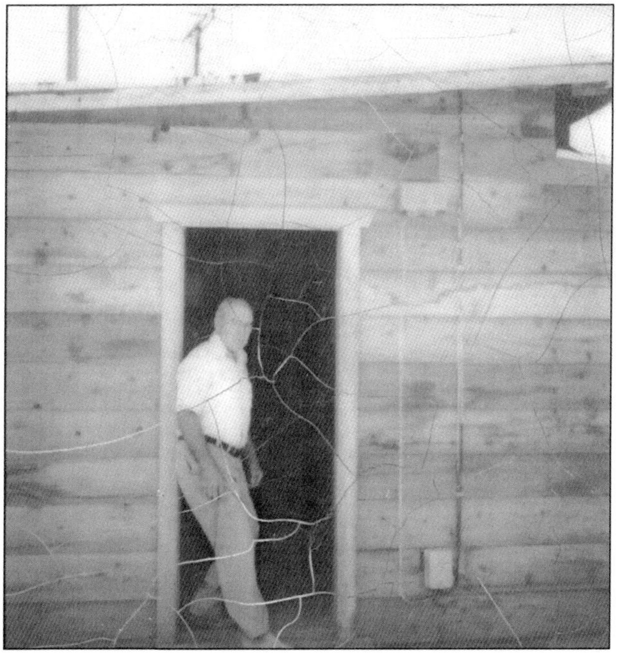

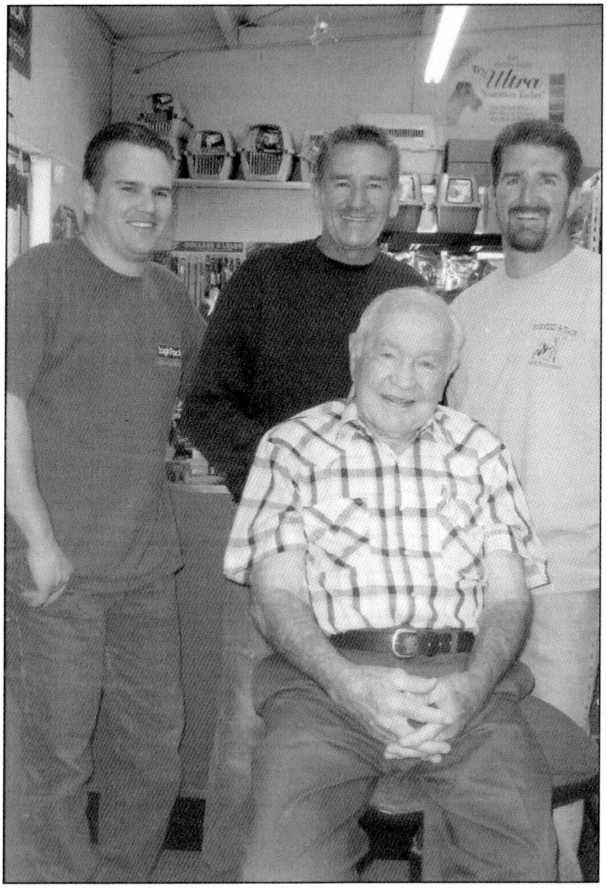

Odie's son and grandsons joined him in the business. Standing behind him in the image at left are his grandsons, Jeremy (left) and Brett (right), and his son, Jerry. Odie continued to work into the 21st century, three decades after opening the store, often doing business with farmers by telephone. He died on June 19, 2008, at the age of 93. (Courtesy of Fox Feed.)

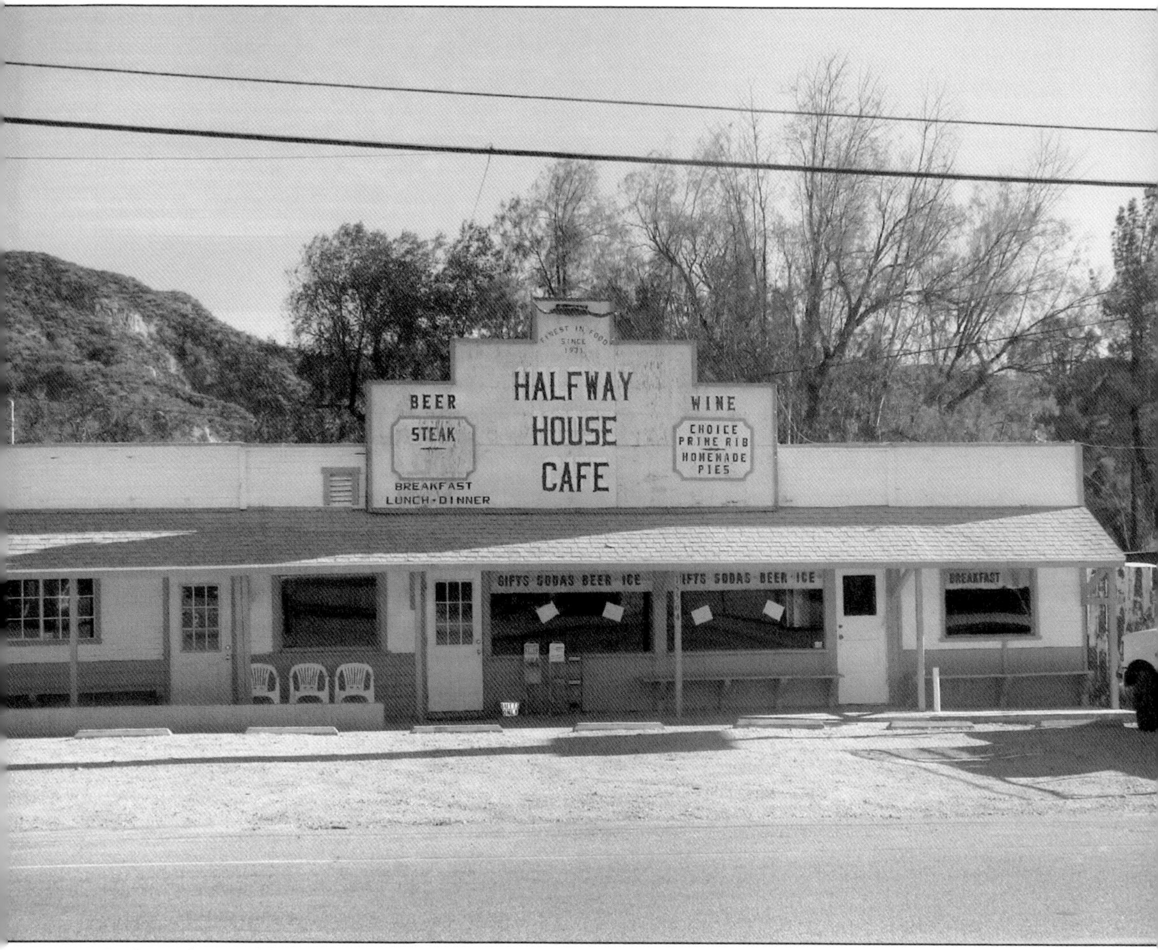

Before the Halfway House Café was established in 1931, the venue was a trading post for farmers coming from Palmdale to meet with Los Angeles marketplace personnel. This led to the café's name, as it was located halfway between Palmdale and Los Angeles. In the 1960s, the Halfway House began to serve as a location for shooting films and television shows. (Courtesy of Halfway House Café.)

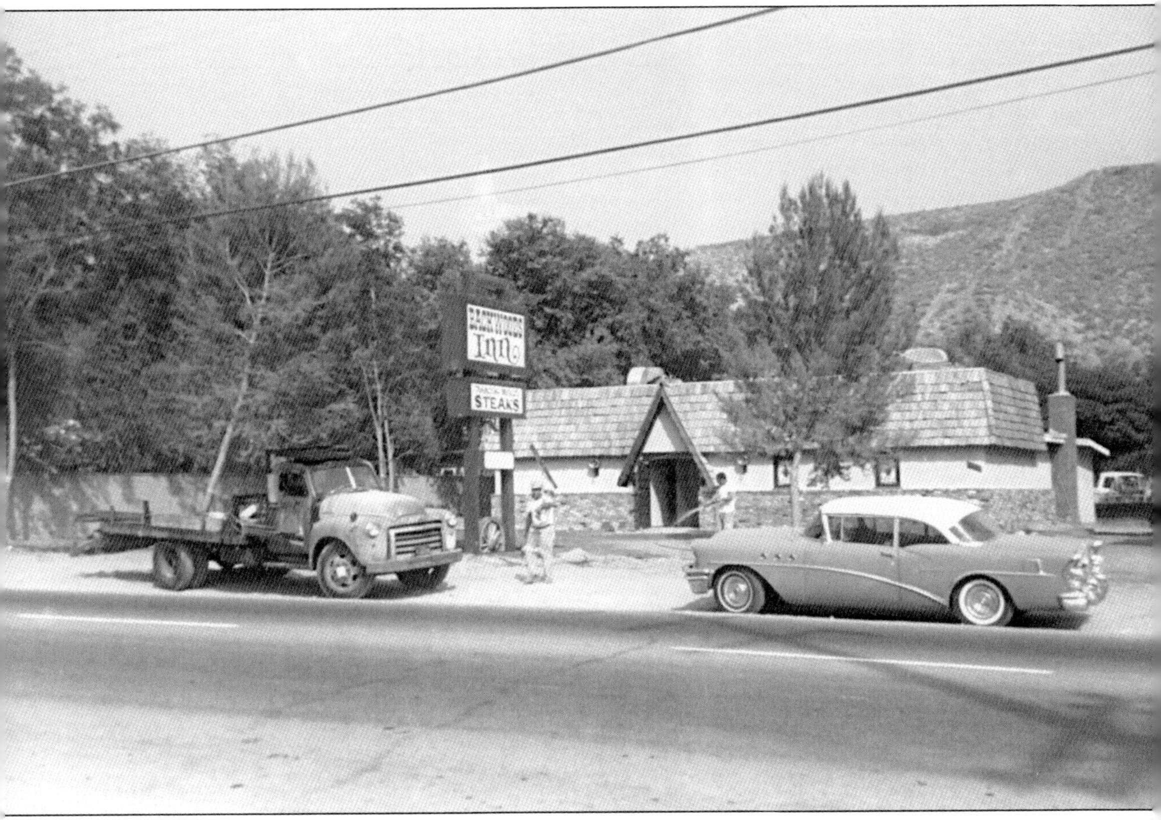

In the mid-1960s, Jerry Woods purchased a house belonging to the Bishop family on Sierra Highway, and Woods chose to convert it into a restaurant. The building is seen here during its reconstruction. Much of the interior was changed, but a fireplace was kept intact for the center of the restaurant's dining room. Woods opened The Backwoods Inn for business in 1966. (Courtesy of Carol Ohler.)

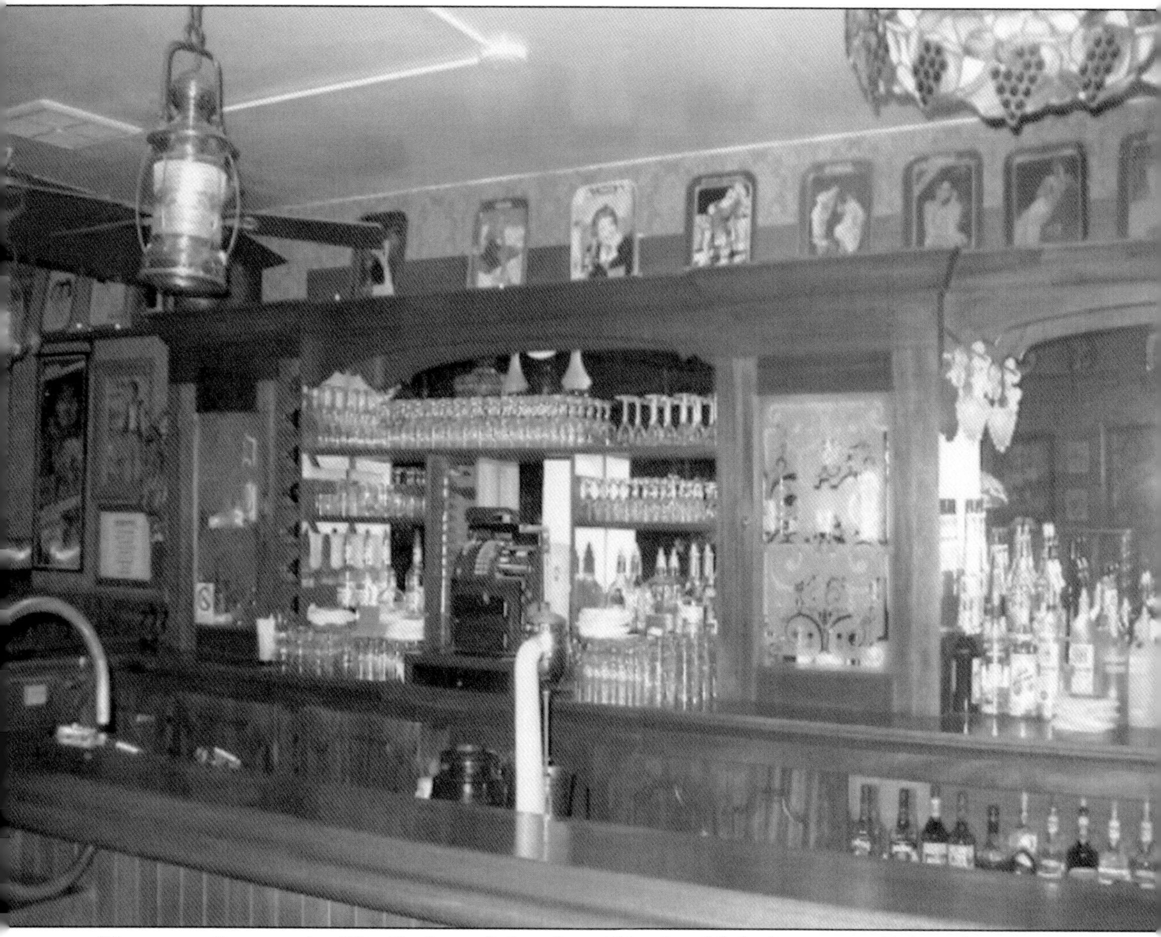

Two years after opening The Backwoods Inn, Jerry Woods sold the business to Bob and Rose Ohler, the sister and brother-in-law of his wife, Lee. The Ohlers took ownership and served as bartender and waitress to keep the business rolling. Rose gathered nostalgic collectibles to decorate the restaurant, as shown in this photograph of The Backwoods Inn's interior. In 1978, she purchased an entire wall from an old drugstore, complete with telephone booth and pharmacy drawers, and the couple added a separate room to the building. (Courtesy of Carol Ohler.)

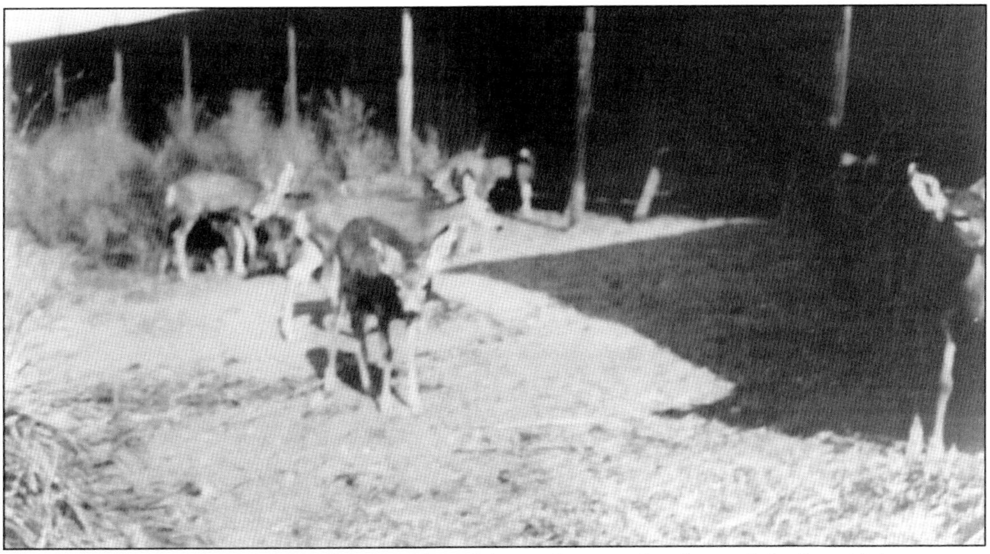

Remi Nadeau, the grandson and namesake of the mule-team freighter of the late 19th century, bought land in Canyon Country and befriended his neighbor, pioneer resident John W. Mitchell of Soledad Canyon. The two men partnered in a cattle-ranching business, and their adjoining ranches became the venue for annual roundups, which were widely attended events in the valley. An even bigger draw was the innovative Nadeau's Deer Farm (above), established in 1927, which became a popular tourist attraction. Nadeau died in 1941, and in 1946, Helm and Earle Schmidt purchased Nadeau's 1,800-acre plot of land and opened the 6-S Ranch Airpark. A 1948 Los Angeles Local Aeronautical Chart revealed a 2,600-foot unpaved runway, and a 1949 chart described a hangar on the south side of the field. The aerial photograph below shows an asphalt runway with a parallel taxiway. The site was located on the northwest side of the intersection of modern-day Whites Canyon and Soledad Canyon Roads. Fun-seeking teenagers from the late 1940s to the late 1950s claimed to have used the facility as a drag strip when it was not in operation. After Helm Schmidt died in 1960, his heirs sold the acreage to developers who then used the land as the site for the tract of homes called North Oaks.

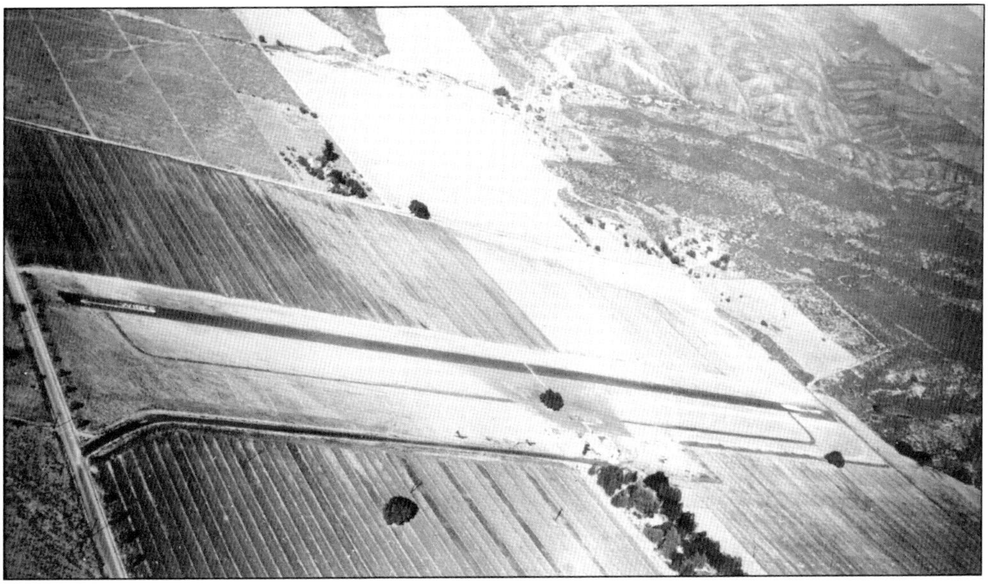

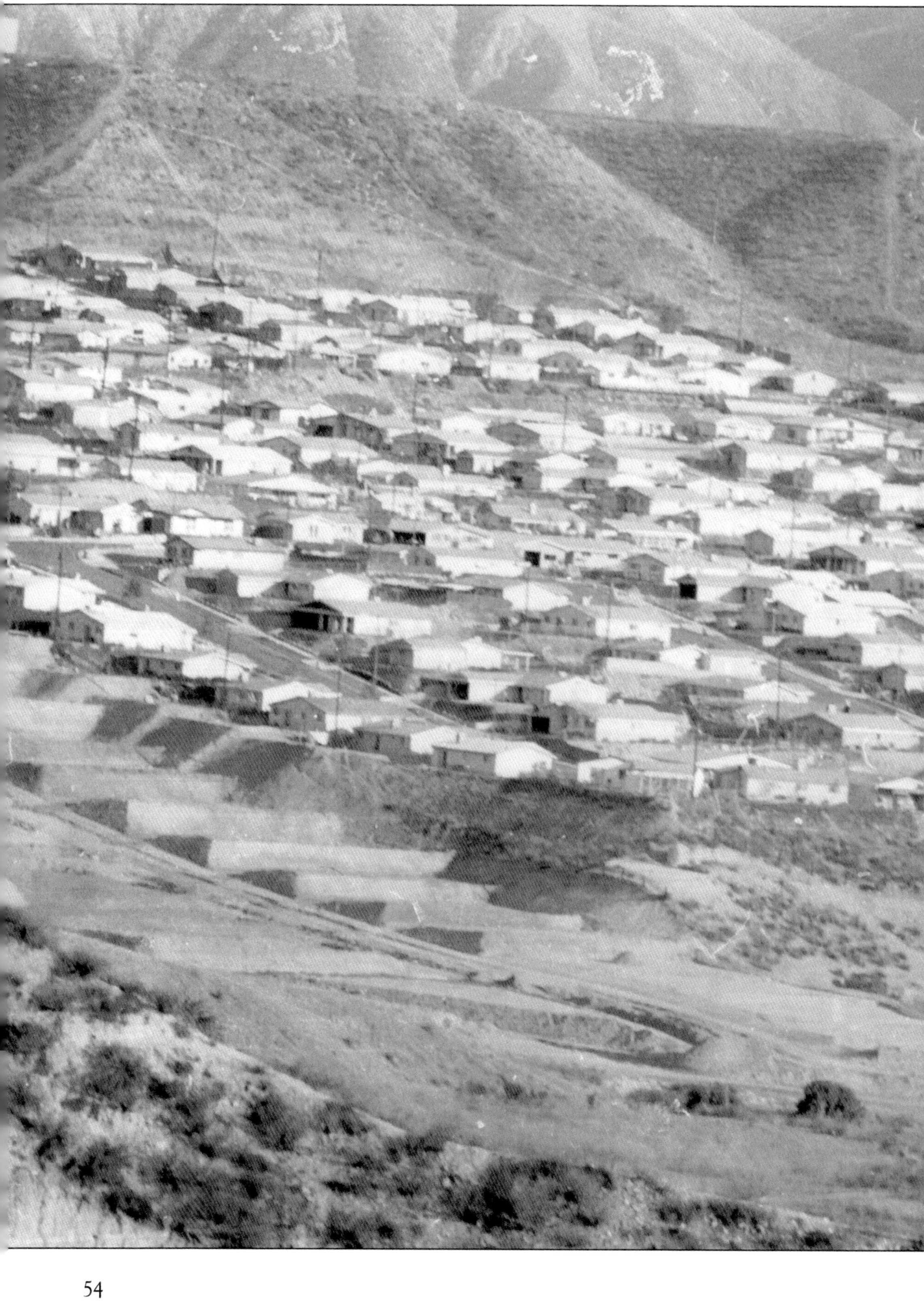

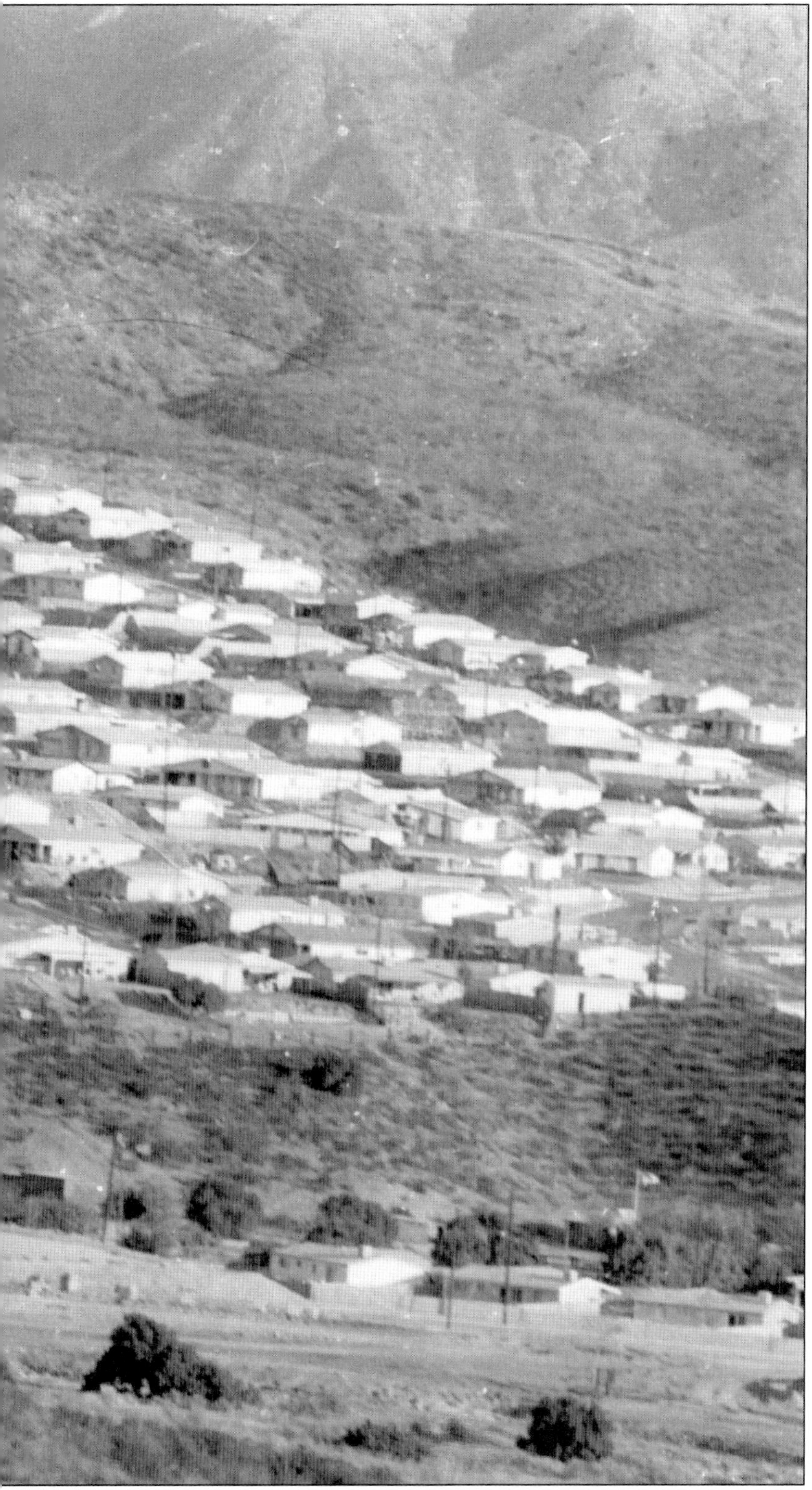

The 6-S Ranch Airpark was closed and sold to J.H. Snyder, a commercial developer, after Helm Schmidt's death in 1960. The land became a new part of history when Snyder developed the North Oaks residential tract, the first housing development in Canyon Country and the second in the Santa Clarita Valley. The first housing tract in the valley had been the 15-home Rancho Santa Clarita tract built by the Bonelli family in 1947 in modern-day Saugus, near Seco (Dry) Canyon. This 1969 aerial view of the North Oaks site was taken from the east side, looking southwest. Nothing is left of the airstrip; in its place are rows of houses.

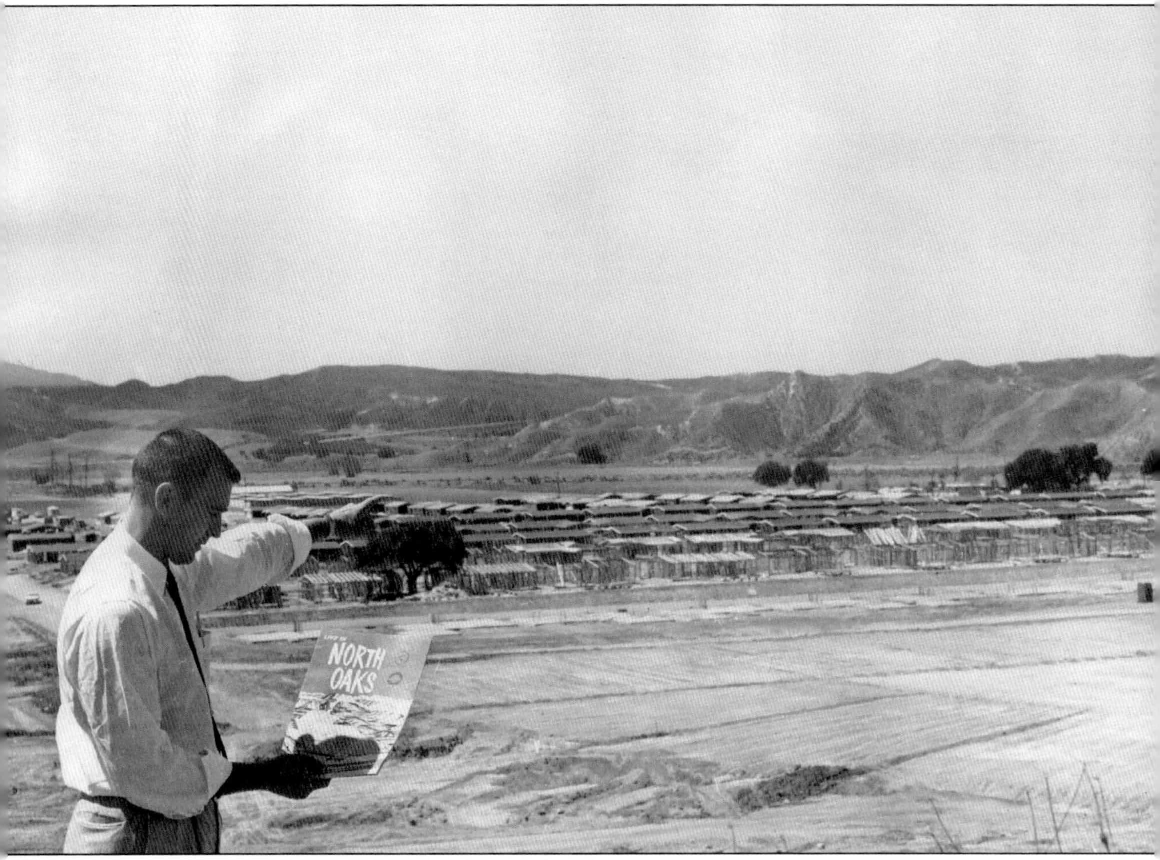

When construction began on the North Oaks housing tract in 1961, the area was called Saugus, but by 1963, it had established a new identity—Canyon Country. The name became official in 1968 when the US Postal Service opened the first Canyon Country post office.

Four

GETTING AN EDUCATION

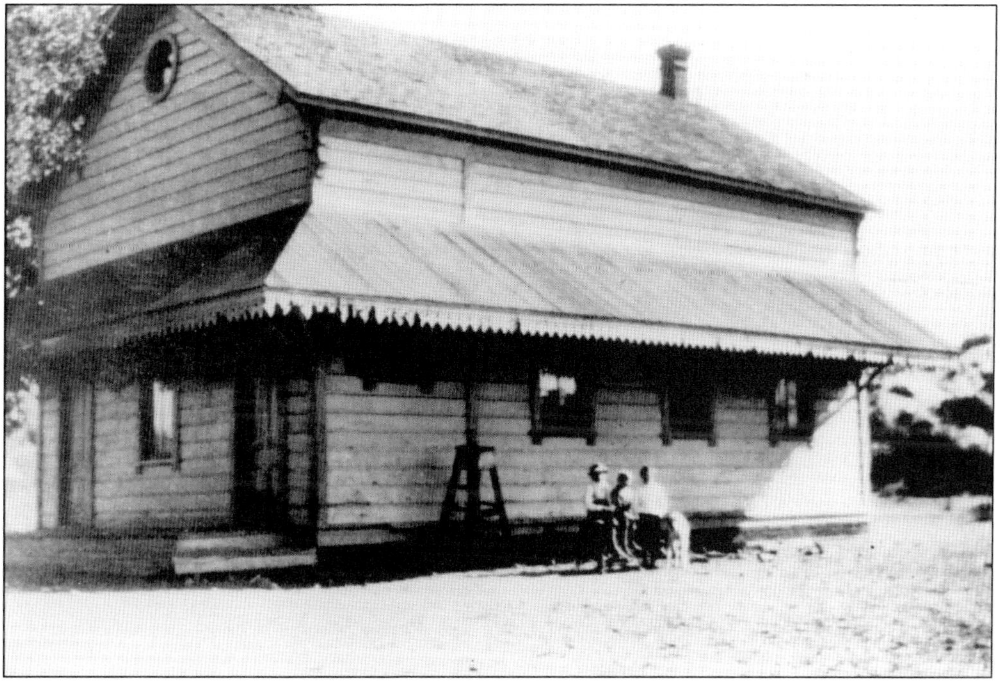

This 1910s image shows the Sulphur Springs School where classes were first held outside of Thomas and Martha Mitchell's adobe house. The one-room schoolhouse accommodated students in eight grades and had a library. In 1940, the building was razed and a larger, modern two-classroom building was erected, housing 65 students in eight grades.

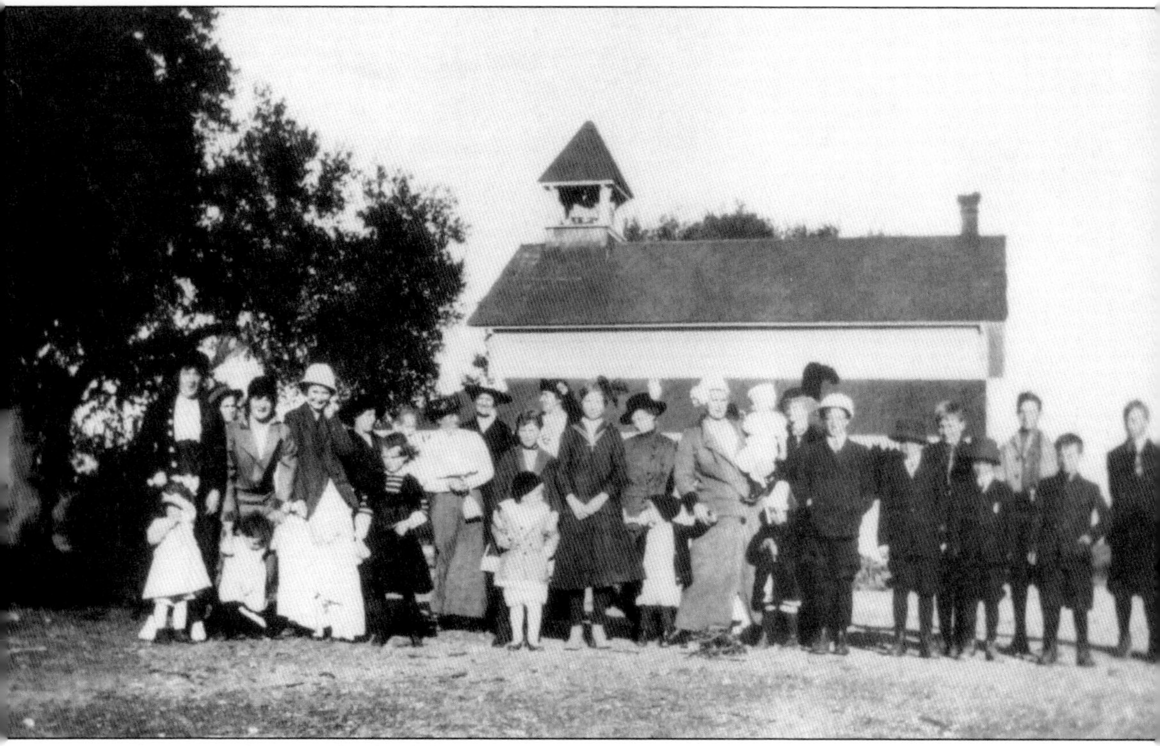

In this 1910s photograph of Sulphur Springs School, students and staff pose next to the building. The pioneering Mitchell family donated the school bell in the tower, which was saved when this building was torn down after the construction of a new school in 1940. District lines were drawn in 1943, after a fire destroyed Mint Canyon Elementary School, and the Mint Canyon District joined the Sulphur Springs School District; the district's name was revised to Sulphur Springs Union School District. In 1945, Sulphur Springs had a total of 138 students and five teachers. District boundaries were originally determined by ridgelines, streambeds, and section lines, but community changes brought about new area distinctions. In the 1970s and 1980s, boundaries changed again when Sulphur Springs acquired portions of the Newhall, Saugus, and Los Angeles City school districts.

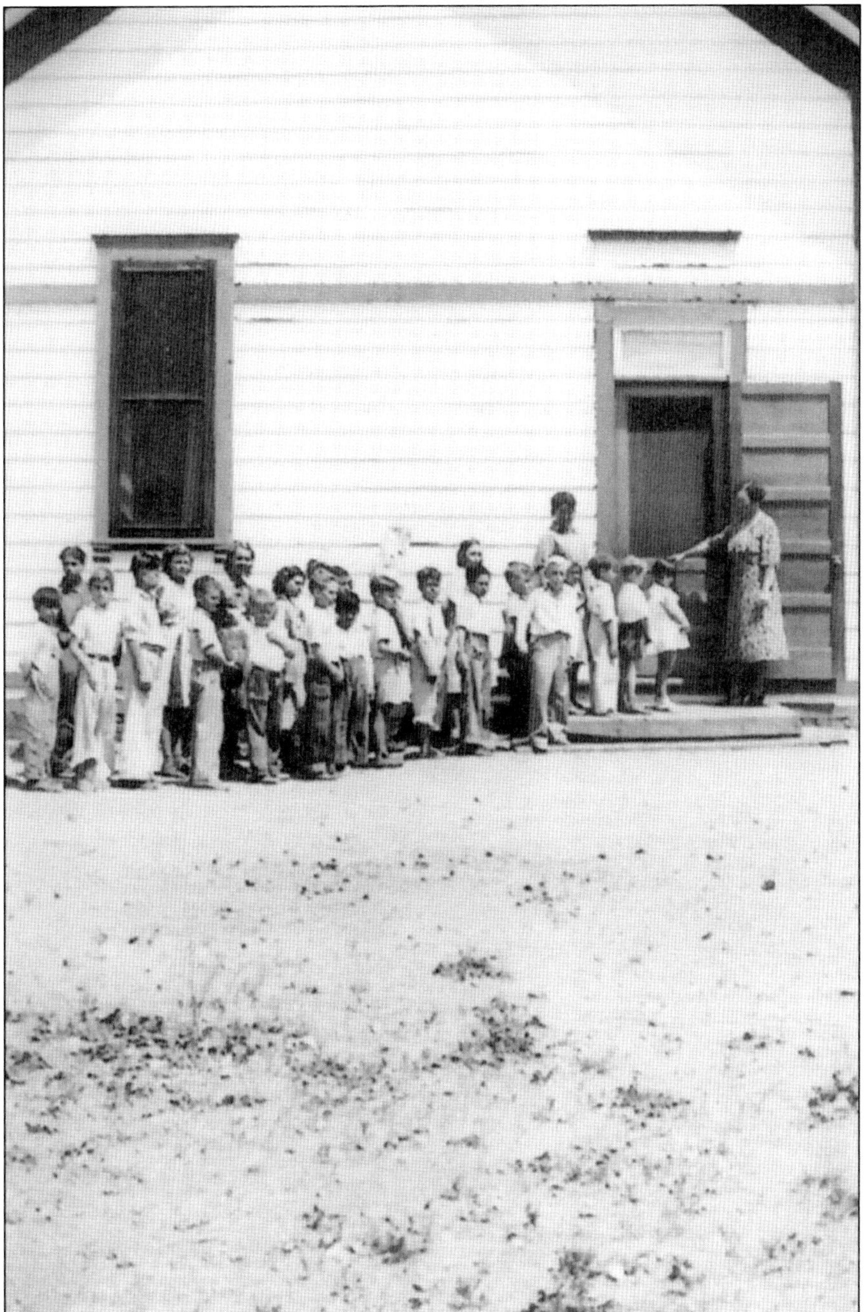

In the one-room Sulphur Springs School, the teacher covered eight grades and taught several members of the same families. In this 1938 photograph, teacher Florence Mitchell displays her reputed strictness while bringing the children inside. Among the students in the image is Mary Warmuth Sathre, who spoke highly of her experience with Mitchell. The instructor advanced Sathre a few grades because she was ahead in her abilities. Sometimes, the Warmuth children would ride a horse-drawn cart to school, and the animal would stay all day and graze until taking the children home at the end of the school day. (Courtesy of Mary Warmuth Sathre.)

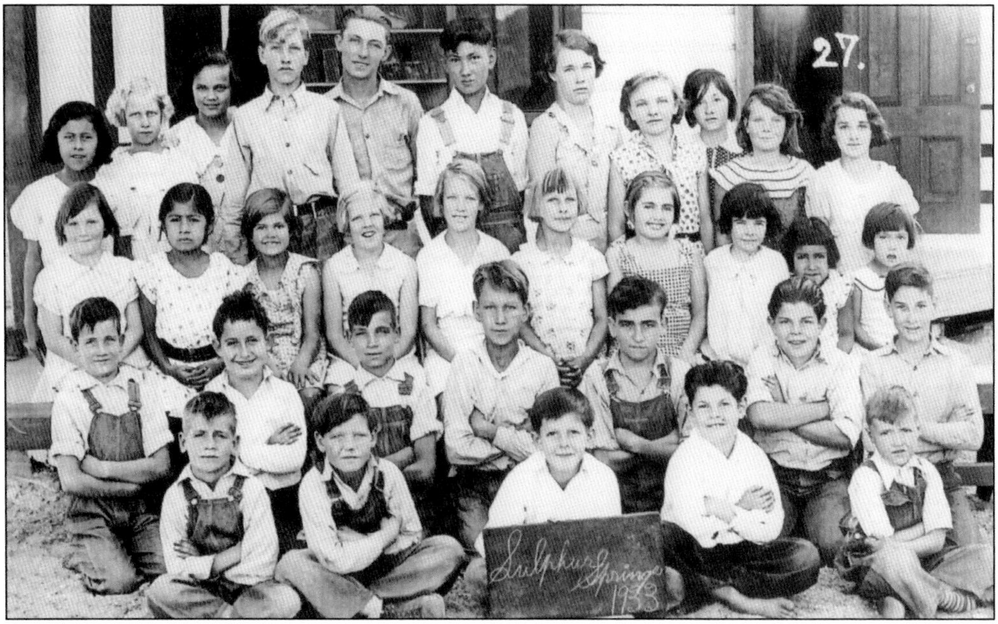

Two Sulphur Springs School classes are pictured on this page. The 1933 photograph above includes, from left to right, (first row) unidentified, David Sleeper, Clem Cox, Murray Cox, and "Cactus Pete" Gere; (second row) unidentified, Mike Bello, unidentified, Henry Warmuth, Leroy Insley, Donald Cox, and unidentified; (third row) unidentified, unidentified, Mildred Gere, Doris Gere, unidentified, Mary Warmuth, Vivian Reed, unidentified, ? Traviso, Lupe Traviso; (fourth row) unidentified, Madeline Warmuth, unidentified, Joseph Warmuth, unidentified, unidentified, unidentified, unidentified, Sybil Bell, Winifred Sleeper, and Marie Gigga. The 1937 photograph below includes, from left to right, (first row) unidentified, ? Cox, unidentified, unidentified, unidentified, Jackie Eisenbrau, Stanley Jones, and Leland Jones; (second row) unidentified, Lupe Traviso, unidentified, unidentified, unidentified, unidentified, unidentified, unidentified, ? Mitchell, unidentified; (third row) Clem Cox, unidentified, Mike Bello, Jack Maddison, Madeline Warmuth, Mary Warmuth, Anna Maddison, Marion Sleeper, and Murray Cox. Teachers had to handle approximately 30 youngsters at a time. (Both courtesy of Mary Warmuth Sathre.)

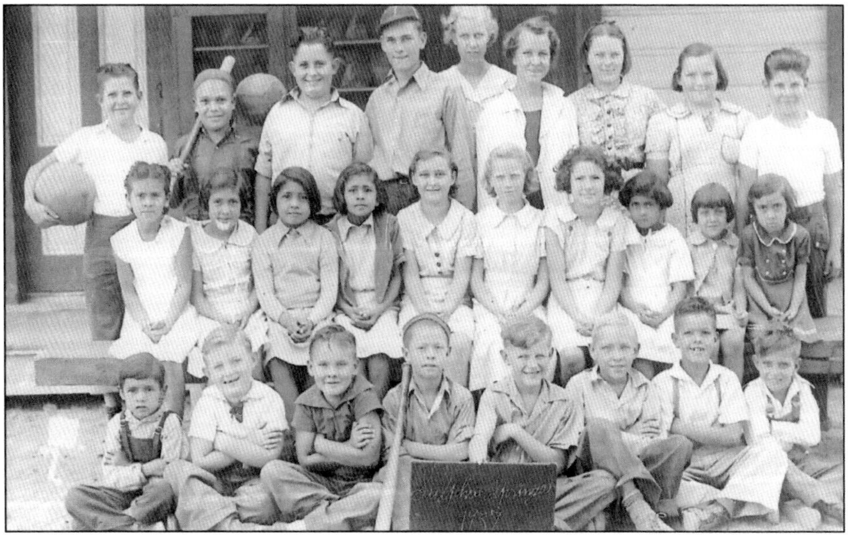

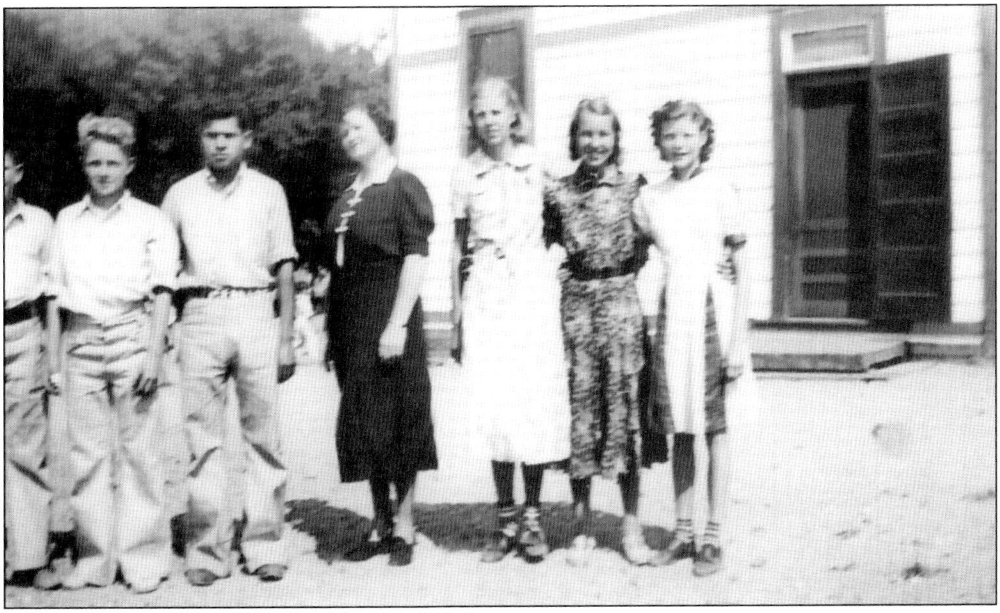

In the above photograph, Florence Mitchell (center) stands with some of her students on graduation day in 1938. To the right of Mitchell are, from left to right, Madeline Warmuth (Davis), Mary Warmuth (Sathre), and their friend and classmate, Darlene. In the image at right, Madeline (left) and Mary (right) stand with their mother, Minnie, at the sisters' graduation from San Fernando High School in 1942; Mary was only 16. It was wartime, and the Warmuth girls worked—Josephine Warmuth (Ramey) at the Bermite Powder Company making shells, and Madeline as a welder. Madeline was featured in the *Los Angeles Times*. After trade school, she was hired by Hughes Aircraft as a welder, then by Lockheed Airfield after the war. Mary Warmuth worked at Bank of America in Newhall and later went to work with Madeline as a timekeeper. (Both courtesy of Mary Warmuth Sathre.)

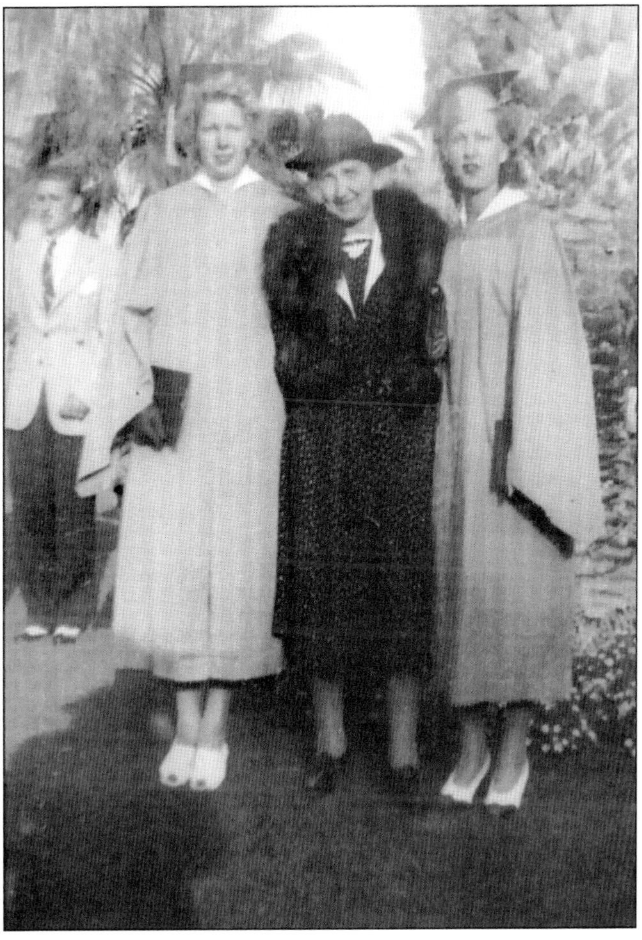

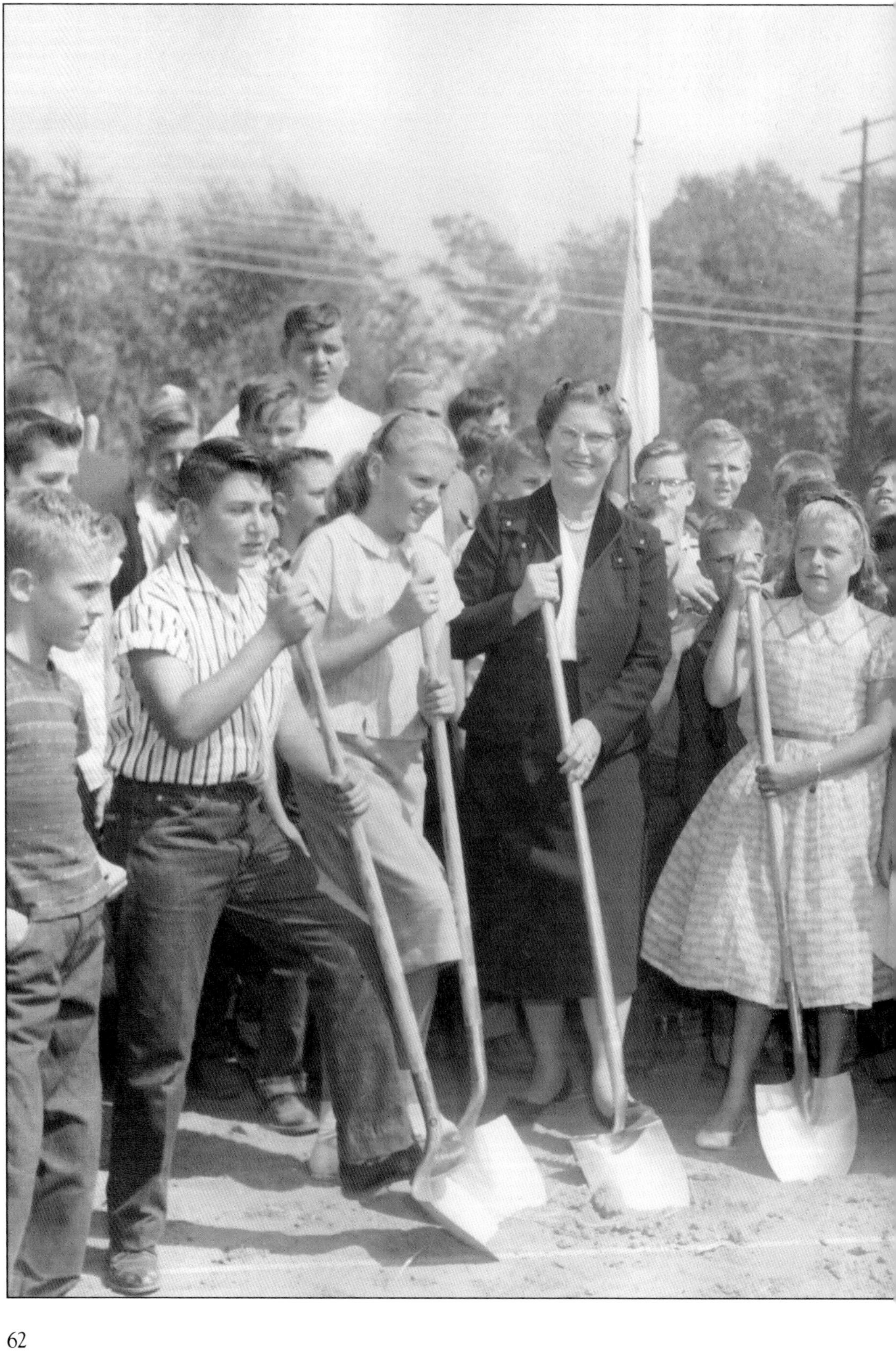

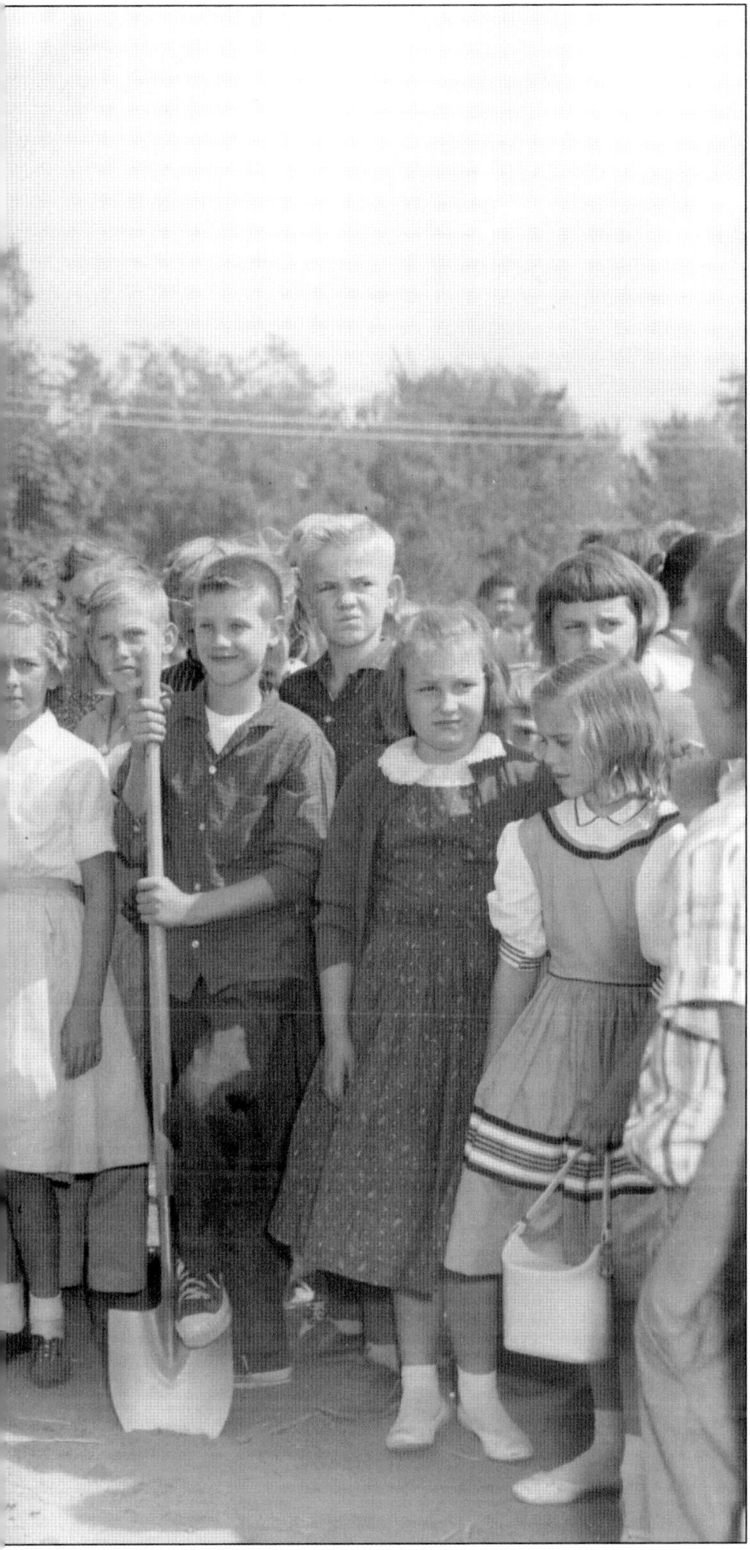

The image on this page shows the August 1, 1963, ground-breaking ceremony for an elementary school named for Canyon Country resident Leona Cox (center). Born in Strassberg, Alsace Lorraine, in France, and arriving in Florida at age three, Cox moved to a 40-acre ranch in Canyon Country (then called Saugus) in 1922 and married Clement Dunbar Cox. After the couple welcomed the births of three sons, Clement died at the start of the Depression, leaving Leona to raise the boys alone. In the 1930s, when a drought reduced the water level in the Santa Clarita Valley, Cox transported water cans to Sulphur Springs School in an Overland touring car. She also took care of the grounds, worked in the library, and was elected to the school board, where she served as clerk. Leona Cox Community School, part of the Sulphur Springs School District, was constructed on the corner of Oakmoor Street and Bernina Avenue for $500,000. (Courtesy of Cathy Cox Kraeger.)

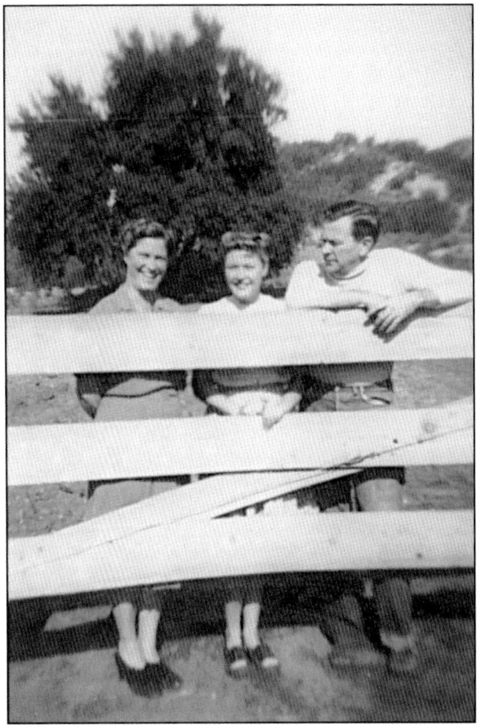

Clement and Leona Cox's son Clem joined the military during World War II and attended California Polytechnic University, San Luis Obispo, while his neighbor and future wife, Paula Palmer, attended the University of Southern California. When Clem and Paula first met, he was 15 and she was 13. The Palmers lived in Hollywood and would go to Canyon Country on weekends to ride horses. Clem and Paula eventually owned a place in Canyon Country, where Paula (center) and her parents posed for this photograph in the 1940s. (Courtesy of Cathy Cox Kraeger.)

Due to an increase in Canyon Country housing in the early 1960s, Sulphur Springs School added 10 new classrooms, and additional school sites were still needed. Mint Canyon School opened in 1963, Leona Cox School opened in 1964, and Soledad Canyon School opened in 1966. The latter school was phased out, and a Regal movie theater was built on its site. This image shows students with two Sulphur Springs Union School District buses. (Courtesy of Joshua Randall.)

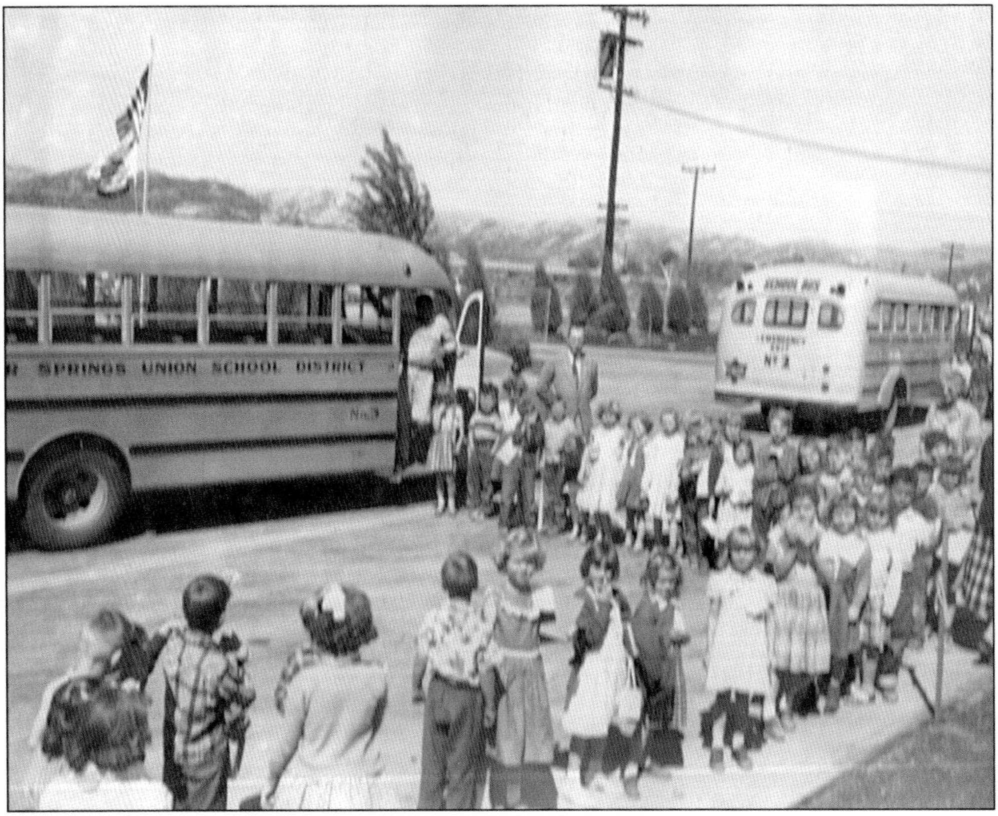

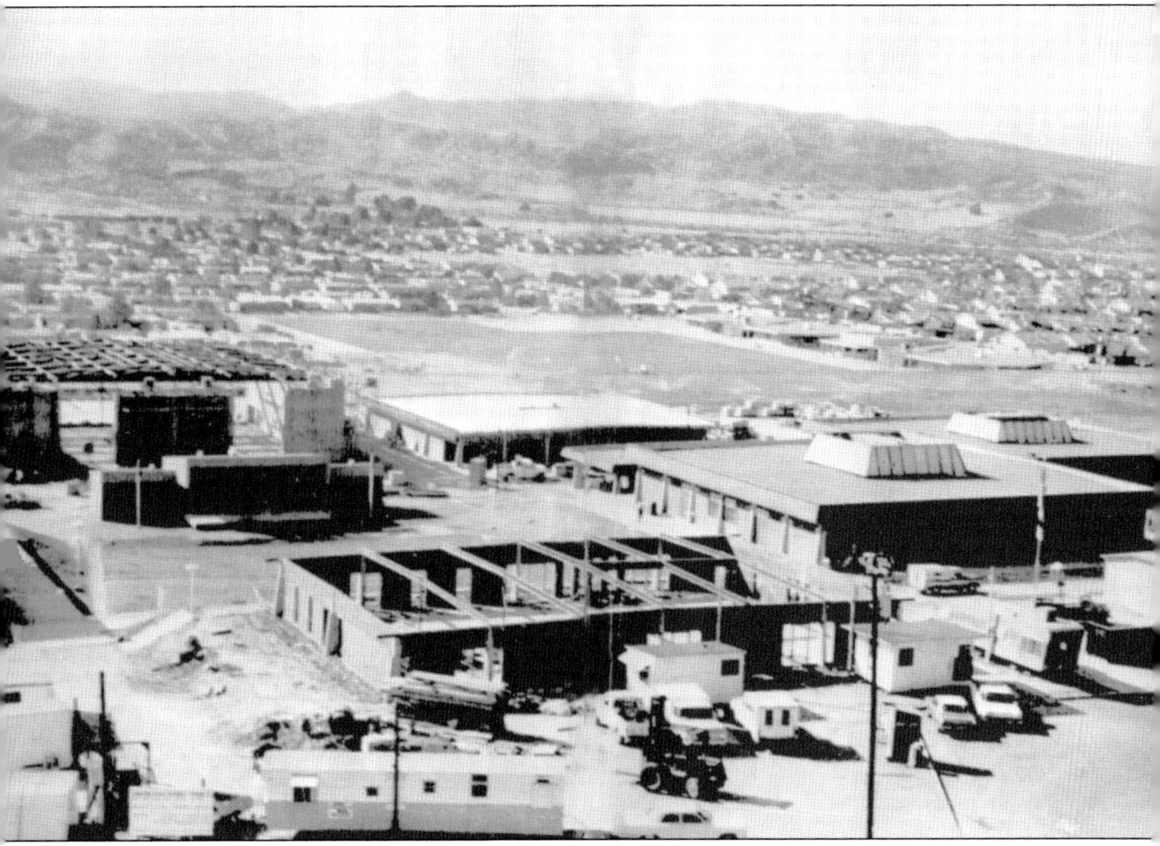

Until the Santa Clarita Union High School District formed in 1945, students from Canyon Country traveled to San Fernando High School. The elementary school districts in the valley petitioned for a secondary school, and when voters approved a bond measure, construction began on the district's first high school on 27 acres in Newhall. Because the school opened in 1946, just three months after the death of actor and school benefactor William S. Hart, the school became William S. Hart Union School. This photograph was taken decades later during construction of the second high school built in the Santa Clarita Valley—Canyon High School. (Courtesy of Gail Pinsker on behalf of William S. Hart Union High School District.)

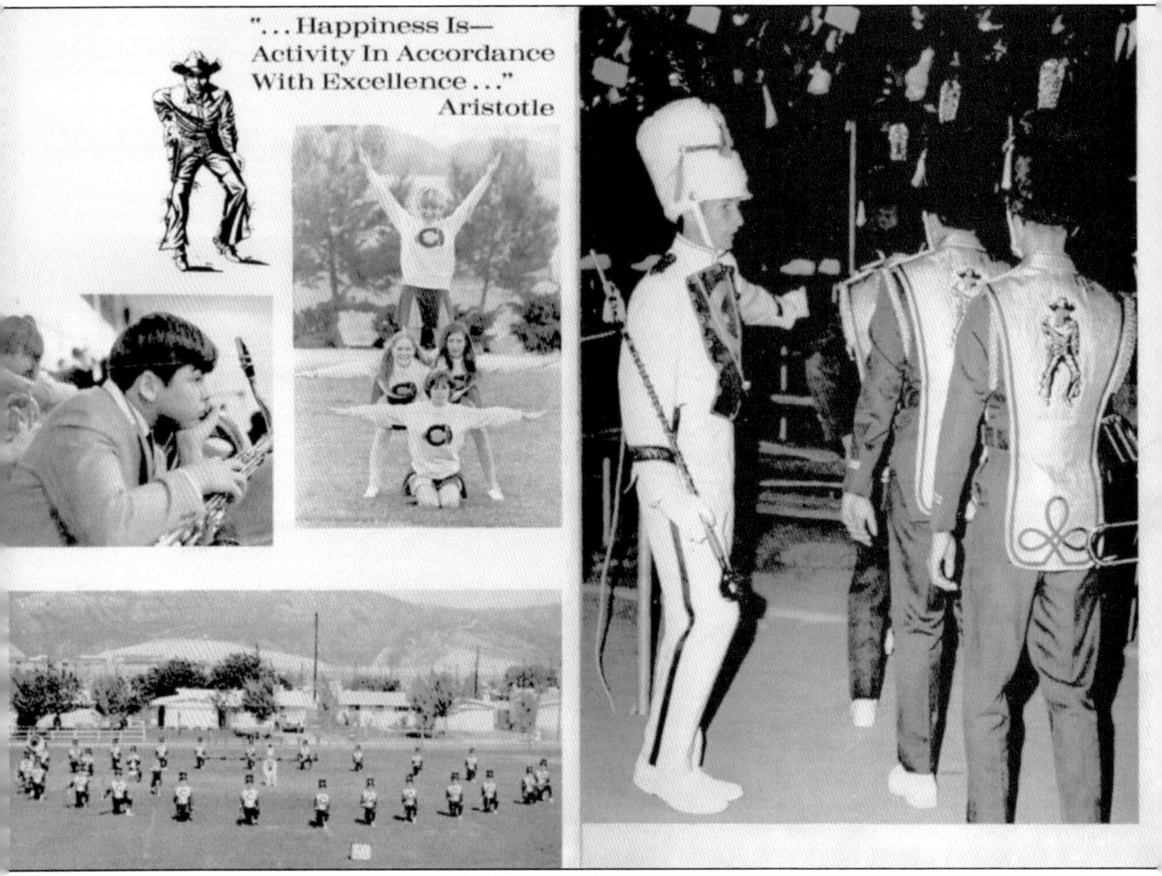

Canyon Country students attended Hart High School until 1968, when Canyon High School opened. These are pages from the first Canyon High School yearbook, which was published in 1969. In 2004, Golden Valley High School was added to the district, drawing from Newhall and Canyon Country neighborhoods. The students from Golden Valley's first freshman class graduated in 2007. (Courtesy of Gail Pinsker on behalf of William S. Hart Union High School District.)

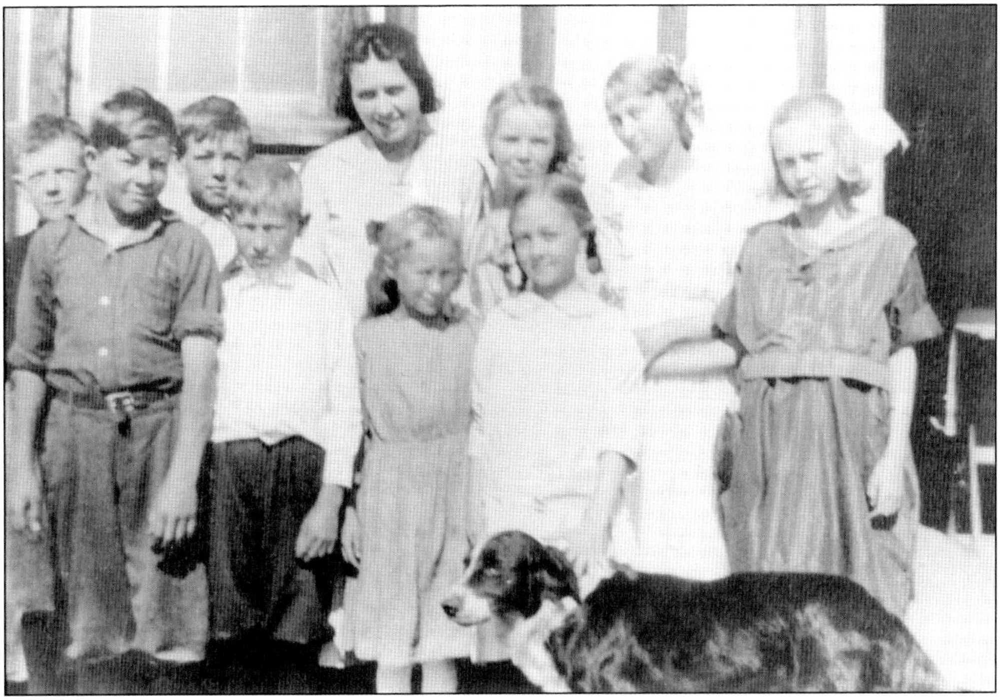

Early in the 20th century, the Sterling Borax Company brought in enough residents to necessitate a school in the Agua Dulce area. These 1914 photographs represent the earliest days of Mint Canyon School. The above photograph depicts the first class, with nine pupils and one large water spaniel. Below, teachers Pansy Barrington (left) and Clara Lang pose in front of the school. The property for the school was donated by Lula Chappel Johnson. A 16-foot-by-16-foot board-and-batten building was constructed. The structure, located in Agua Dulce, stood until 1943, when it burned down. Johnson's daughter, Mary Johnson, married Leslie Wright, whose sister-in-law was Agua Dulce teacher Clara Lang.

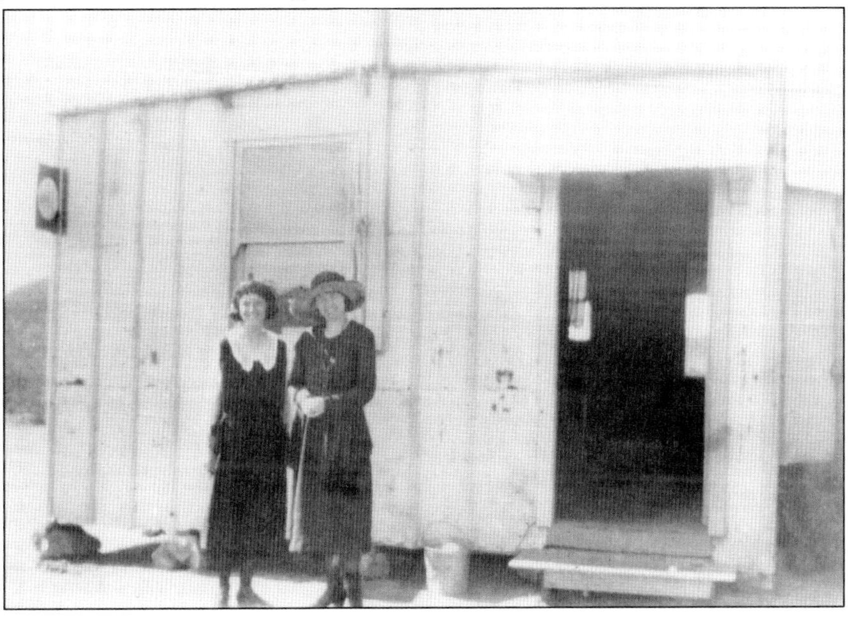

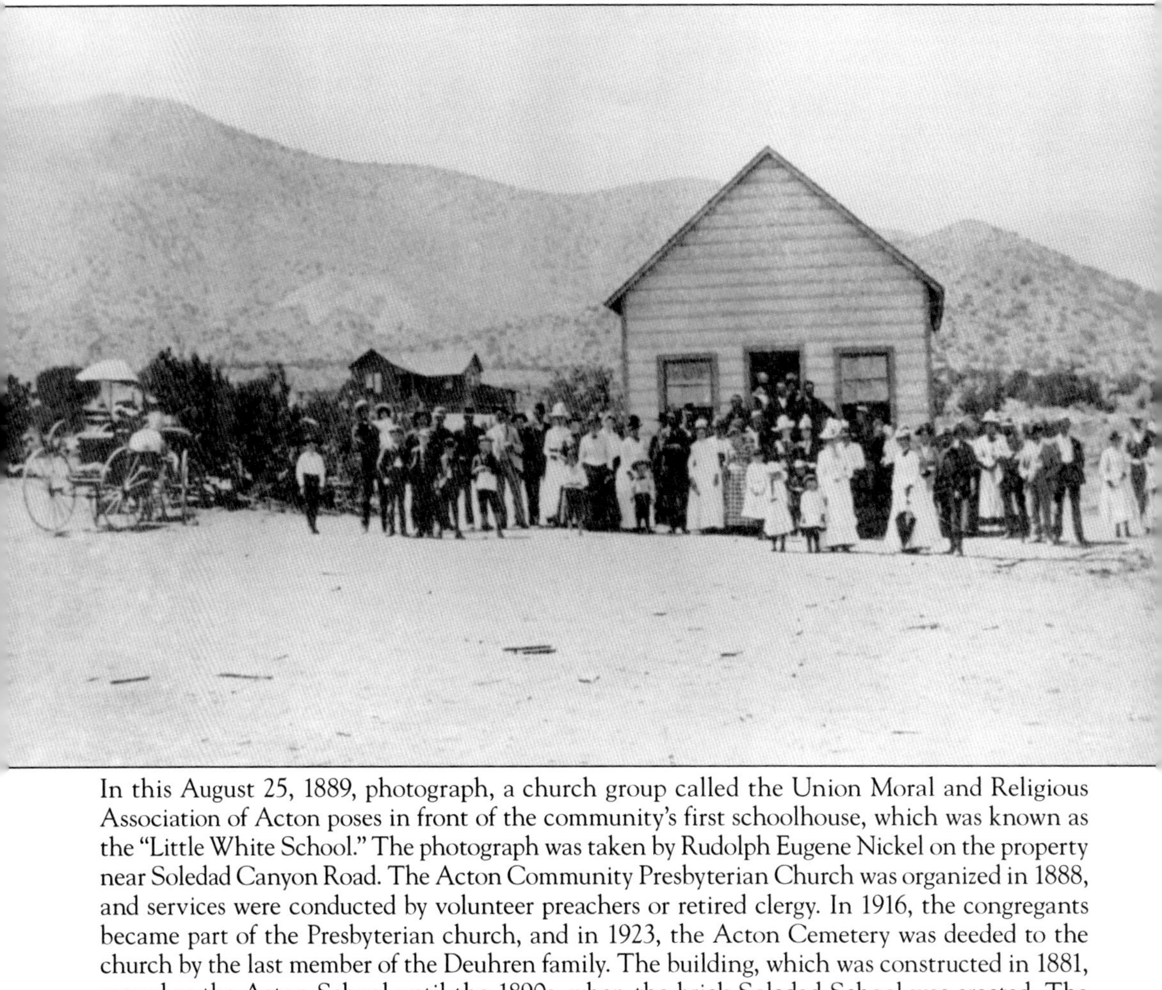

In this August 25, 1889, photograph, a church group called the Union Moral and Religious Association of Acton poses in front of the community's first schoolhouse, which was known as the "Little White School." The photograph was taken by Rudolph Eugene Nickel on the property near Soledad Canyon Road. The Acton Community Presbyterian Church was organized in 1888, and services were conducted by volunteer preachers or retired clergy. In 1916, the congregants became part of the Presbyterian church, and in 1923, the Acton Cemetery was deeded to the church by the last member of the Deuhren family. The building, which was constructed in 1881, served as the Acton School until the 1890s, when the brick Soledad School was erected. The historical building was updated in 1988 for the church's 100th anniversary.

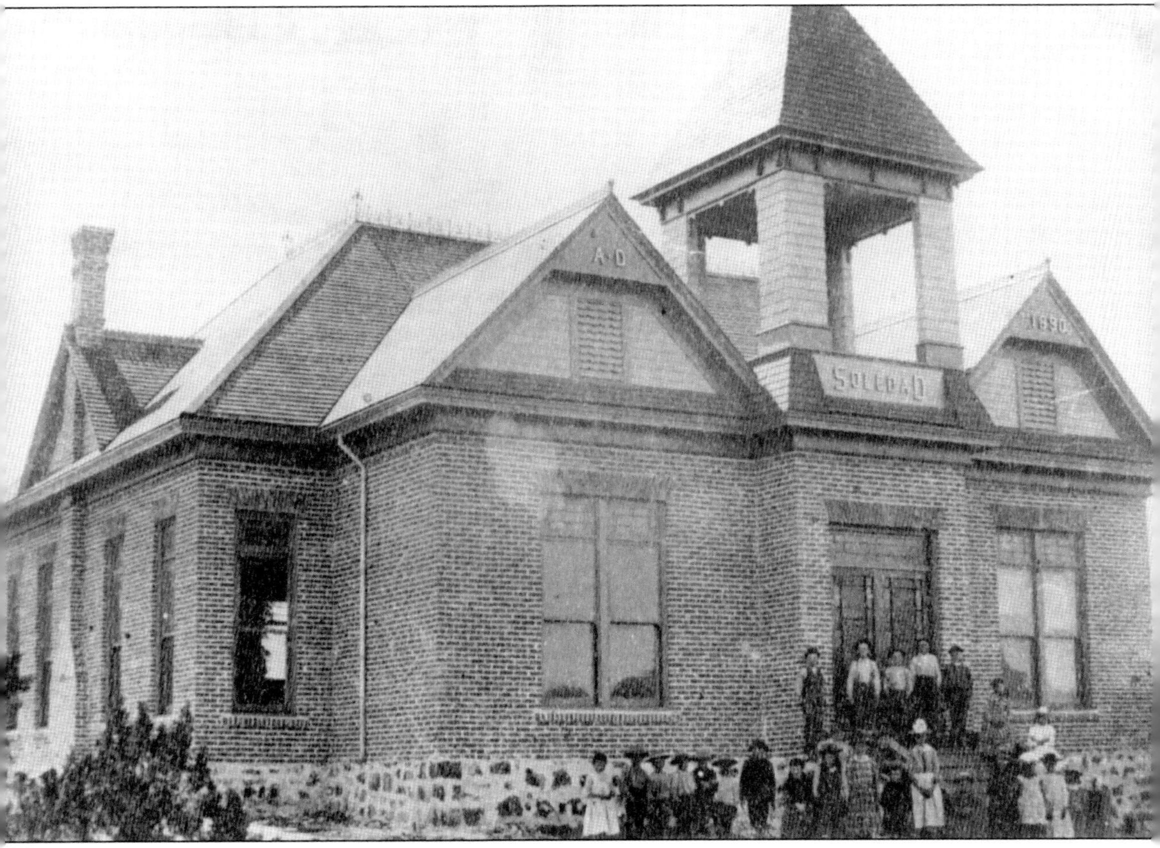

A few decades after the establishment of Sulphur Springs School, the growing community warranted a separate school in the Acton area. This early-20th-century photograph of Soledad School shows the second schoolhouse, which was made using homemade bricks in 1890. This replaced the earlier, one-room wood schoolhouse. It reportedly cost $4,000 to construct and opened with approximately 45 students, with Mattie Adams serving as teacher. This brick building became a farmhouse in the 1930s, when a larger school was erected at a different site in Acton.

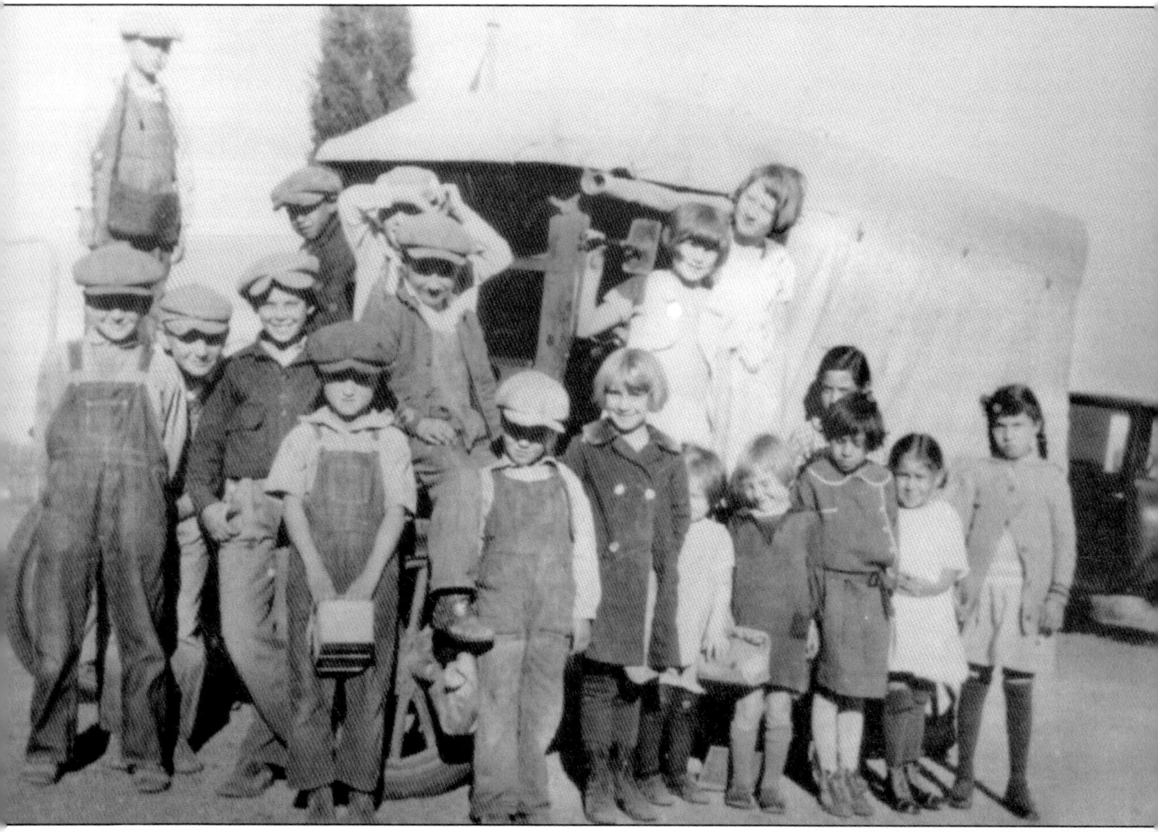

The Acton children who lived some distance from the school took a school bus driven by resident Gilla Kennedy, whose husband, John, was the first stationmaster in Ravenna. The bus she drove is pictured here with several riders on a school day in 1926. Of the 18 students, two are her children, Hugh and Bill.

Five

In the Limelight

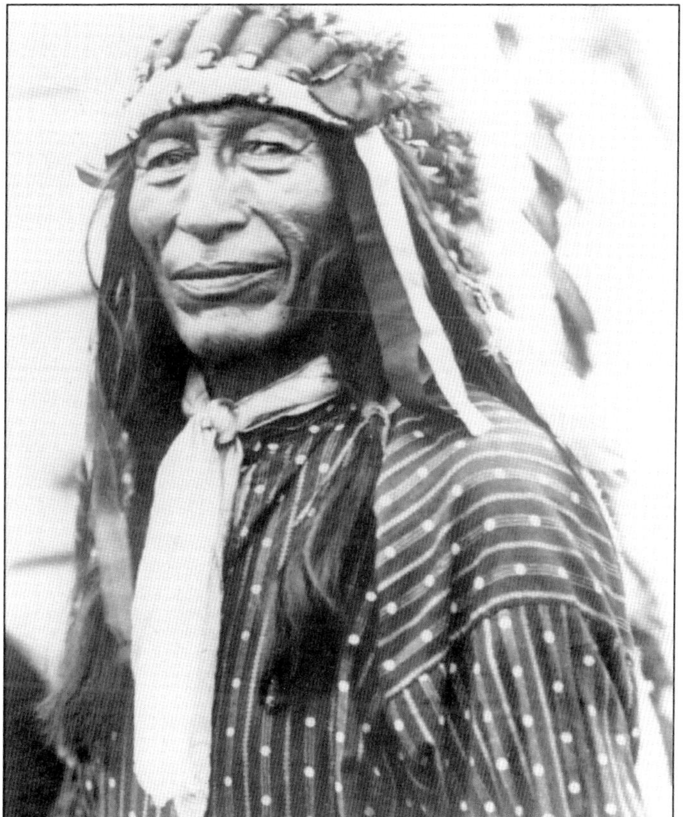

Like most towns, Canyon Country has seen its share of widely known individuals pass through the area. In addition, many significant persons and notable personalities have called the area home. One of the most widely seen faces is that of Sioux chief Iron Tail, who lived in the Canyon Country area in the early 20th century. The face on the Buffalo nickel, also known as the Indian Head nickel, was reportedly a composite based on the faces of numerous Native Americans, including Chief Iron Tail. The copper-nickel 5¢ coin was minted by the US Treasury from 1913 to 1938.

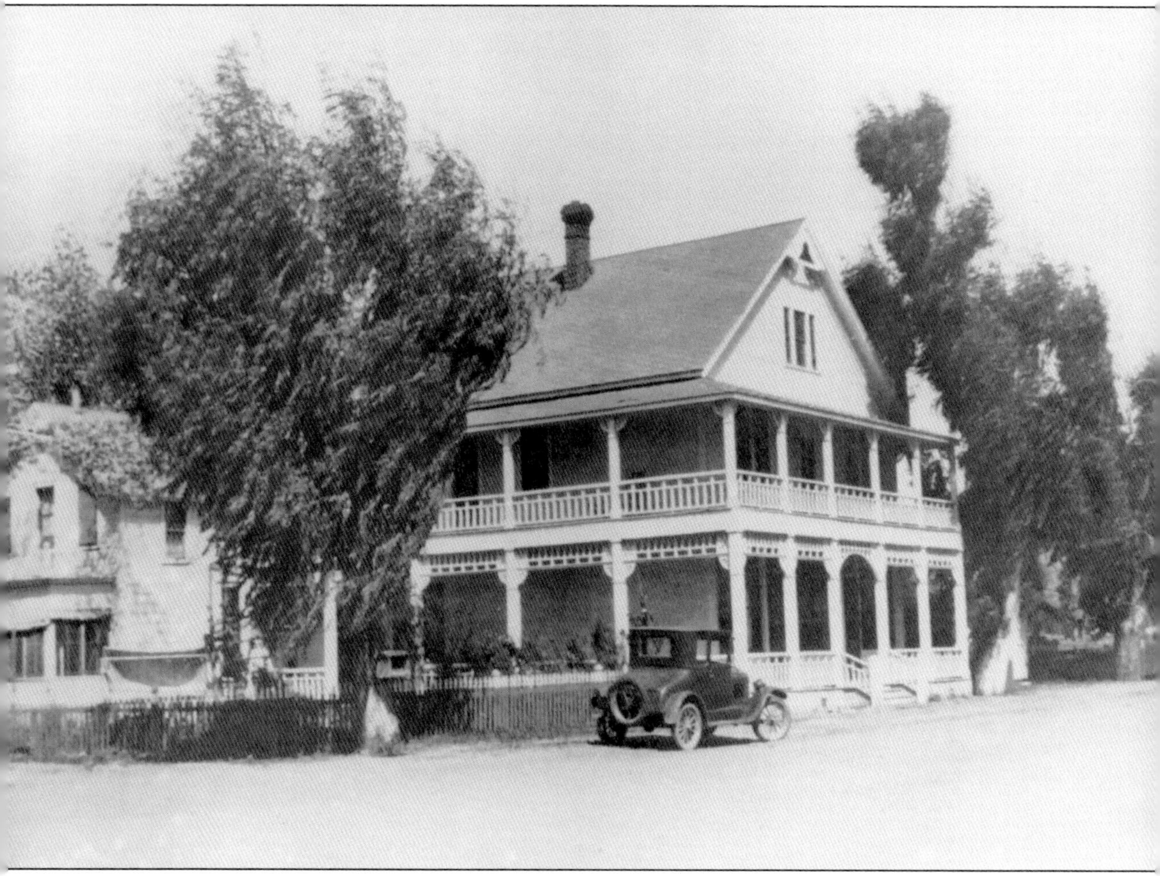

Rudolph Eugene Nickel built the Acton Hotel, the two-story Victorian building pictured here, in 1890. Nickel was the second resident of Acton and the first postmaster in the town. In 1888, Nickel moved the Soledad post office into his general store, which he built, and lived with his family in a residence above the store. In 1891, Nickel began publishing the first newspaper in the area, *The Acton Rooster*. That same year, the entrepreneur also established the first water company in the Santa Clarita Valley—Acton Water Works. Nickel moved out of the area in 1900, when he was appointed the port warden of San Francisco Harbor by Gov. Henry T. Gage. Nickel died in 1922.

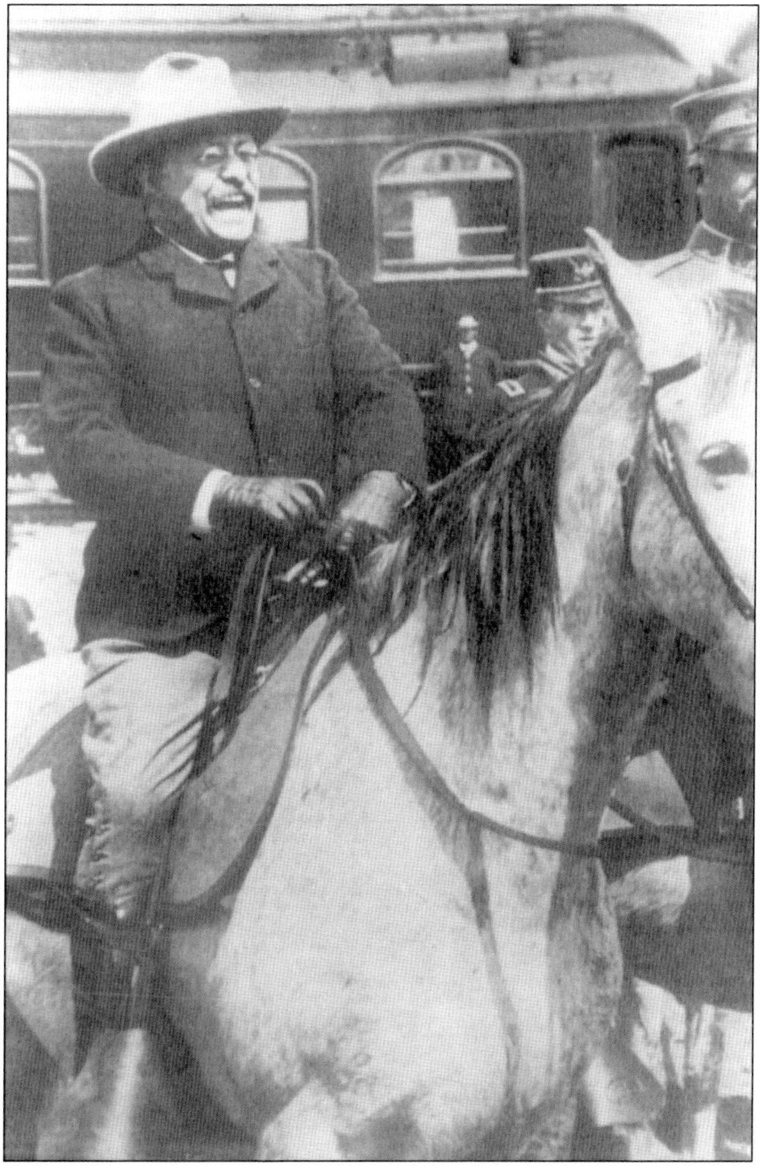

The Acton Hotel welcomed distinguished guests such as Pres. Theodore Roosevelt, pictured above at the train station on a visit in May 1903. Roosevelt stayed at the hotel while visiting his friend and political ally, California governor Henry T. Gage. Roosevelt reportedly enjoyed a meal at the Saugus Café, ordering a New York steak, and was heard claiming that the food was "splendid." The 26th president was elected and served two terms, from 1901 to 1909. Known as an outdoorsman and naturalist, Roosevelt also traveled to Yosemite to encourage the preservation of natural resources. Some of the Soledad Canyon's most successful gold mines were owned by Gage, a Los Angeles attorney and businessman who became the governor of California in January 1899. In 1877, Gage's Red Rover Mine saw action and continued until 1940, producing about $550,000 in gold. Gage's New York Mine was operational beginning in the 1880s, and Gage's son, Francis, eventually changed the name of the mine to "The Governor." The elder Gage arrived in California in 1874, eventually owning a 1,100-acre ranch where he raised horses and farmed oranges, grapes, and walnuts.

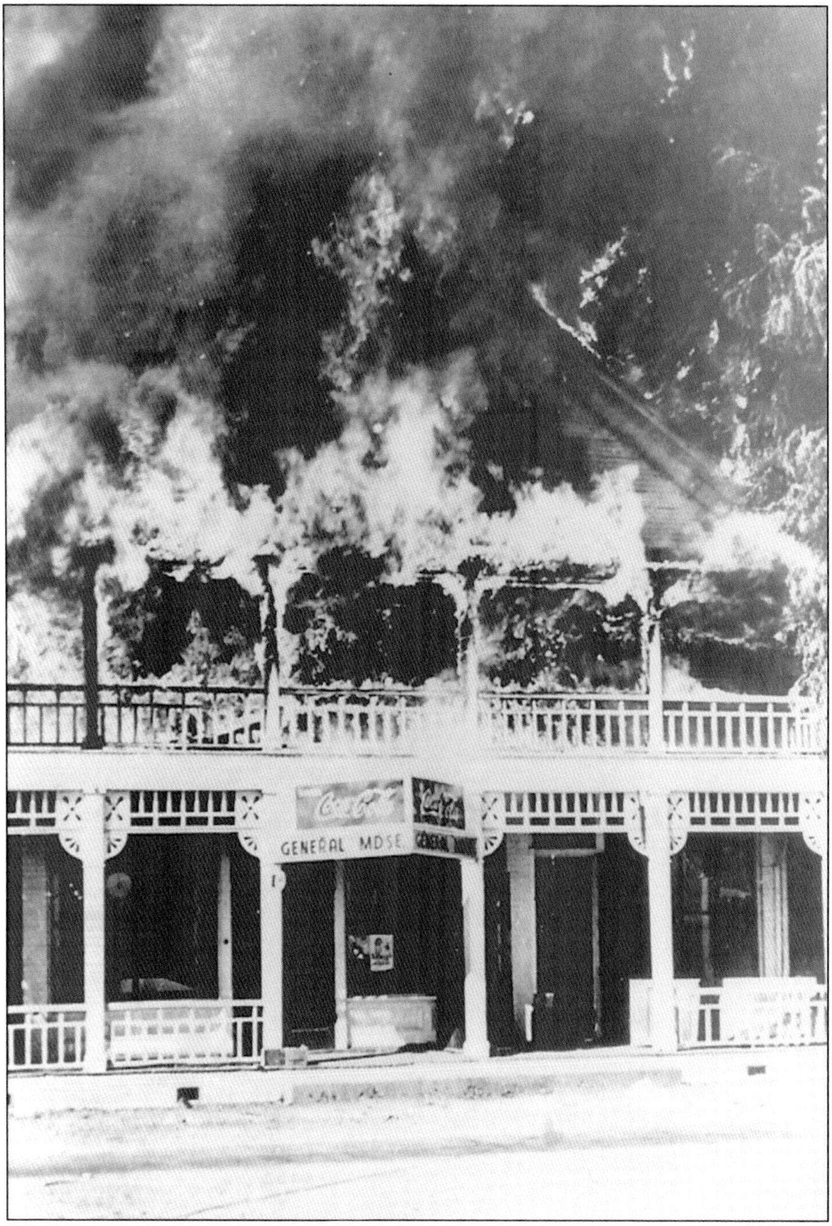

The Acton Hotel, built in 1890, also housed a store and the Acton post office. It nearly burned to the ground on the night of October 19, 1945, after a suspicious fire started in the attic. At that time, the hotel was owned by Samuel Schorr, who, upon returning from military service, found a number of articles missing from the hotel. Schorr accused Clarence Rush, the manager/postmaster he had hired, of stealing. Rush was arrested and arraigned, then released on $2,000 bond just one day before the fire started. The firemen's pumpers were hooked up to a large water tank just across the road, but it was too late to save the structure. Firemen and citizens, including the postmaster's wife, got all of the post office materials out of the building. Grand theft charges were brought against Rush by Schorr, who filed the complaint in Soledad District Court. Charges of misappropriation of goods and merchandise in the amount of nearly $10,000 were later dropped for lack of evidence.

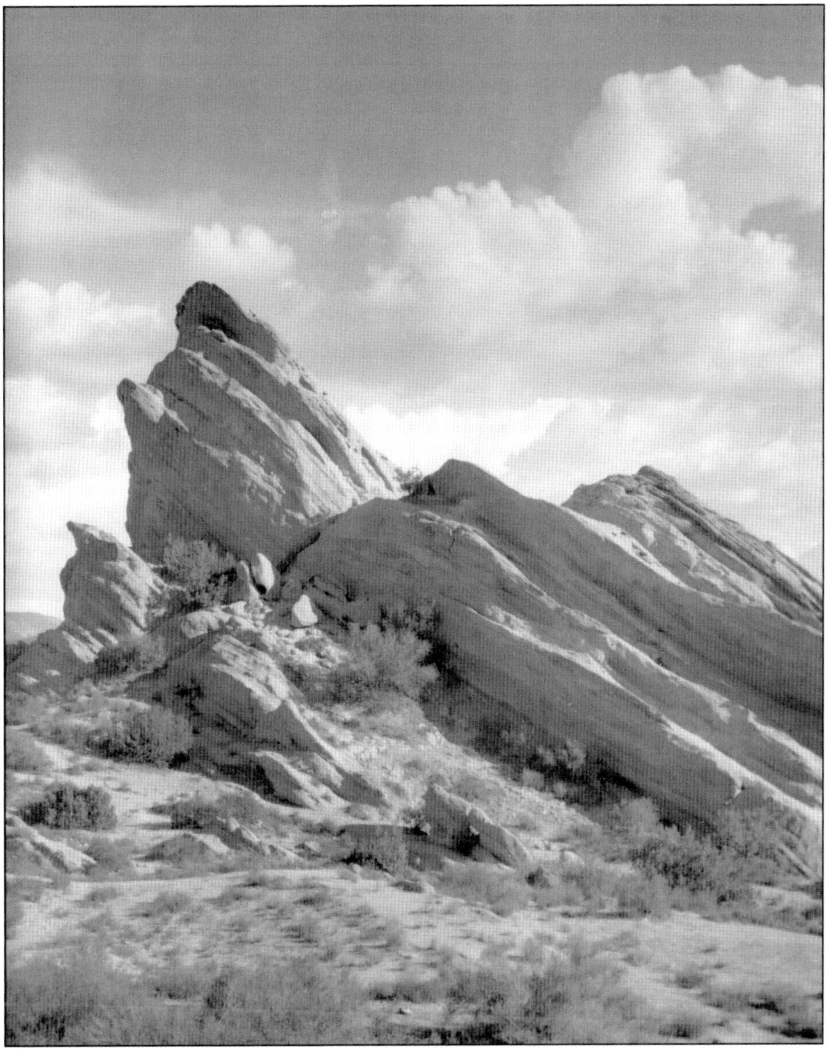

The dramatic hogback ridges of Vasquez Rocks in Agua Dulce are believed to be the result of earthquakes and volcanic forces dating back to millions of years ago. The site was named for notorious bandit Tiburcio Vasquez, who was found guilty of murder and hanged in 1875. The area became a government-owned entity beginning in 1970 and was added to the National Register of Historic Places in 1972. The park gained acreage in 2001, when the Bureau of Land Management deeded over 155 acres to Vasquez Rocks in a horseback ceremony with Los Angeles County supervisor Michael D. Antonovich. Almost a century before that, however, Vasquez Rocks was homesteaded by Henry Krieg, whose deed was signed in 1919 by Pres. Woodrow Wilson. Krieg built cabins and rented them out to visitors. He also constructed a dam to act as a water source for residents, which also created a swimming hole. The innovative Krieg also designed an early solar heating system using a pipe and a metal barrel on a platform. It heated the shower for Agua Dulce schoolteacher Grace Heath, who lived in one of Krieg's cabins. Krieg was known for distilling whiskey during Prohibition and pressing grapes for wine. Krieg's property was near the AAA Ranch, which stood for the owners—Jefferson Asher and his sons Jefferson Jr. and Thomas, who built a vacation home in 1935. Beekeeper James T. and Mary Dyer lived in one of Krieg's cabins, where Mary died in 1945. She was buried in the Mitchell-Dyer Cemetery on the pioneer family's property, but Krieg, his sister, and others were buried at Vasquez Rocks.

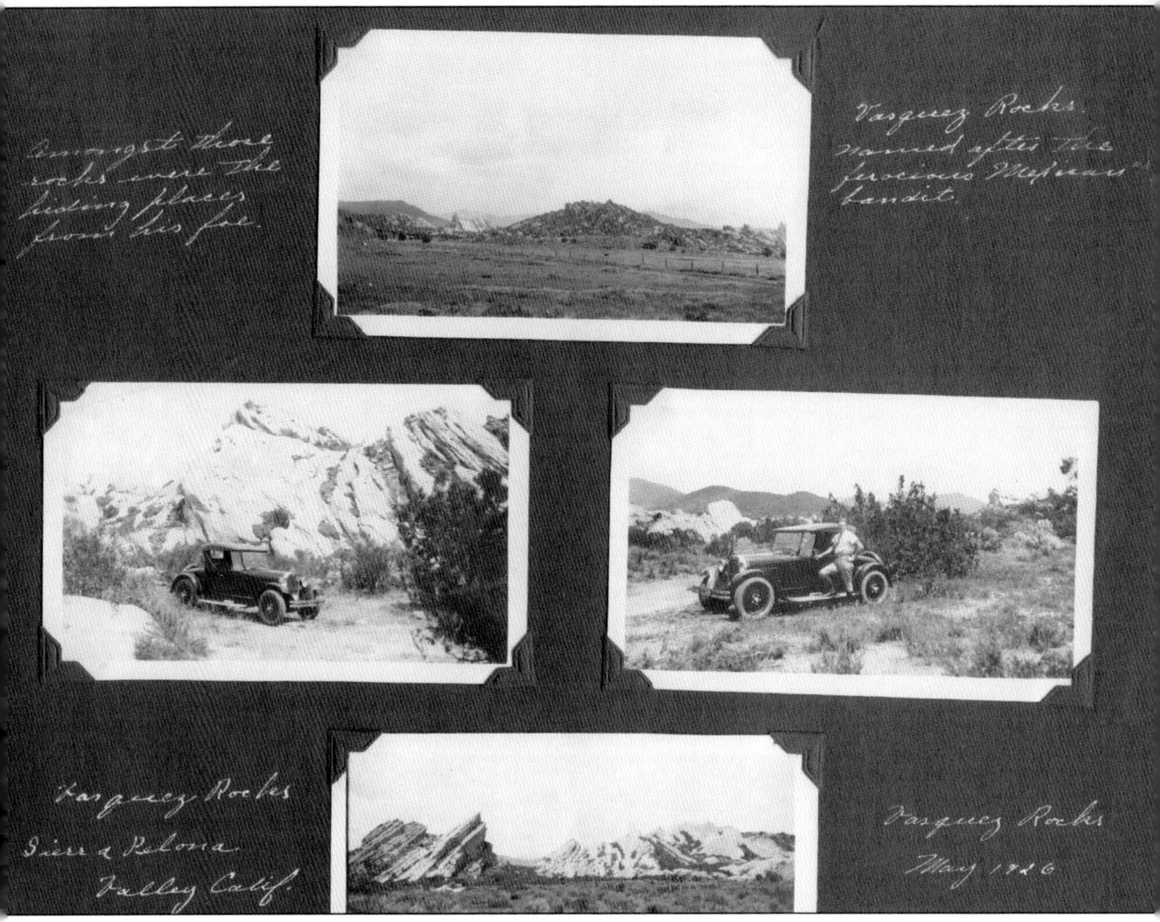

The dramatic appearance of Vasquez Rocks led to it becoming more than just a residence for the Krieg family. When Krieg's descendants turned ownership of the land over to Los Angeles County, it became Vasquez Rocks Natural Area and Nature Center. Throughout changes in ownership, its dramatic rock tower formations attracted visitors who enjoyed hiking, horseback riding, and picnicking. Homesteader Henry Krieg's caretaker would charge 25¢ for admission to "The Rocks." It was also a venue for Hollywood filmmaking, and this brought in location fees for Krieg. The earliest film shot at the site was a movie starring Rudolph Valentino. Other productions filmed at Vasquez Rocks include the film *Apache*, with Burt Lancaster, and the television shows *Star Trek* and *The High Chaparral*. Hollywood was partly responsible for the name "Vasquez Rocks," which took root after the 1920 movie *The Mask of Zorro*, which had a title character said to be based on outlaw Tiburcio Vasquez. Pictured here is a page, dated May 1926, from a scrapbook created by a visitor to Vasquez Rocks. The visitor identifies the area as "Sierra Pelona Valley, Calif." and writes, "Vasquez Rocks. Named after the ferocious Mexican bandit."

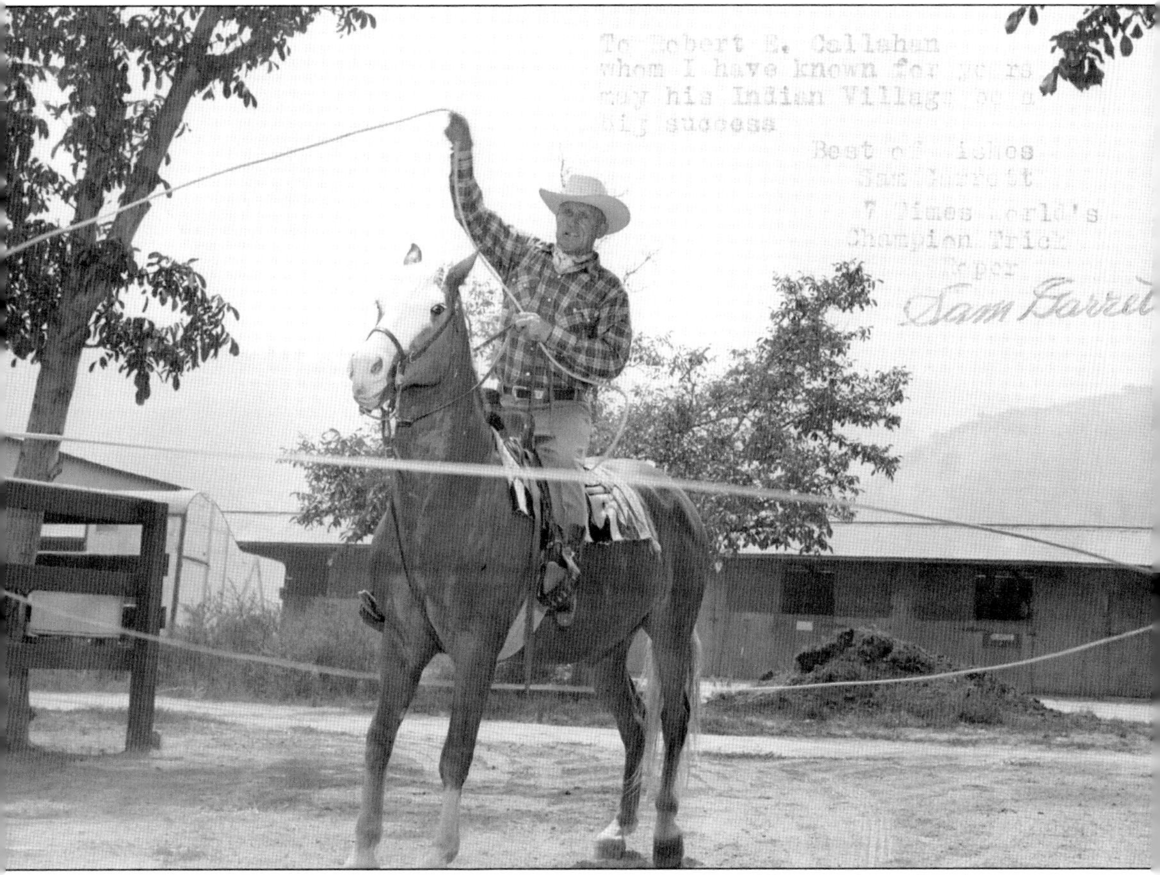

In addition to being a champion trick roper, Sam J. Garrett, pictured here in the mid-20th century, did some film acting and stunt work, beginning with silent movies in the 1920s. He starred in more than 90 films, including *Flying Lariats* in 1931, and taught several Hollywood celebrities how to trick rope, including actress Debbie Reynolds. He spent decades in the rodeo circuit, performing steer wrestling, steer roping, and calf roping in addition to mastering tricks. In 1985, Garrett was inducted into the Rodeo Hall of Fame at the National Cowboy & Western Heritage Museum in Oklahoma.

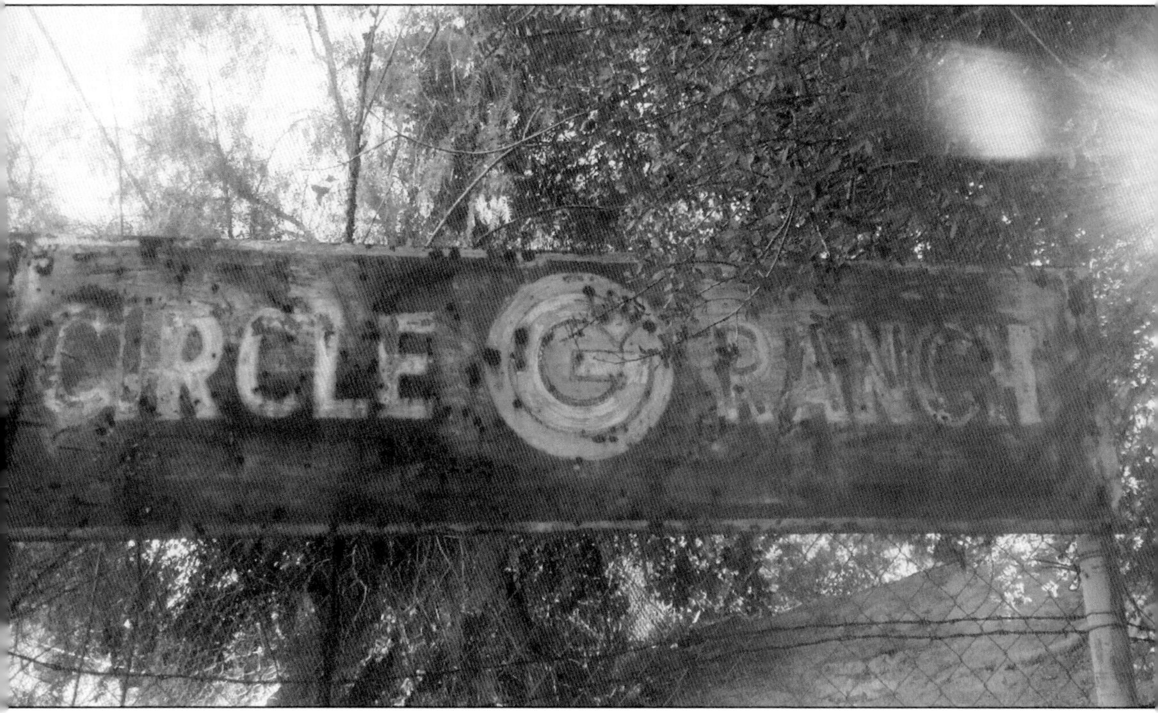

Sam Garrett and his wife, Ruby, were performers in the early 20th century. The couple moved to Sand Canyon around 1940, settling on land near Live Oak Springs Canyon and Sand Canyon Roads and calling it the Circle G Ranch. Sam, born in Mulhall, Oklahoma, on December 8, 1892, was a professional trick roper who traveled with Buffalo Bill's Wild West Show, Texas Cattle Theatrical Show, Pawnee Bill's Show, and the Barnum & Bailey Circus. He began trick roping at the age of 14 at the Miller Brothers 101 Ranch in Oklahoma and was discovered by vaudeville performer and humorist Will Rogers, who taught Garrett several rope tricks and techniques. Garrett was a world champion trick roper at Cheyenne Frontier Days seven times from 1916 to 1926. He was a headlining act at the Madison Square Garden rodeo for four years during World War I. The Sand Canyon property owned by Sam and Ruby, the Circle G Ranch, was sold around 1963 and developed into tract housing. After the housing construction, all that remained from the Garretts' property was the signage seen here, but "Circle G" was incorporated into the name of a street within the tract. The Garretts had one daughter, Maxine. The couple eventually moved to Fallbrook, California, where Sam J. Garrett died on April 4, 1989, at the age of 97.

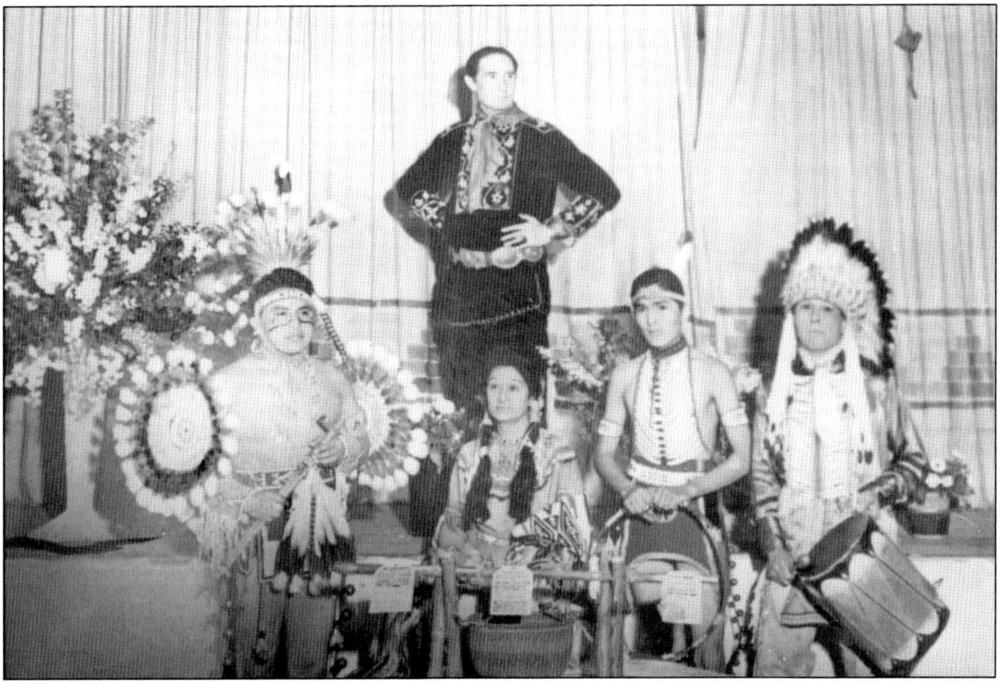

Entertainer and novelist Robert E. Callahan owned Mission Village, a Western-themed amusement park in Los Angeles. When the construction of the Santa Monica Freeway on Interstate 10 displaced the operation in the 1960s, Callahan moved the Indian village to Sierra Highway in Canyon Country (then called Saugus). It was renamed Callahan's Old West Trading Post, and the area was sometimes referred to as Outlaw Canyon. The attraction brought people and events from the Old West to life with shows featuring Native Americans such as those one pictured above. Callahan was an aficionado of Native American culture, a fact that contributed to Callahan's choice of shows and use of Native American actors. In the photograph at right, actor Gary Cooper is awarded an honorary membership into the Sioux Nation, which he received in Canyon Country.

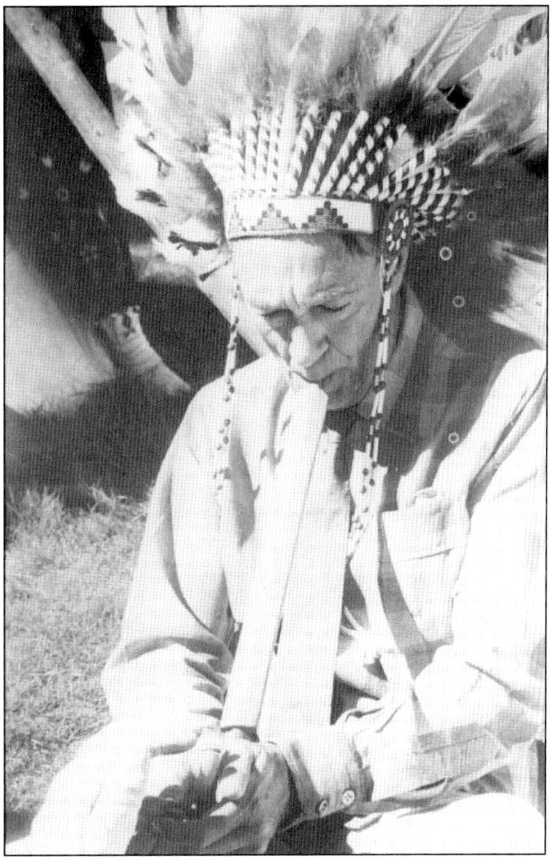

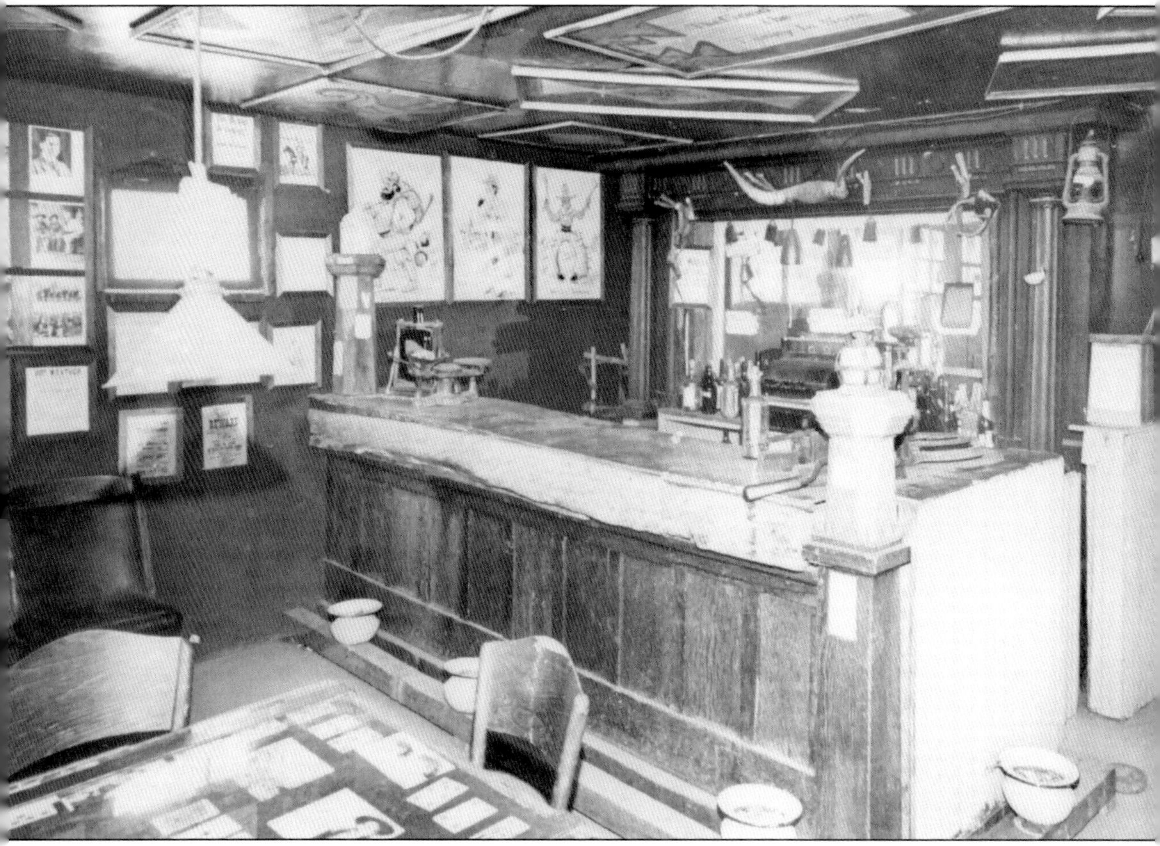

Robert E. Callahan's Old West Trading Post was a tourist attraction on US Route 6, but the village was also a museum that housed authentic western artifacts, including (as shown here) the table purportedly used by Wild Bill Hickok when he was shot to death in Deadwood, Dakota Territory, in 1876. Callahan used to say, "We not only entertain you, we educate you."

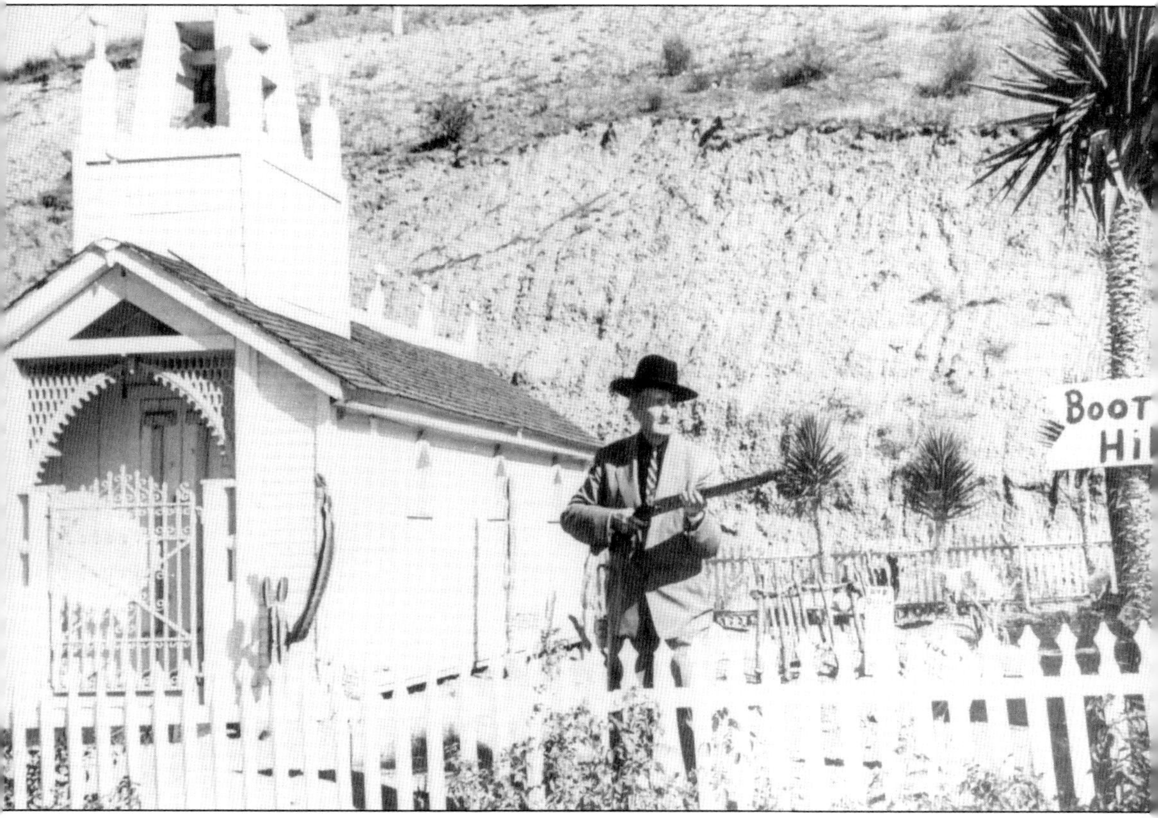

This chapel, built by Robert E. Callahan in 1926, is a model of the building at Rancho Camulos, the site many claimed to be the setting for the popular novel *Ramona*, written in 1884 by Helen Hunt Jackson. After Callahan's death, his widow, Marion Callahan, donated several buildings to the Santa Clarita Valley Historical Society, including this chapel and a red schoolhouse, as well as a number of historical artifacts. They were placed with other significant buildings at Heritage Junction Historic Park in Newhall.

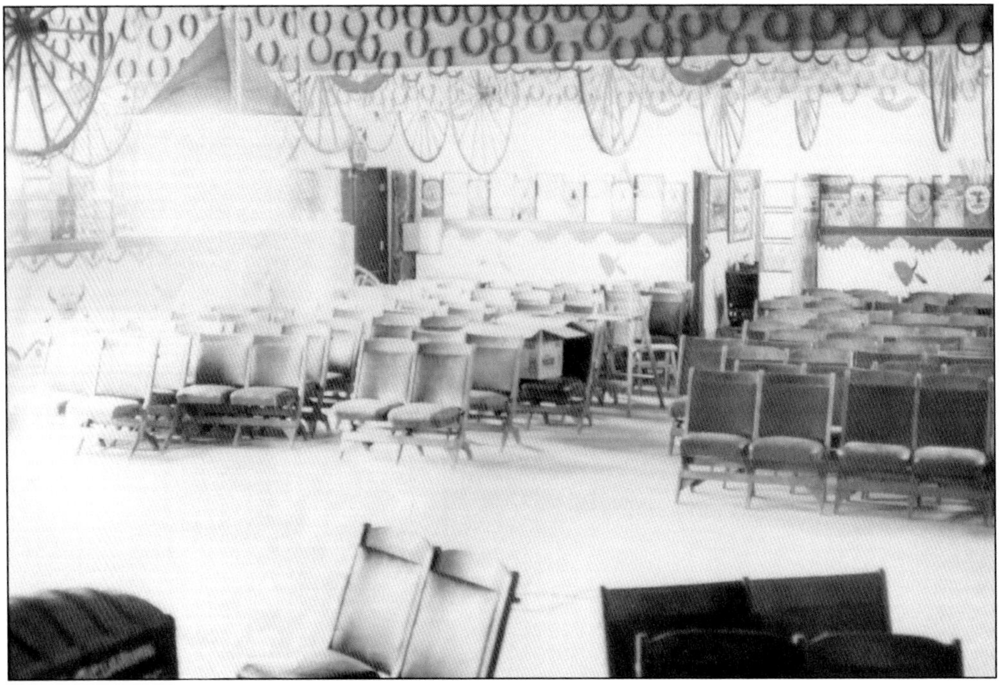

The 15-acre Old West Trading Post drew thousands of visitors every weekend with its mock gunfights, outdoor bar, picnic areas, Indian museum, stage shows, and other attractions. Founder Robert E. Callahan was considered a key to its popularity, but he was in a debilitating accident just four years after moving his attraction to Agua Dulce. Robert and his wife, Marion, operated the attraction for another decade and began renting out the facility for private parties. The theater seating (pictured above and below) was a good fit for local community theater group Canyon Theatre Guild, which moved into the buildings in 1986. The group's first live productions were in Newhall, at The Rafters, and in the William S. Hart High School auditorium beginning in 1970. (Both courtesy of Patti Finley.)

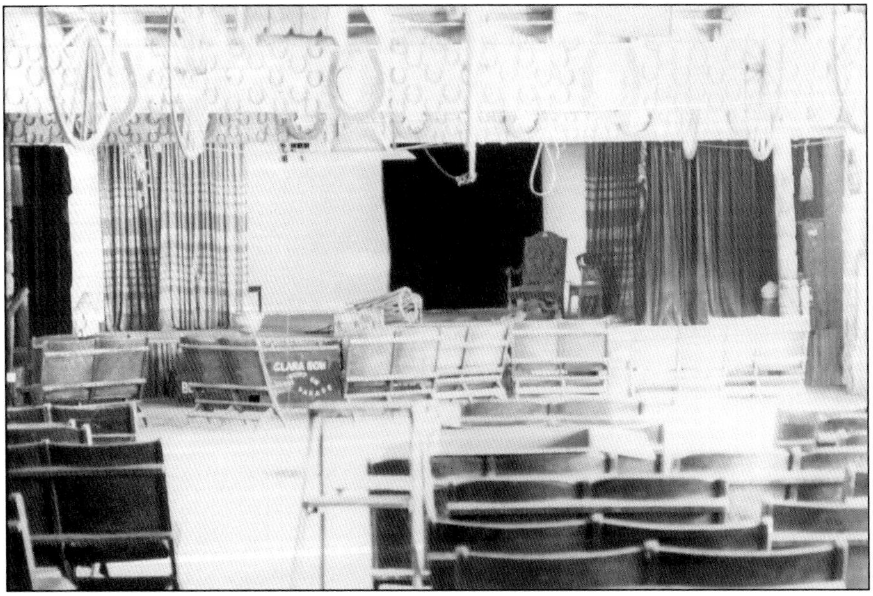

Prior to moving into the former Callahan's Old West Trading Post in 1986, the community theater group Canyon Theatre Guild pleased weekend audiences in schools and worked out of the Storefront Playhouse in the shopping center where the Canyon Country post office was located. The dancers below were part of an act in a Broadway review when Cindi Gallegos, owner of Dance Studio 84, headed the theater. They are, from left to right, Carla Hunt, Liz LaBelle, Cindi Gallegos, and Marsha McLean, who later became a Santa Clarita City Council member and mayor. In 1996, while Timothy Ben Boydston held the reins at the Canyon Theatre Guild, it was moved to newly revitalized downtown Newhall. (Both courtesy of Patti Finley.)

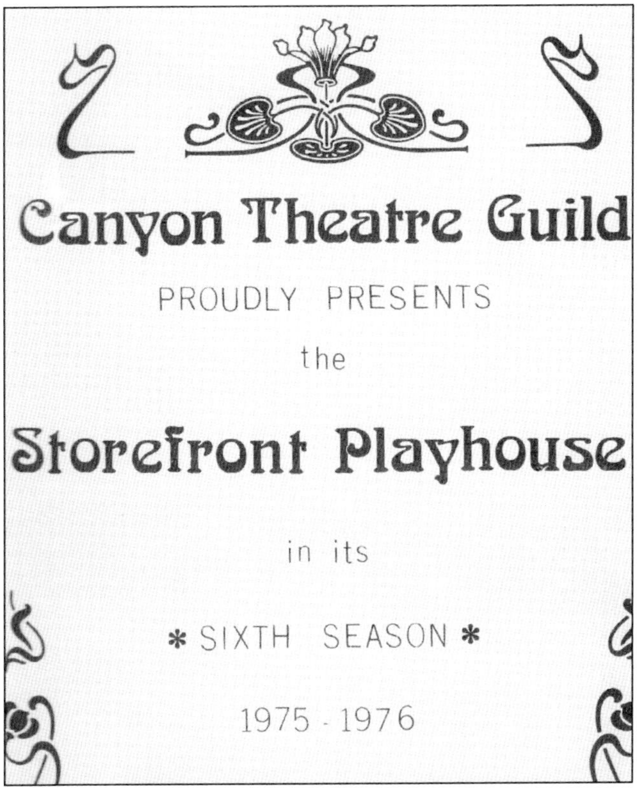

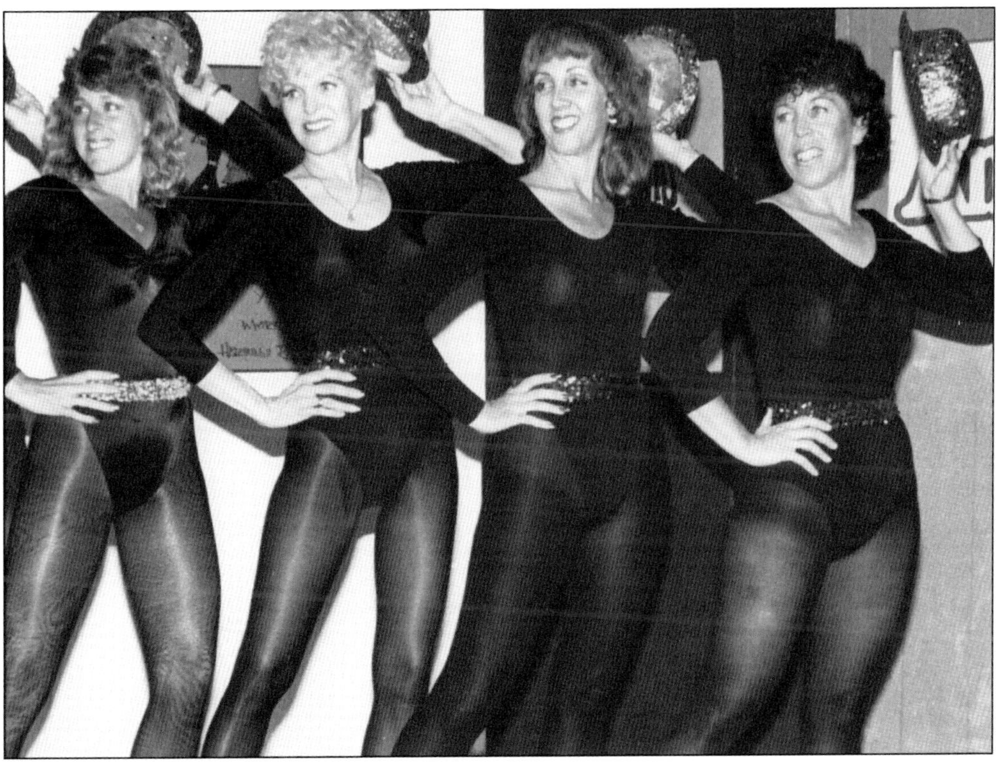

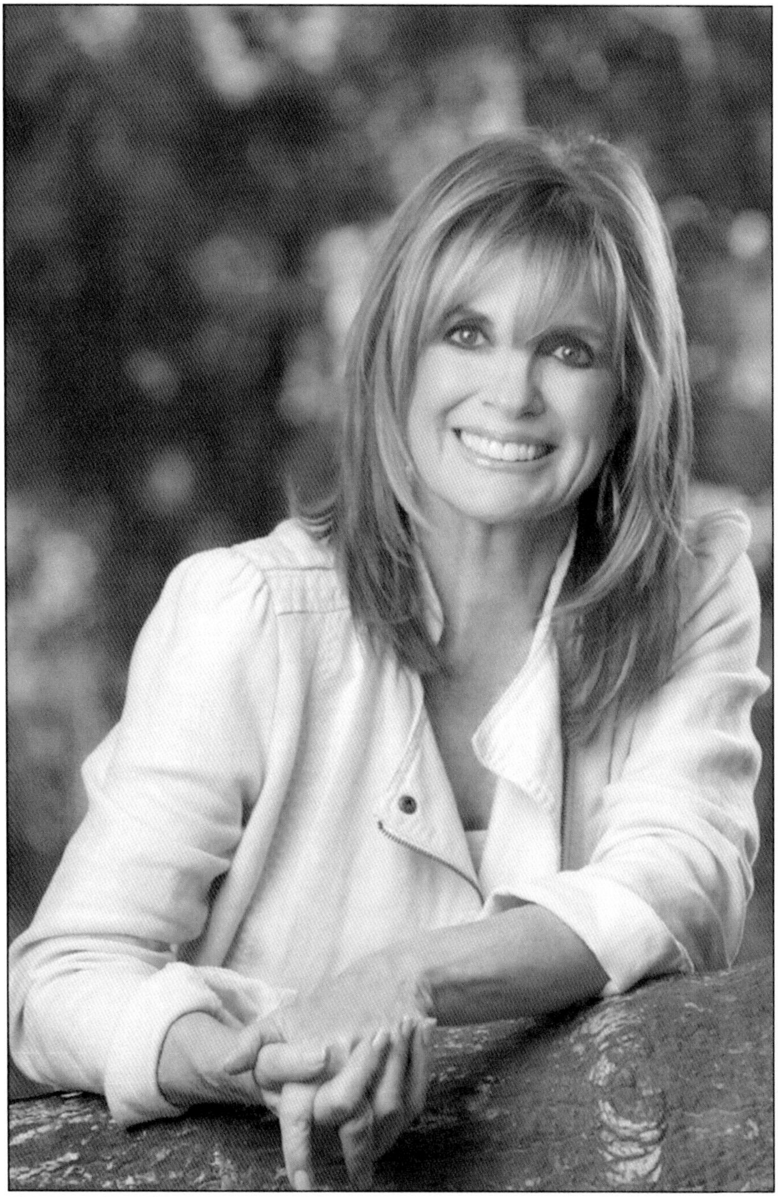

When Linda Gray bought property in Canyon Country in 1969, it was almost a decade before she would become a household name for her role as Sue Ellen Shepard Ewing on the CBS television series *Dallas*. Gray's fame took a backseat when she ran errands or visited Sulphur Springs Community School, where her two children, Jeff and Kehly, attended. Attention from fellow residents multiplied, however, in the summer of 1980, when Gray was the only actor on *Dallas* who knew the answer to the question, "Who shot J.R.?" The famous cliffhanger from the show's previous season prompted constant inquiry, but Gray's professional vow of secrecy meant she could not divulge the answer. She continued acting and traveling abroad for stage roles, and from 1997 to 2007, she served as a United Nations goodwill ambassador. Gray was persuaded by her husband, Ed Thrasher, art director at Warner Bros. Records, to move to the Canyon Country property when it was just a plot on a dirt road. Gray says it was a move she "would never regret." (Courtesy of Jeffrey Lane & Associates on behalf of Linda Gray.)

John Elwin "Jack" Lilley moved to Canyon Country in 1958. Born in Texas, he was a cowboy who followed his father, John, into the stunt business as a teenager in the 1940s. After serving in the US Navy, Lilley began his career as a stuntman, joining the Screen Actors Guild in 1955. He worked on Walt Disney's *Zorro* television series as a double for Cesar Romero beginning in 1956 and created some of his best memories while working on *The High Chaparral* and *Bonanza* television shows. Many years later, he would work alongside his two sons. In the image below, Lilley (center) is with his sons Clay (left) and Clint "Burkey" on the set of the 1993 television movie *Bonanza: The Return*. (Both courtesy of Jack E. Lilley; below, with permission from Andrew J. Klyde.)

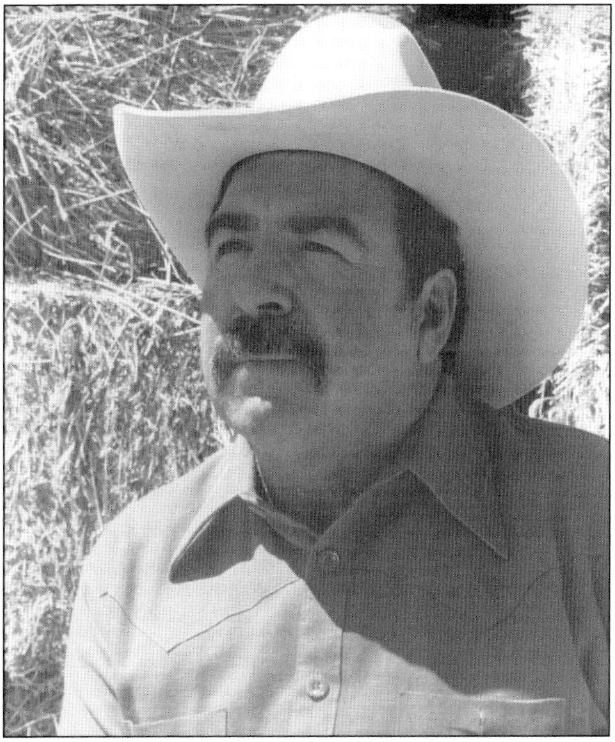

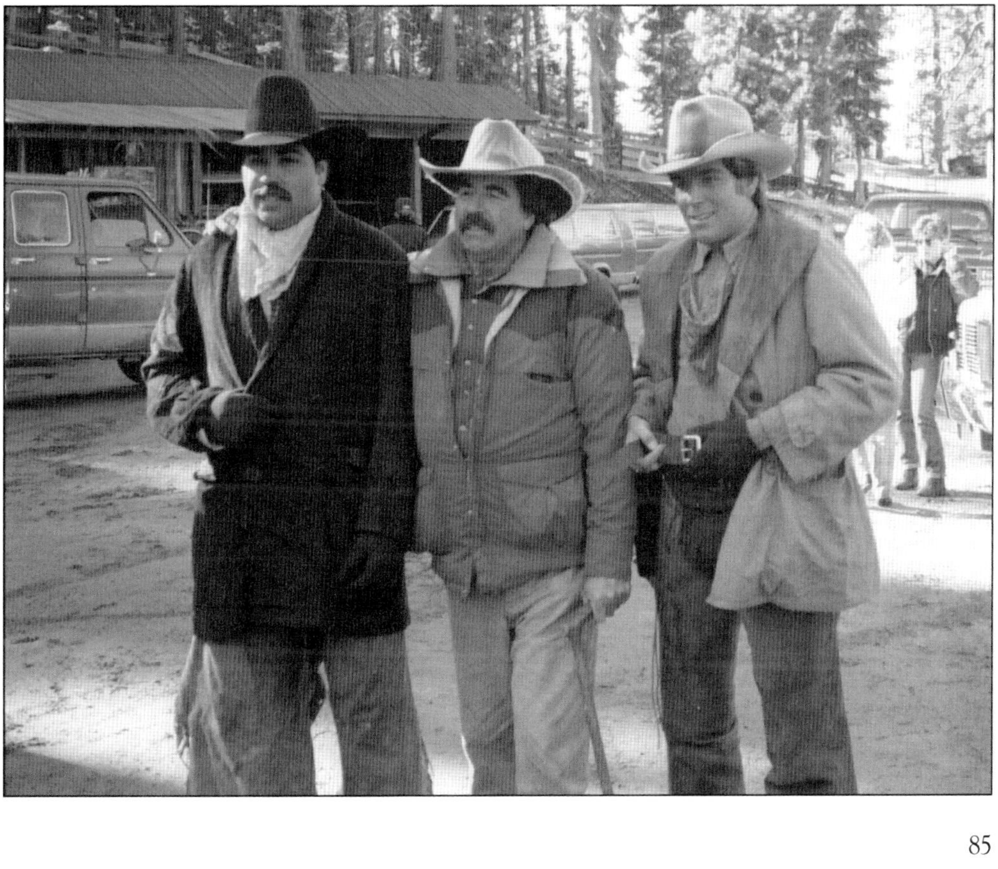

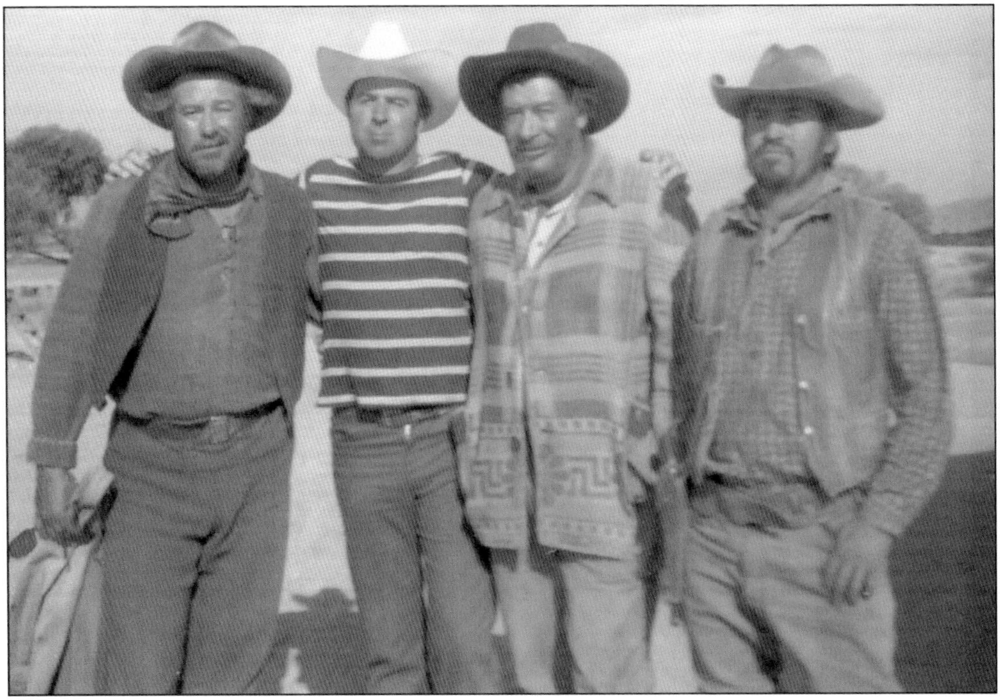

Jack Lilley became so prolific in the industry that his fellow cast members ranged from Marilyn Monroe to Michael Landon. Actor Brian Keith was his son's godfather. In the above photograph, Lilley (second from left) poses with Pancho Villa's son, Frank Villa Jr. (far left), while they were both doing stunt work on a Western in 1968. In the image below, Lilley (center) poses with actors Billy Crystal (left) and Jack Palance while shooting the 1991 movie *City Slickers*. (Above, courtesy of the Lilley family; below, printed with permission from Warner Bros. Entertainment, Inc.)

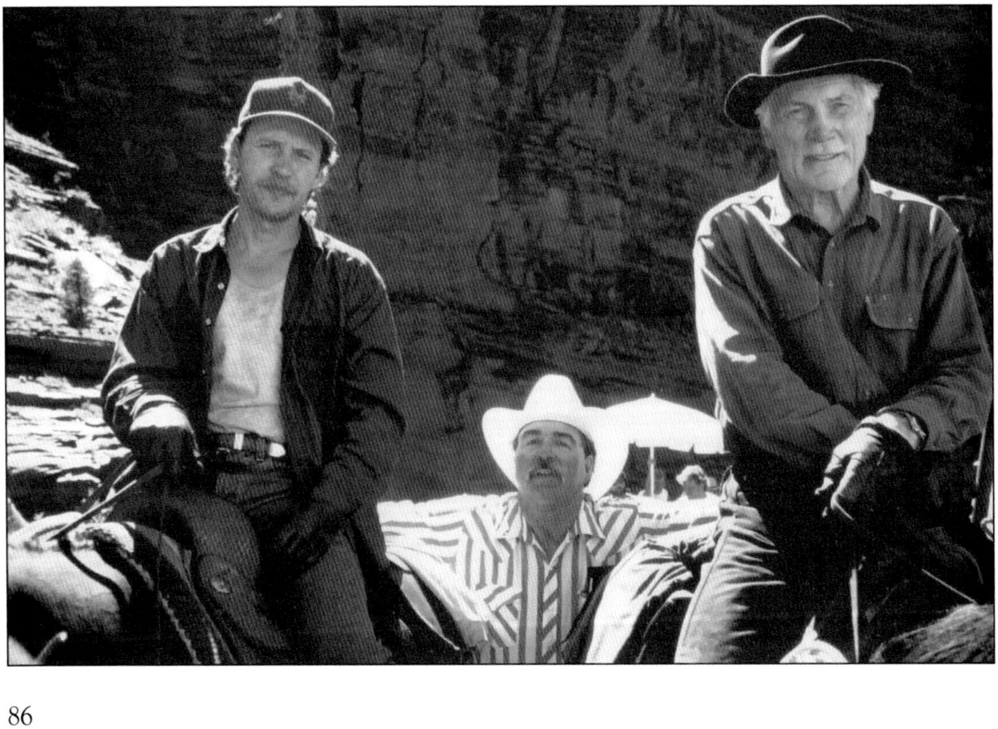

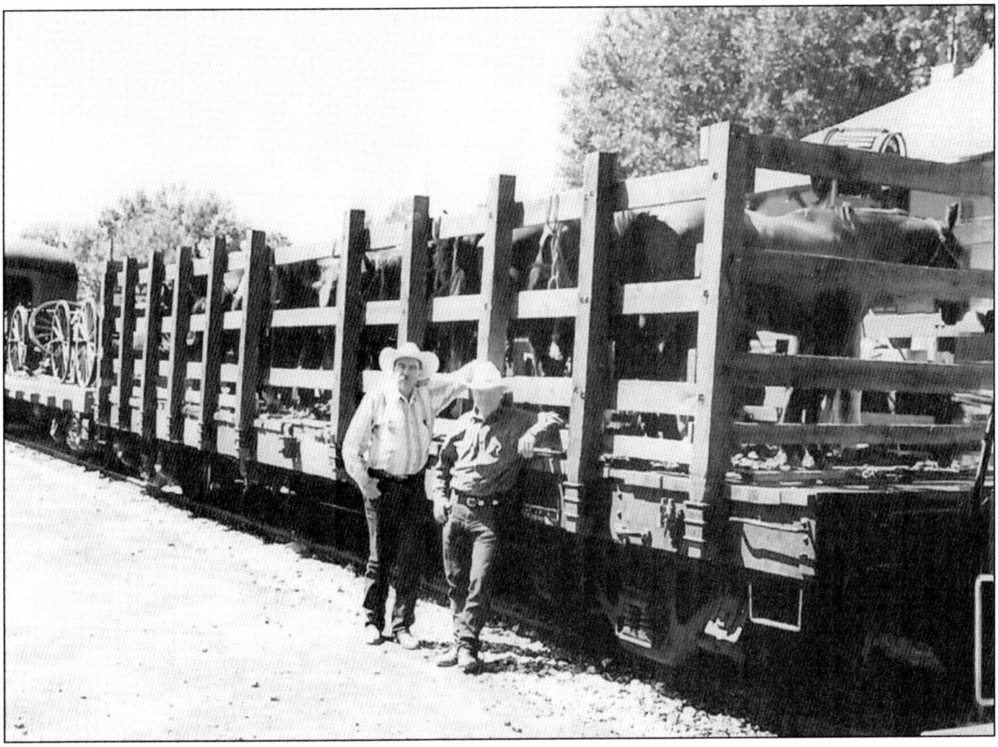

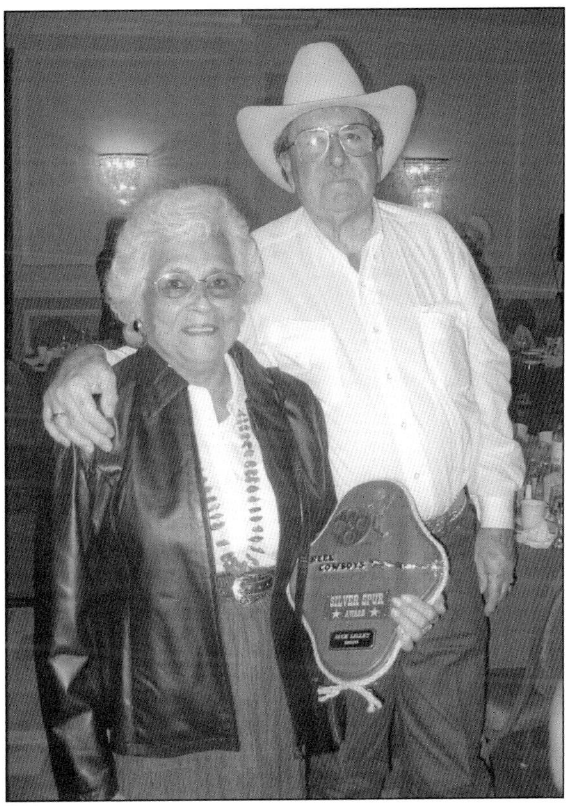

Jack Lilley's father, John, raised and traded quarter horses, so, from the earliest days, the Lilleys were relied upon for their expertise with animals. As Jack left more of the actual stunt work to the third and even fourth generations of Lilleys, he expanded his business, providing horses and other animals to locations for filming. In 1989, the Lilleys launched Movin' On Livestock, through which they were hired as wranglers, supplying horses and wagons to production companies. Above, Jack (left) stands next to a wagonload of horses with his friend, Dan Spaethe. Jack's wife, Irene, would sometimes go on location, even appearing on film in *Streets of Laredo*, in which she portrayed a governor's wife. Irene accompanied Jack when he received a Silver Spur Award from Reel Cowboys in 2010 (pictured at right). She was also with him when the City of Santa Clarita awarded him a star on the Walk of Western Stars in Newhall in 2008. (Both courtesy of the Lilley family.)

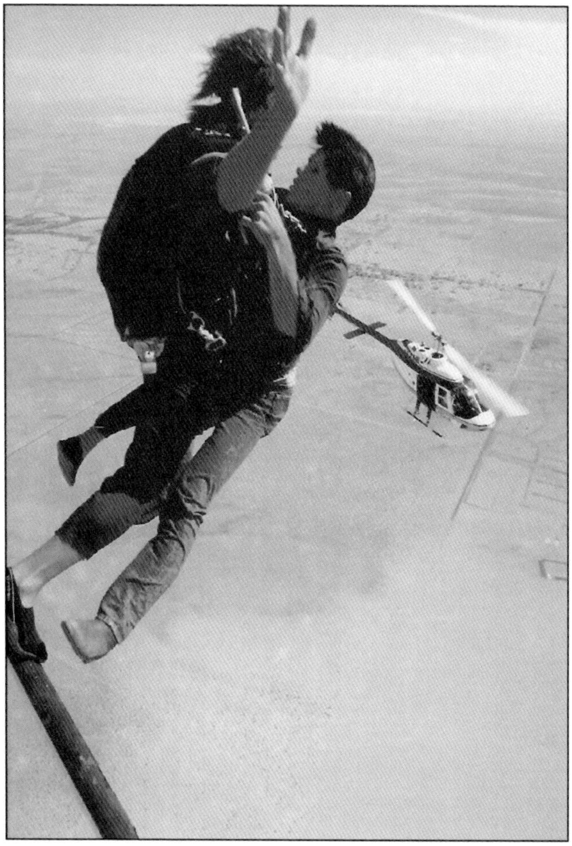

In the photograph at left, Jeff Habberstad (right), a stunt double for actor Keanu Reeves, and fellow skydiver Jim Wallace, doubling for actor Patrick Swayze, execute a scene on the strut of a helicopter in California City, California, for the movie *Point Break* in 1991. As stunt coordinator on the 1999 feature film *The Sixth Sense*, Habberstad (second from left in the image below) shared his vision with director M. Night Shyamalan (far right) for a scene involving his wife, Debbie Habberstad (left), in a near miss with a car on the streets of Philadelphia. *The Sixth Sense* was one of several films Habberstad worked on with Shyamalan. (Both courtesy of Deborah Habberstad.)

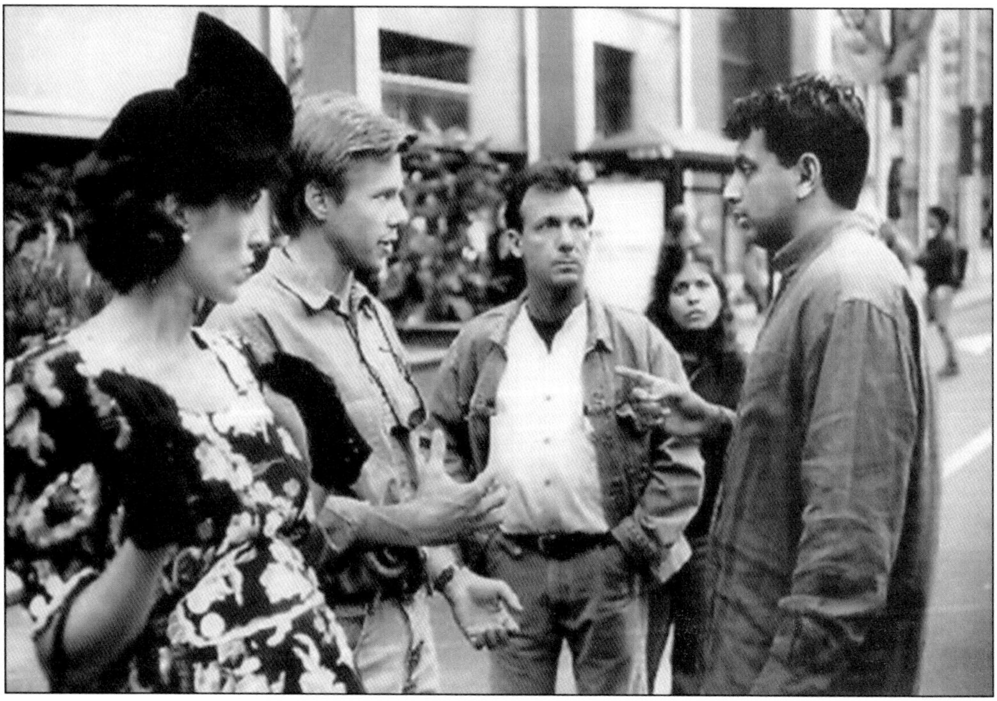

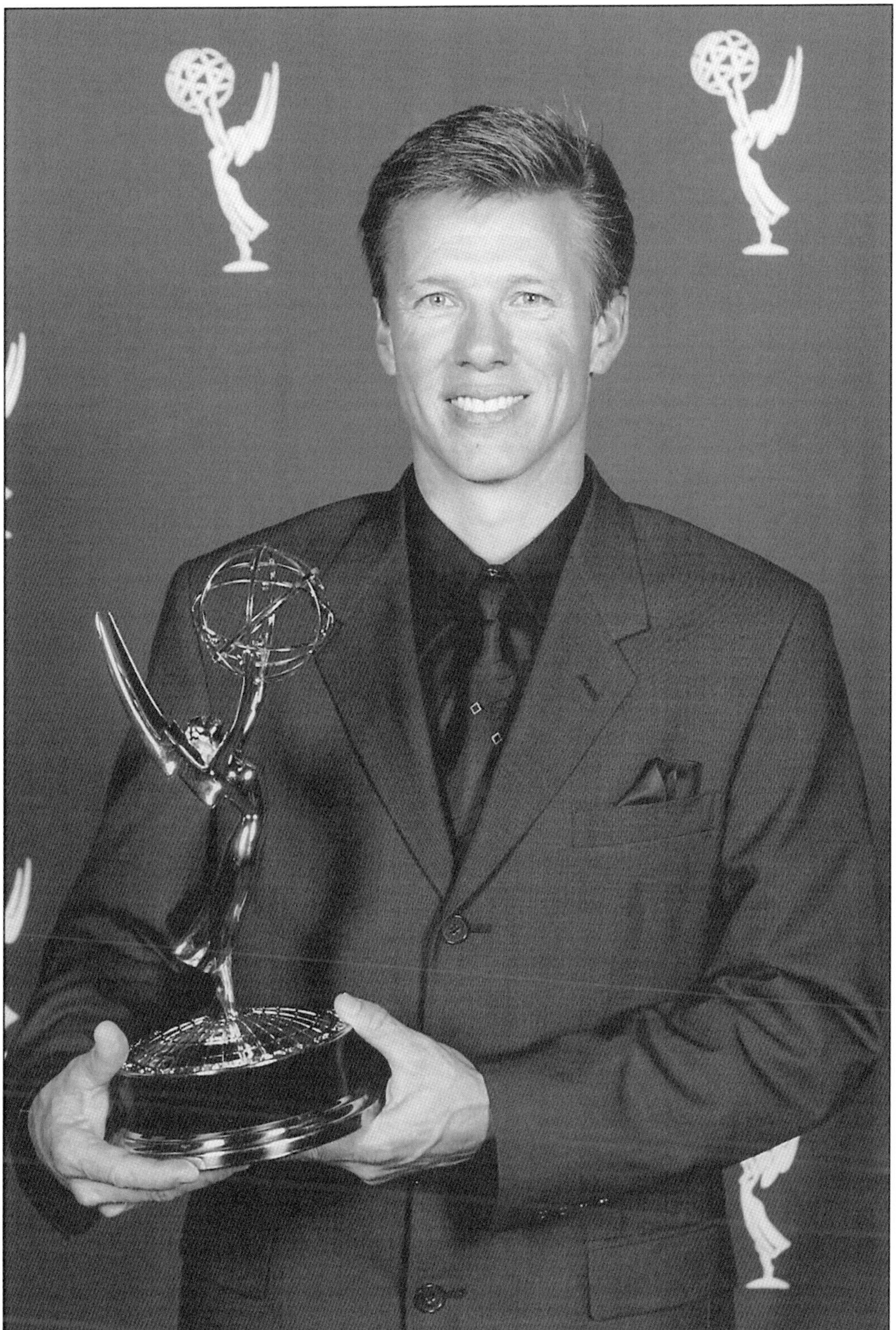

Emmy Award winner Jeff Habberstad moved to the Santa Clarita Valley in 1990. He and his wife, Debbie, and three children—Trevor, Shane, and Allie—all performed stunts and joined other entertainment industry professionals when they moved to Sand Canyon. Here, Habberstad holds one of the first Emmys given out for the category of Outstanding Stunt Coordination, which he won for his work on the ABC drama *Alias*—specifically, for the 2003 episode called "The Telling." (Courtesy of the Habberstad family.)

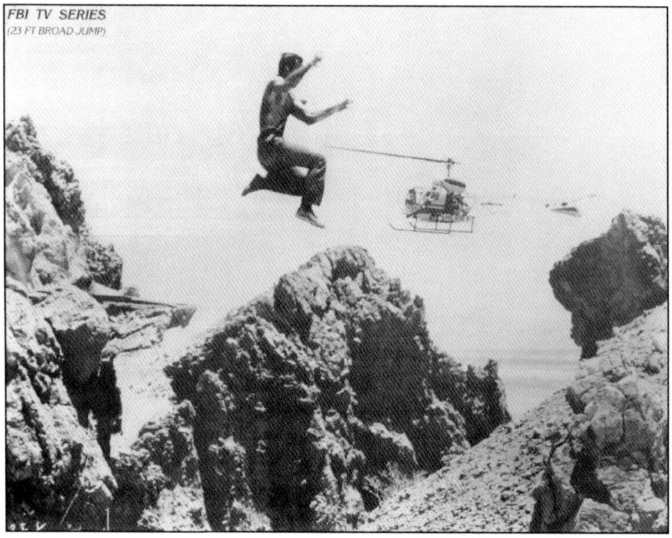

Loren Janes, who cofounded the Stuntmen's Association of Motion Pictures and Television in 1961, had a stunt career that lasted for almost 50 years. He began his career with an 80-foot dive off of a cliff in a 1954 Esther Williams movie. His background in gymnastics and diving prepared him for scenes such as this 23-foot broad jump in the television series *The F.B.I.*, which aired from 1965 to 1974. (Photograph printed with permission from Warner Bros. Entertainment, Inc.)

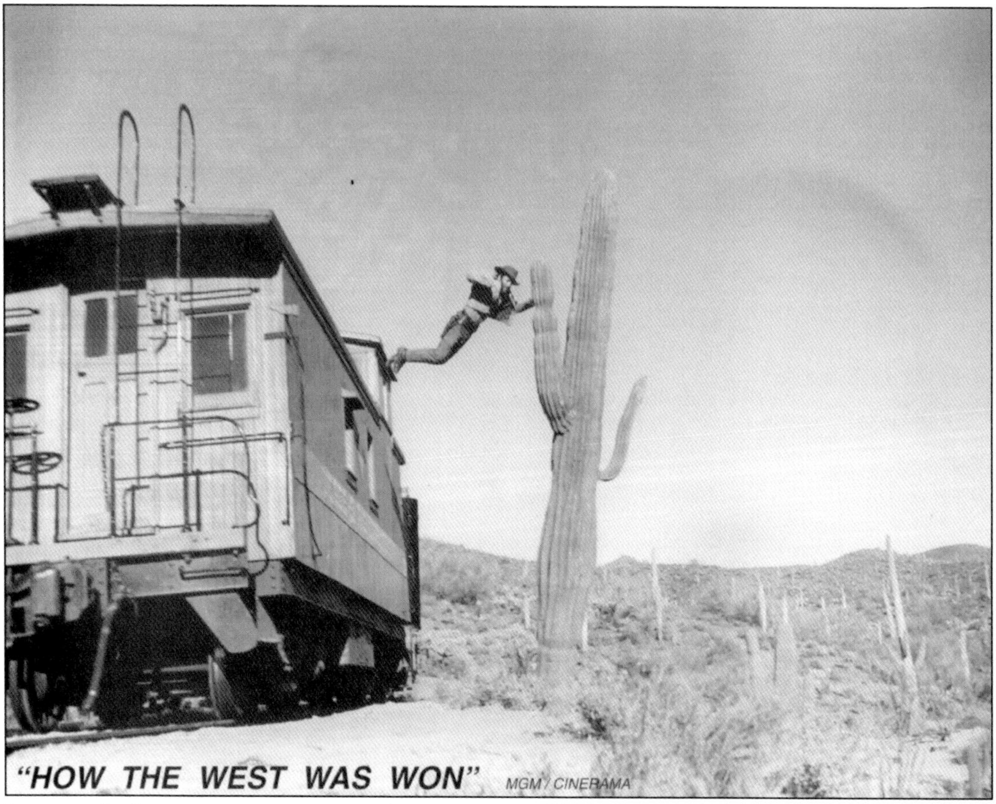

Janes worked as a stunt actor or coordinator in more than 500 movies and over 2,200 television shows, including *The Ten Commandments* (1956) and several *Batman* movies. Jumping off of a train—as Janes is doing in this photograph from the set of *How the West Was Won*—was one of many stunts Janes performed in Westerns ranging from *The Oklahoman* to *Blazing Saddles.* (Photograph printed with permission from Warner Bros. Entertainment, Inc.)

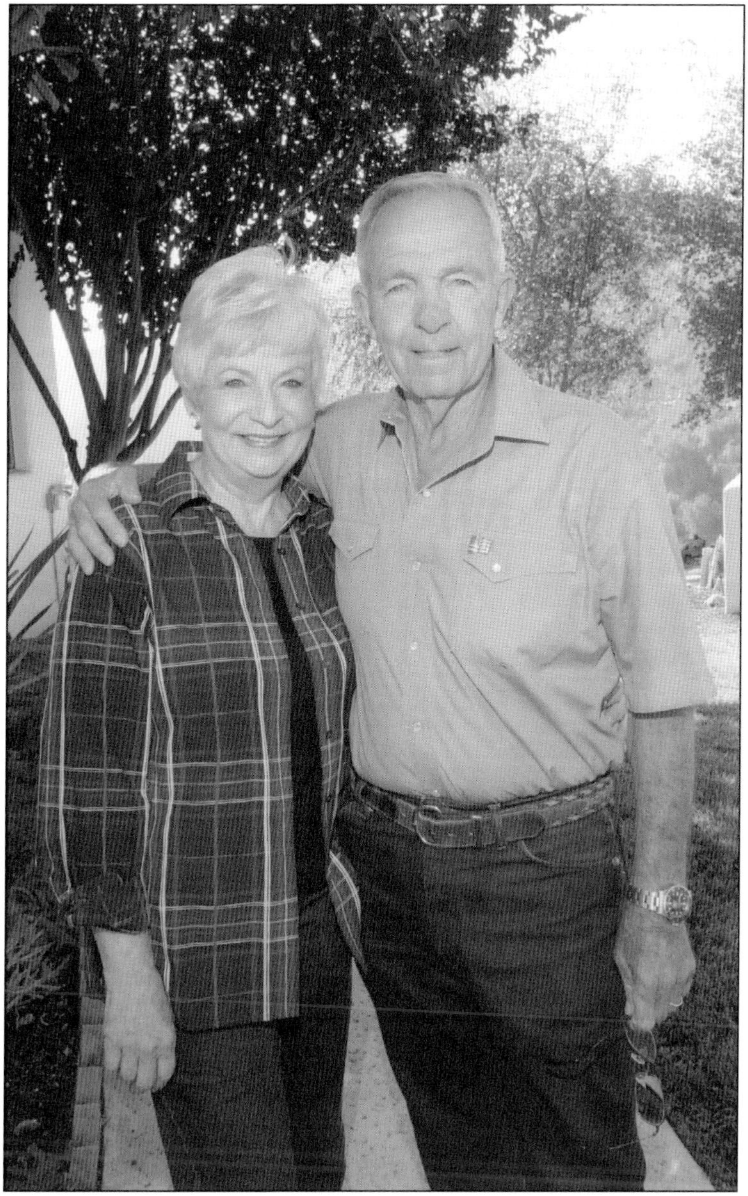

Loren Janes moved to Canyon Country in 1967, before the construction of California State Route 14 (the 14 Freeway). He was at home during the 6.6-magnitude Sylmar earthquake in 1971, when parts of the Santa Clarita Valley became virtually inaccessible, and telephone service was discontinued. Actor Steve McQueen, for whom Janes served as a stunt double for 23 years, rode a motorcycle through rubble to arrive at the stuntman's house to offer assistance. Janes recalled that it was McQueen's ability to leave Canyon Country and seek help that brought a helicopter to airlift an expectant mother to a hospital. In retirement, Janes moved to a home near Bear Divide with his wife, concert pianist Jan Sanborn (pictured above with Janes). Among his numerous recognitions is the 2001 Golden Boot award, given by the Motion Picture & Television Fund for contributions to Western films; Janes joined such previous honorees as Roy Rogers and Gene Autry. In 2010, Janes received a Lifetime Achievement Award from the Taurus World Stunt Awards. Janes also has a star on the Walk of Western Stars in Santa Clarita. (Courtesy of Loren Janes.)

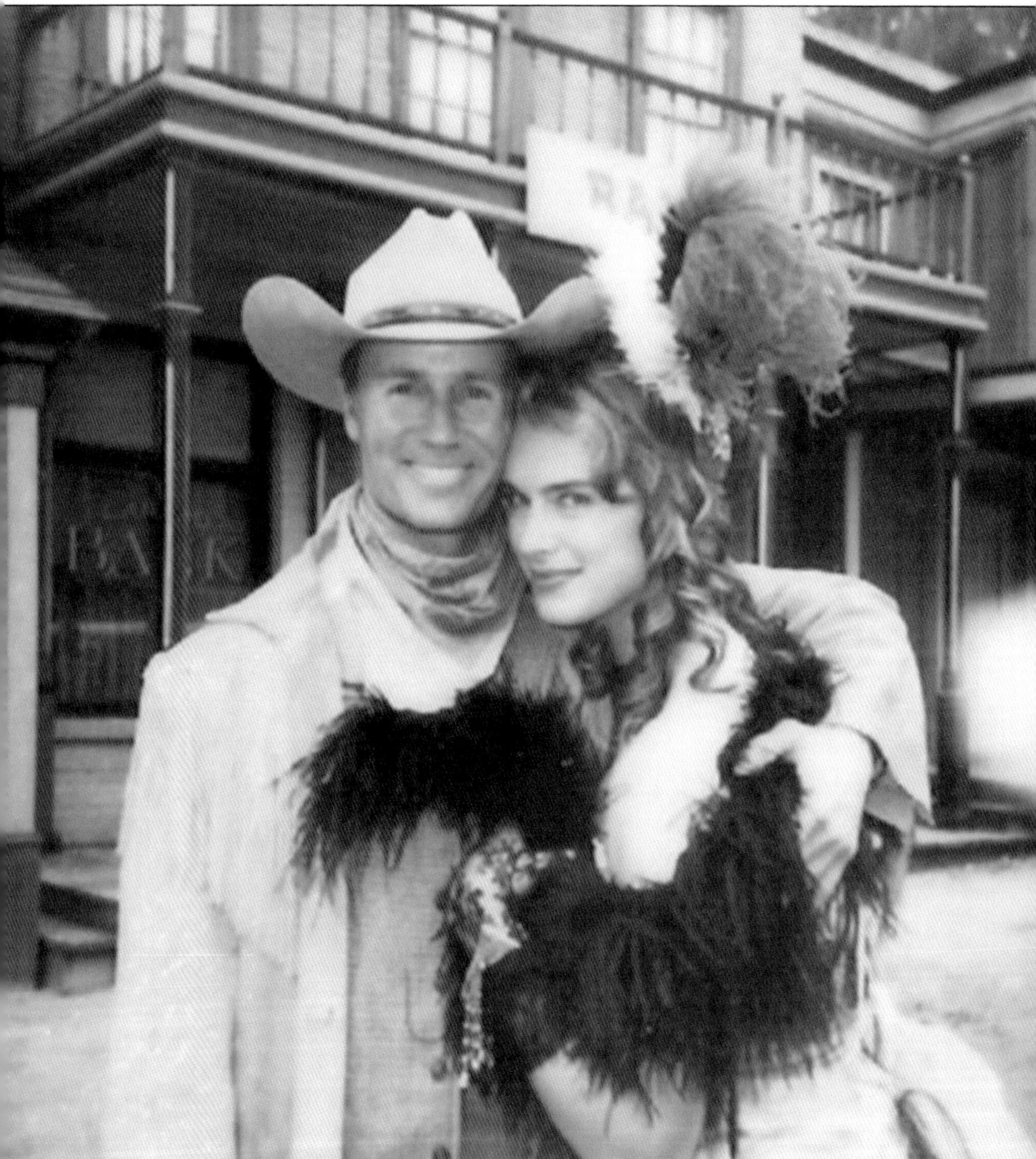

Before his move to Canyon Country in 1989, Craig Branham already had a lot on his resume. The Tombstone, Arizona, native was a four-time All-American athlete in college, and while competing for Pima Community College in Tucson, he set a national record in the decathlon. After Branham entered and won a male model of the year contest, he ended up with a New York City agency and eventually worked in Europe, appearing in prêt-à-porter fashion shows in Paris. Branham worked for Armani, Guess, Girbaud, and became the fit model for the late Gianni Versace, traveling with the designer. He is pictured here in 1996 with actress Brooke Shields during a break in an acting role on the show *Suddenly Susan*. (Courtesy of Craig Branham.)

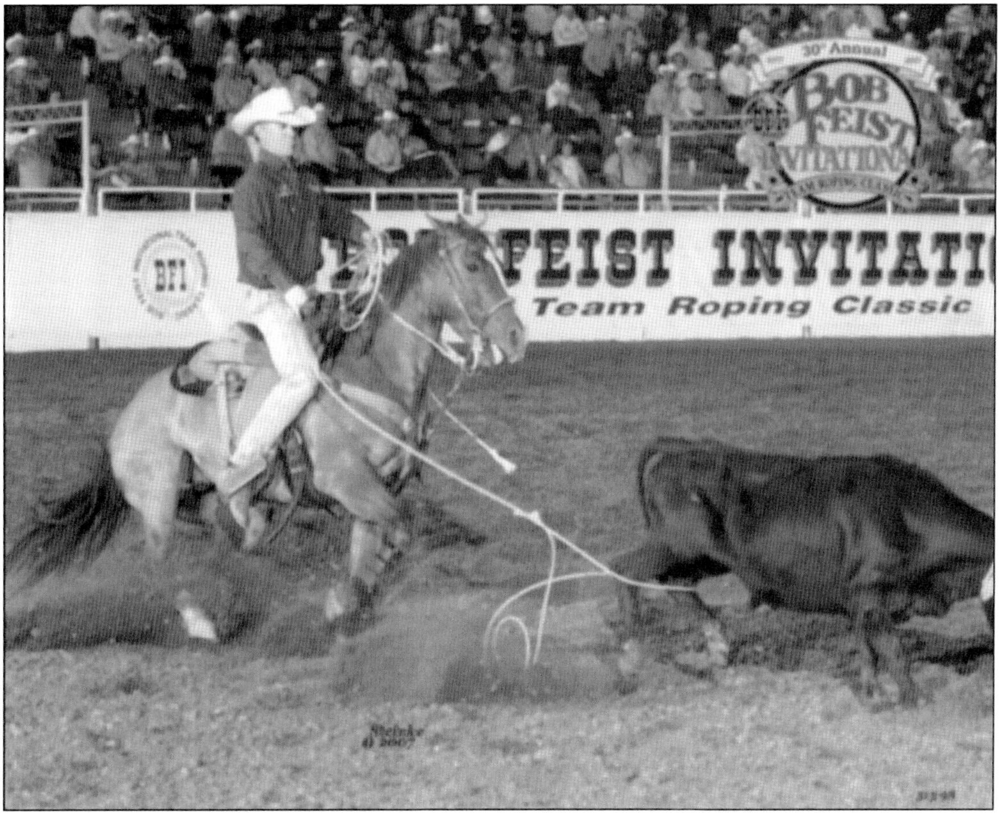

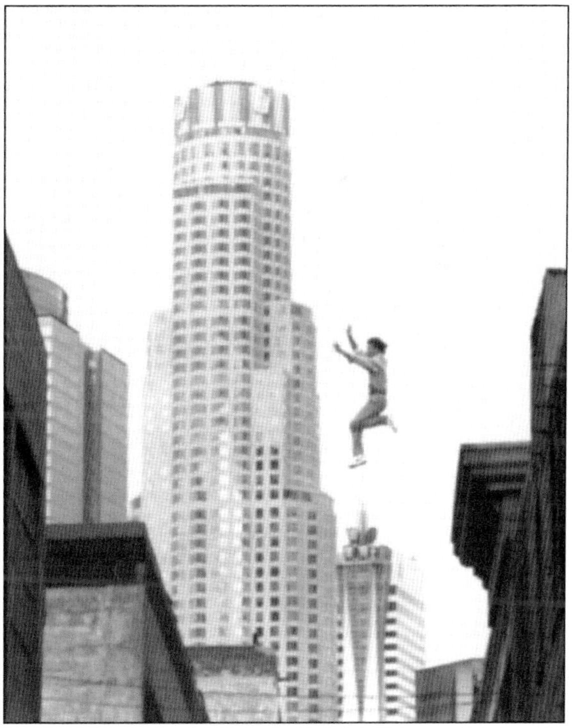

The photograph at right shows Craig Branham doing stunt work on a commercial that aired during the Super Bowl. In 1991, Branham became a part of the television show *American Gladiators* and won the show's championship that same year. Also in 1991, he appeared in *People* magazine as one of their "50 Most Beautiful People." At times, Branham returned to an activity he had enjoyed since he was a child in Arizona: rodeo competition. In the Professional Rodeo Cowboys Association (PRCA), Branham earned the Rookie of the Year award in 1999 for team roping. He competed in PRCA rodeos for several years, including the Bob Feist Invitational Rodeo (above). (Both courtesy of Craig Branham.)

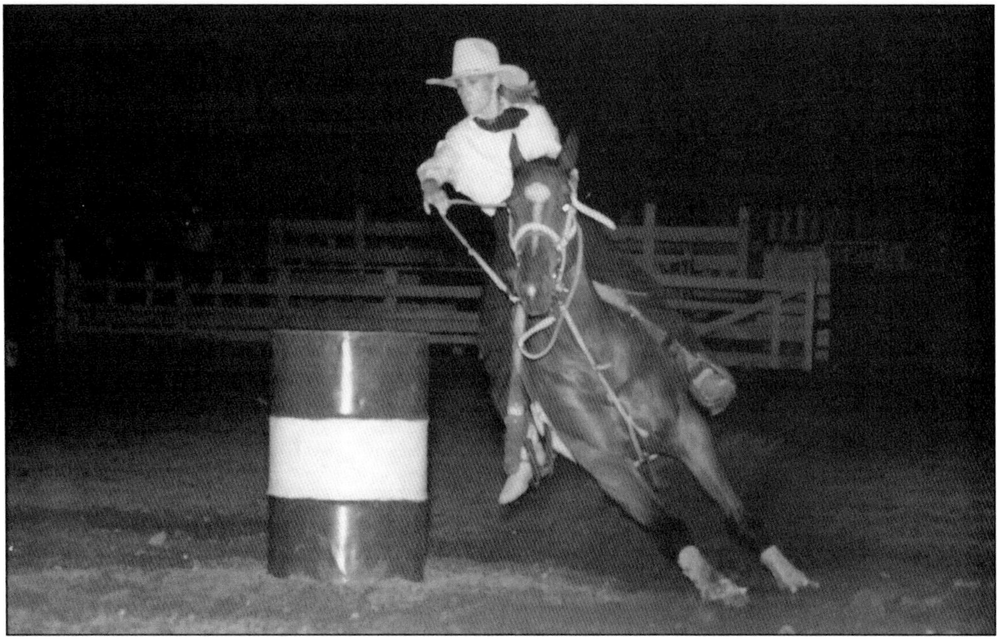

When Tracy Keehn moved to Canyon Country with her family in 1972, she made use of the area's wide open spaces for horseback and dirt-bike riding. At the age of 13, she began team roping and barrel racing (pictured above). Keehn attended Sulphur Springs Community School, Sierra Vista Junior High School, and Canyon High School, then entered the field of stunt acting, later bringing her mother and her children into the same line of work. Tracy met Jeff Dashnaw while doing stunt work, and they settled in Agua Dulce, raising four sons and one daughter—all participants in junior rodeos, motorcycle races, and Little League. Jeff advanced to stunt coordinating and second-unit directing, while the children—J.J., Nick, Chad, Jake, and Jessie—gained stunt experience. The Dashnaw kids were stunt doubles in movies like *Spy Kids*, while Jeff and Tracy doubled for such actors as Steven Seagal and Kim Basinger. Pictured below are, from left to right, Chad, Nick, Jake (in front), Jeff, Tracy, and J.J. at A Day in the Dirt Motocross Grand Prix in 2008. (Both courtesy of Tracy Keehn-Dashnaw.)

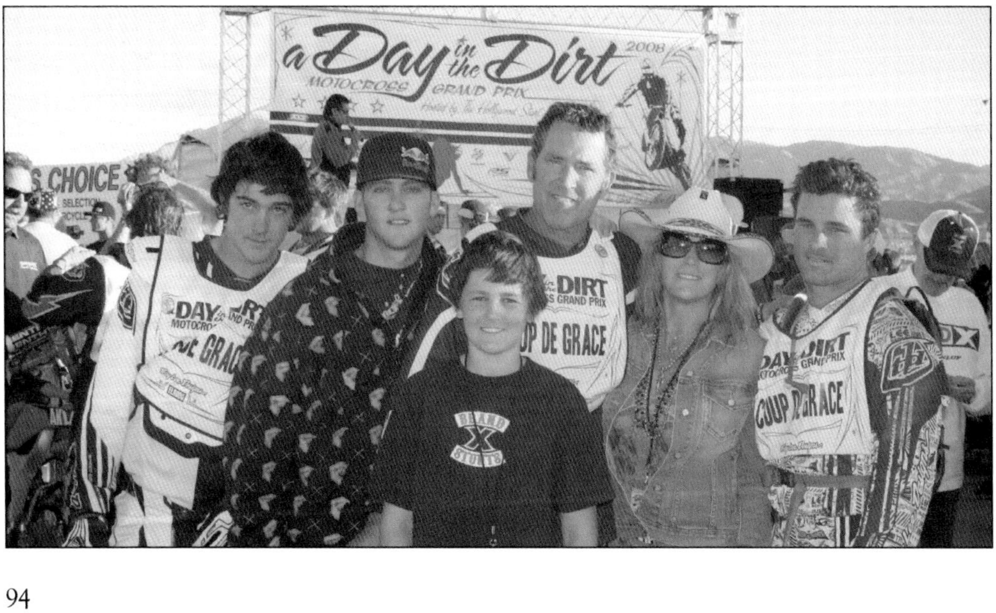

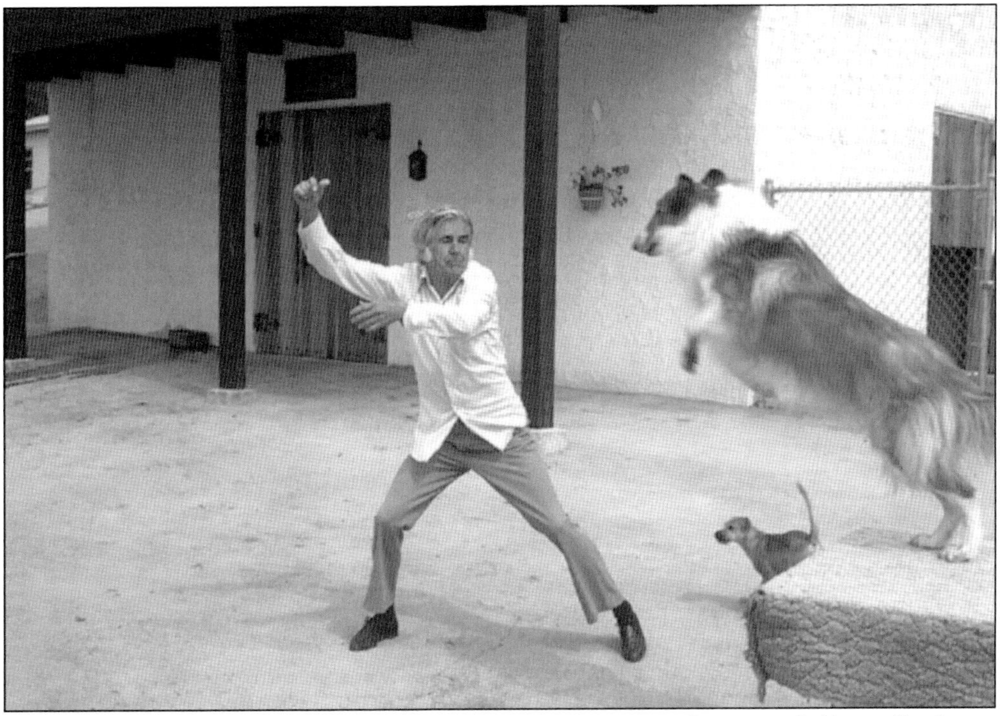

In 1955, Rudd Weatherwax spotted a property in Canyon Country that reminded him of his home state of New Mexico, so he bought it and built a house, kennels, and livestock outbuildings. In this image, Weatherwax is training one of many generations of Lassies that he bred, trained and handled. Rudd previously trained many other Hollywood dogs, including Skippy, who played Asta in the *Thin Man* movie series in the 1930s. (Courtesy of Robert W. Weatherwax.)

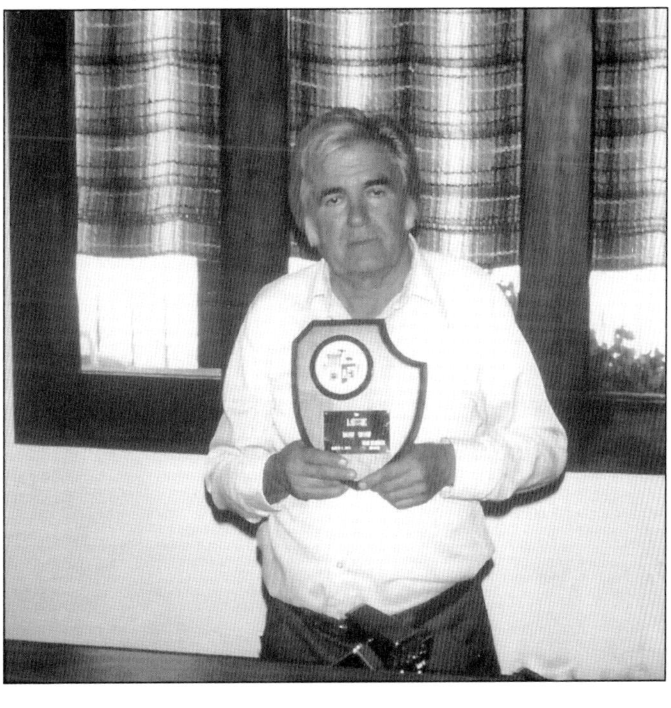

The image at right shows Rudd Weatherwax with an award he received in 1974 from mayor Tom Bradley and the City of Los Angeles for his work with Lassie. (Courtesy of Robert W. Weatherwax.)

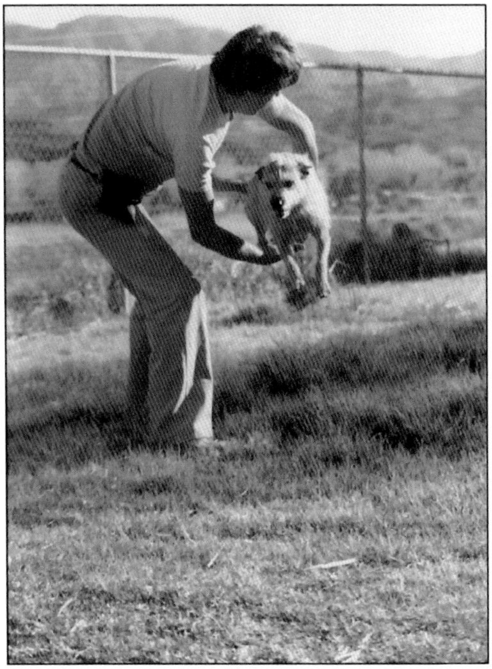

Rudd Weatherwax's son, Robert "Bob" Weatherwax, also entered the dog-training business; in the photograph at left, he is working with one of his dogs, Corky, a mixed breed who appeared in print ads, the *Newhart* series, and the movie *Down and Out in Beverly Hills*. In addition to his appreciation for the open space for the kennels, Bob enjoyed participating in recreational activities in Canyon Country; in the image below, he poses with his motorcycle and Lassie VIII. Bob and Lassie VIII were on the cover of the 1993–1994 local telephone directory, and the US Postal Service would deliver fan mail addressed to "The Lassie House" to Bob's residence. After Bob and his dogs moved away, the Weatherwax home, located on Soledad Canyon just east of Sand Canyon, was destroyed by a seasonal wildfire around 2007. (Both courtesy of Robert W. Weatherwax.)

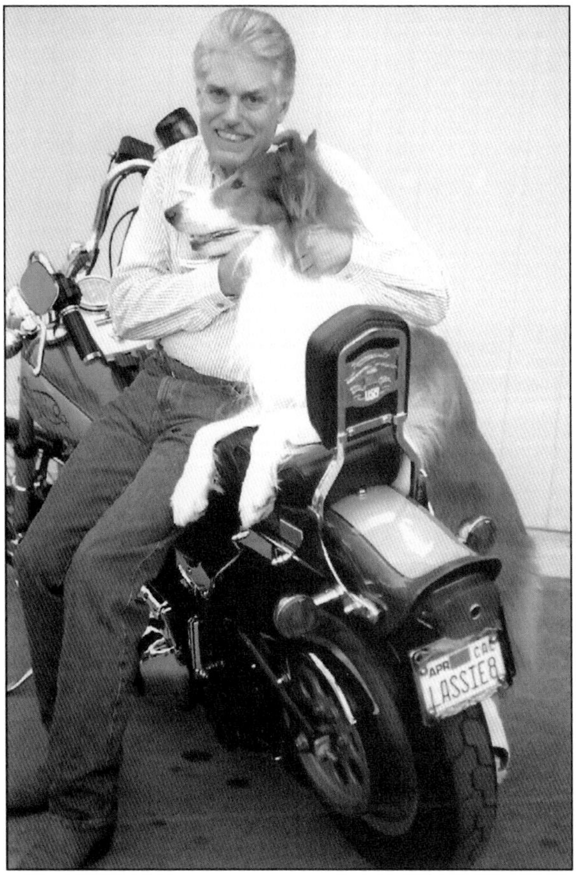

The Roar Foundation, founded in 1983 by actress Tippi Hedren, was created to help abandoned and abused exotic felines at the Shambala Preserve in Acton. Shambala grew to become home to over 50 big cats, including lions, tigers, cougars, black and spotted leopards, servals, bobcats, Asian leopard cats, and a jungle cat. As a true sanctuary, Shambala never buys, breeds, sells, or trades animals, and does not subject them to commercial use but instead allows them to live out their lives in dignity. Hedren, best known for her role in Alfred Hitchcock's *The Birds*, was prompted to establish the animal sanctuary when the Acton site was created for the 1981 film *Roar*, a film Hedren coproduced and starred in with her daughter, Melanie Griffith. In the photograph at right, Hedren is pictured with her cat, Antonio, named for her son-in-law, Antonio Banderas. The two tigers shown below, Thriller and Sabu, were moved from the late Michael Jackson's Neverland Ranch to the Shambala Preserve. (Both photographs by Bill Dow.)

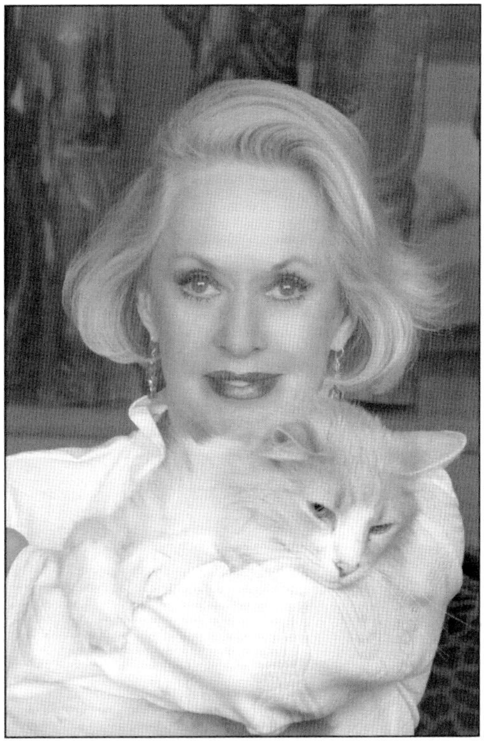

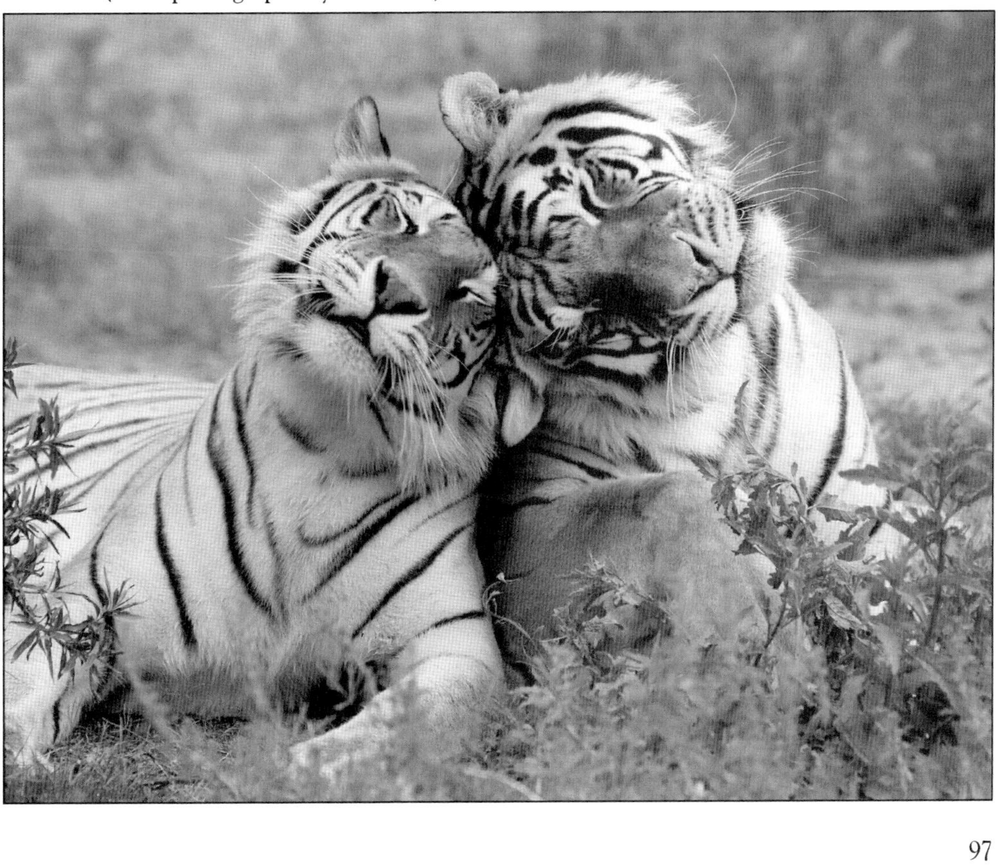

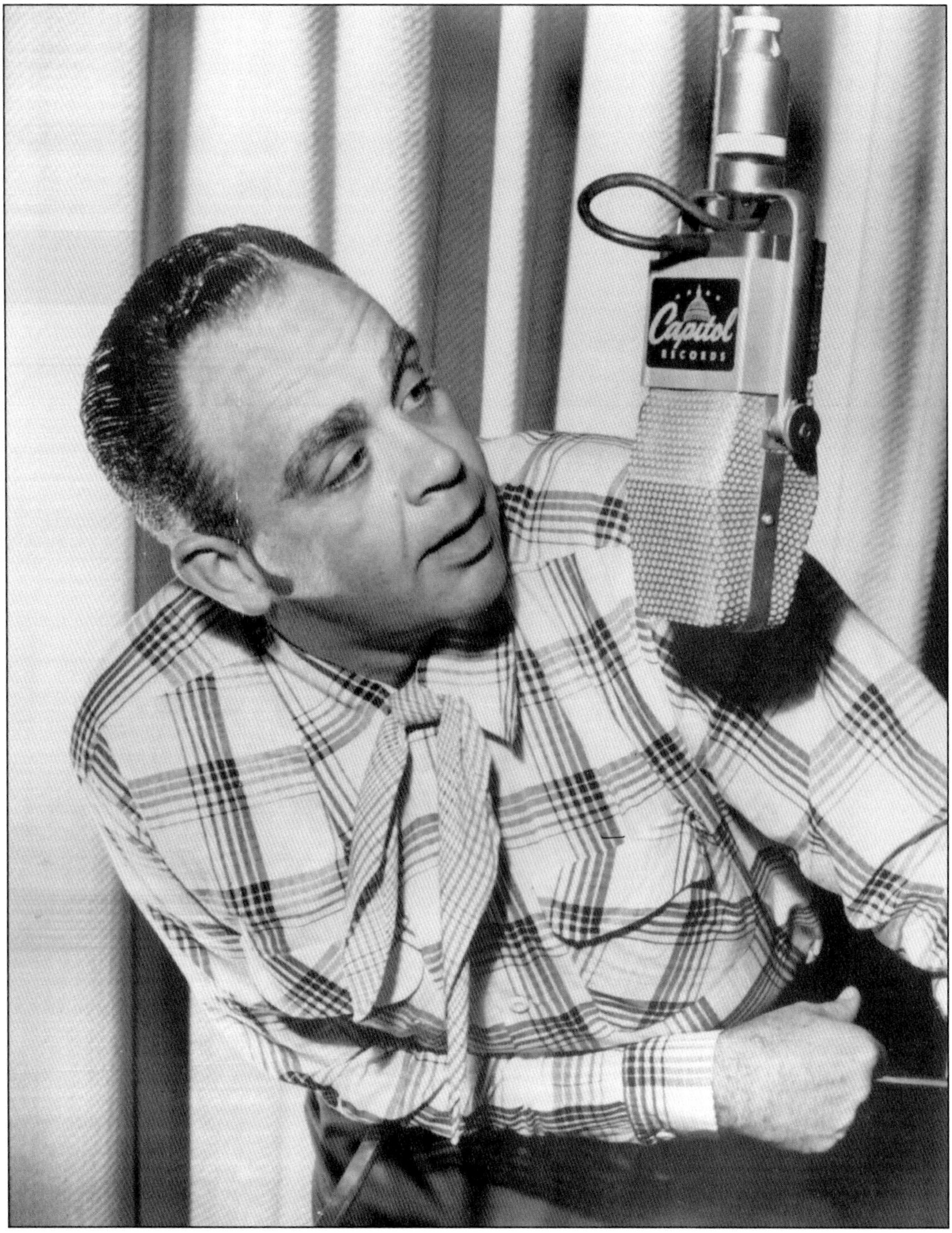

Cliffie Stone was already a country music legend when he and his family moved to Canyon Country from Toluca Lake in 1956. Stone's contribution was wide-ranging, including as a bassist, disc jockey, radio/television host, talent manager, music publisher, songwriter, and executive at Capitol Records, where this photograph was taken. He began performing at age 16, when he played bass on Stuart Hamblen's radio show using the name Cliffie Stonehead. Later, when he had his own radio show, he was on 28 stations in California, which led to his induction into the Country Music Disc Jockey's Hall of Fame in 1979. Stone received a star on the Hollywood Walk of Fame in 1989 and was inducted into downtown Newhall's Walk of Western Stars in 1990. He also earned a place in the Country Music Foundation's Country Music Hall of Fame in 1989. (Courtesy of Steve Stone.)

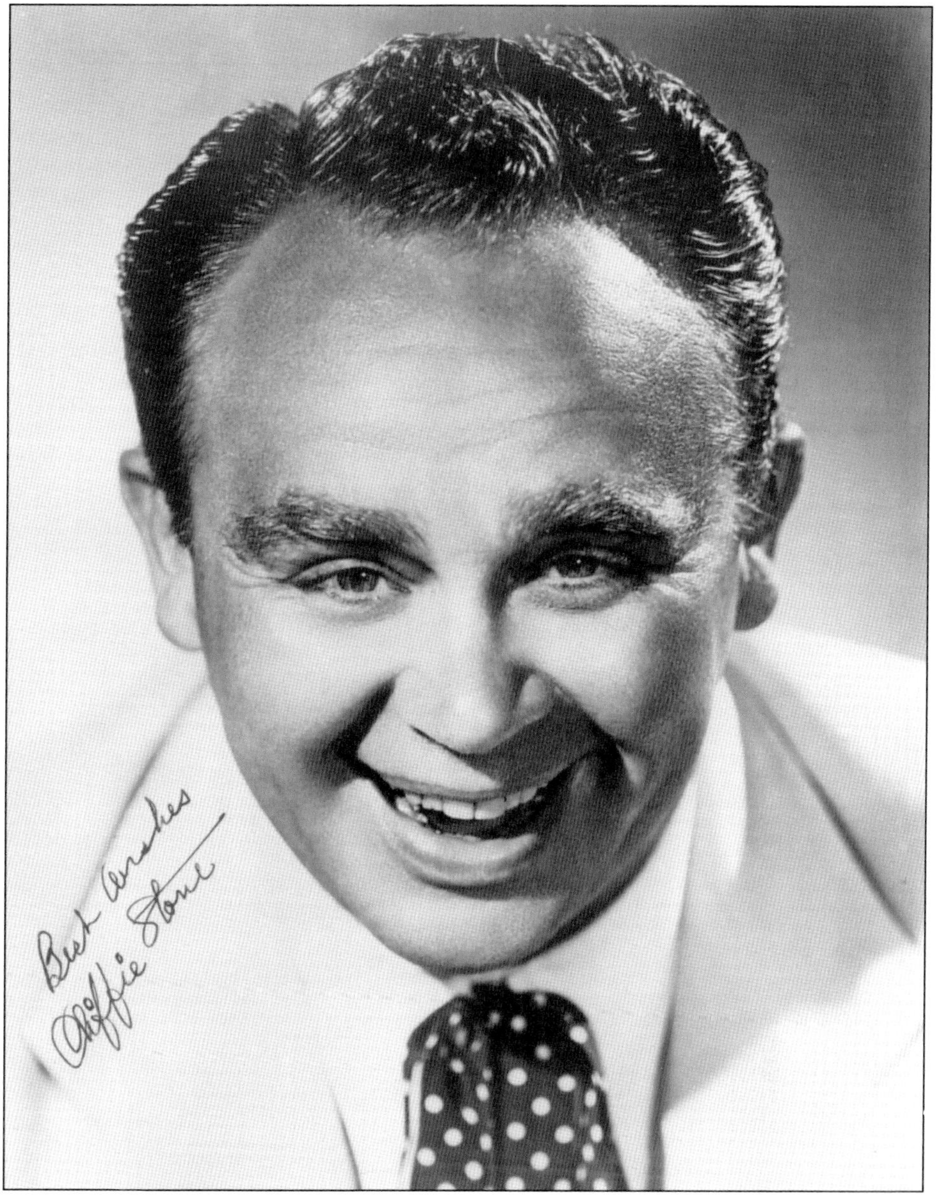

Born Clifford Gilpin Snyder on March 1, 1917, to Nina Belle and Clifford H. Snyder in Stockton, California, Cliffie Stone grew up in Burbank, enjoying football, acting, and music. Clifford Snyder Sr. was a successful musician known as "Herman the Hermit." Pictured here in 1954, Cliffie Stone hosted *Dinner Bell Round Up*, a lunchtime radio show that became the Saturday night television show *Hometown Jamboree*, which aired from 1949 to 1960. It was the launching pad for musicians including Johnny Cash, Barbara Mandrell, and Marilyn Tuttle, and it featured appearances by Liberace and Elvis. Stone never missed a broadcast in all the Saturday nights it was televised. It was canceled when Stone began managing Tennessee Ernie Ford's burgeoning career. Because Stone was one of the Academy of Country Music's founding fathers, the ACM's Pioneer Award was named "The Cliffie" after Stone's death. In Stone's 64-year career, he also wrote two books: *Everything You Always Wanted to Know About Songwriting but Didn't Know Who to Ask* and *You Gotta Be Bad Before You Can Be Good*. (Courtesy of Steve Stone.)

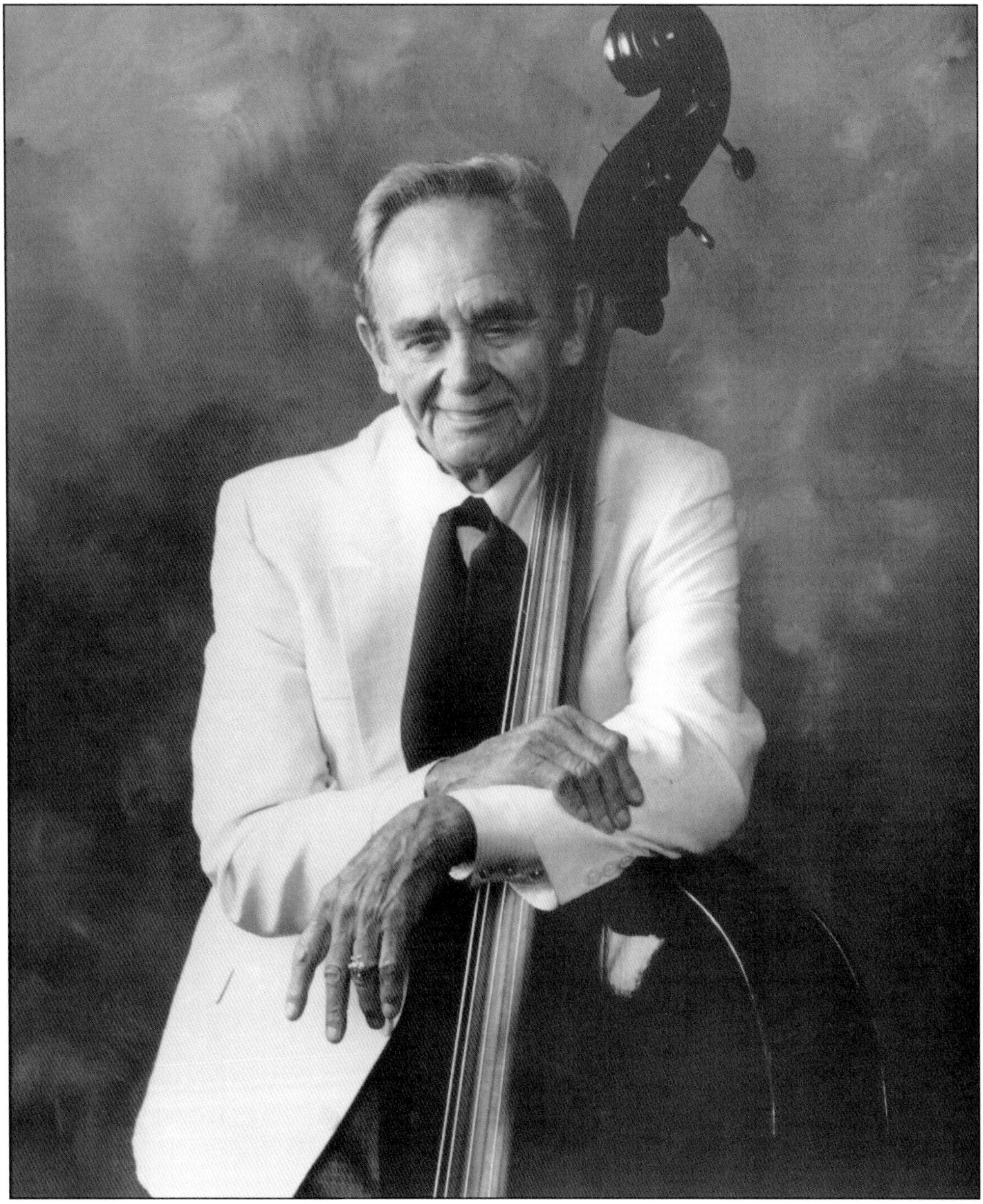

Cliffie Stone and his wife, Dorothy, and their children—Linda, Steve, Curtis, and Jonathan—moved onto 18 acres in Sand Canyon when it was still called Saugus. All of the children attended local schools, including Sulphur Springs School and William S. Hart and Canyon High Schools. Dorothy worked with the 4-H Club and twice led the Sulphur Springs choir to the state championships, where it once earned second place. Stone posed for this photograph with his bass fiddle in 1992, reflecting the early days of his six-decade career as a studio musician. After Dorothy passed away in 1989, Cliffie stayed in Canyon Country and later married songwriter Joan Carol Snyder. Cliffie died in 1998. (Courtesy of Steve Stone.)

Six

Solitude Battles The Elements

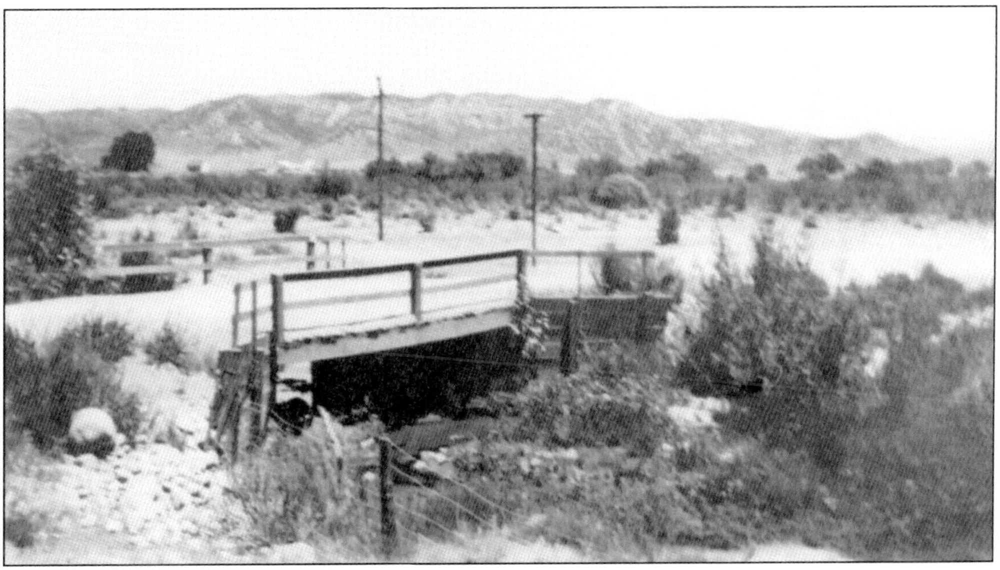

While enduring the natural course of things, whether it be periodic droughts or annual wildfires, Canyon Country and its surrounding communities have proven strong and flexible enough to survive the setbacks. Memorable events include the Great Flood of 1938, of which stories were told about the results of the 10 inches of rain Los Angeles received in just a few days. Mary Warmuth Sathre, a Canyon Country resident from the 1920s to the 1940s, recalled seeing flooding in Sand Canyon at times throughout her childhood. The worst storm she could remember caused water to flood out of the road like an underwater spring near Sand Canyon and Live Oak Springs Road, and she saw local resident Ace Cain's swimming pool rise up as the water table rose. This photograph, taken in Canyon Country in 1912, is labeled, "Crossing the Soledad Creek, out of Saugus." Warmuth Road, where Mary's family lived, required crossing the river in Sand Canyon. When the river was at its highest levels, the children would pile into a wagon and a horse would pull them across to get them to school.

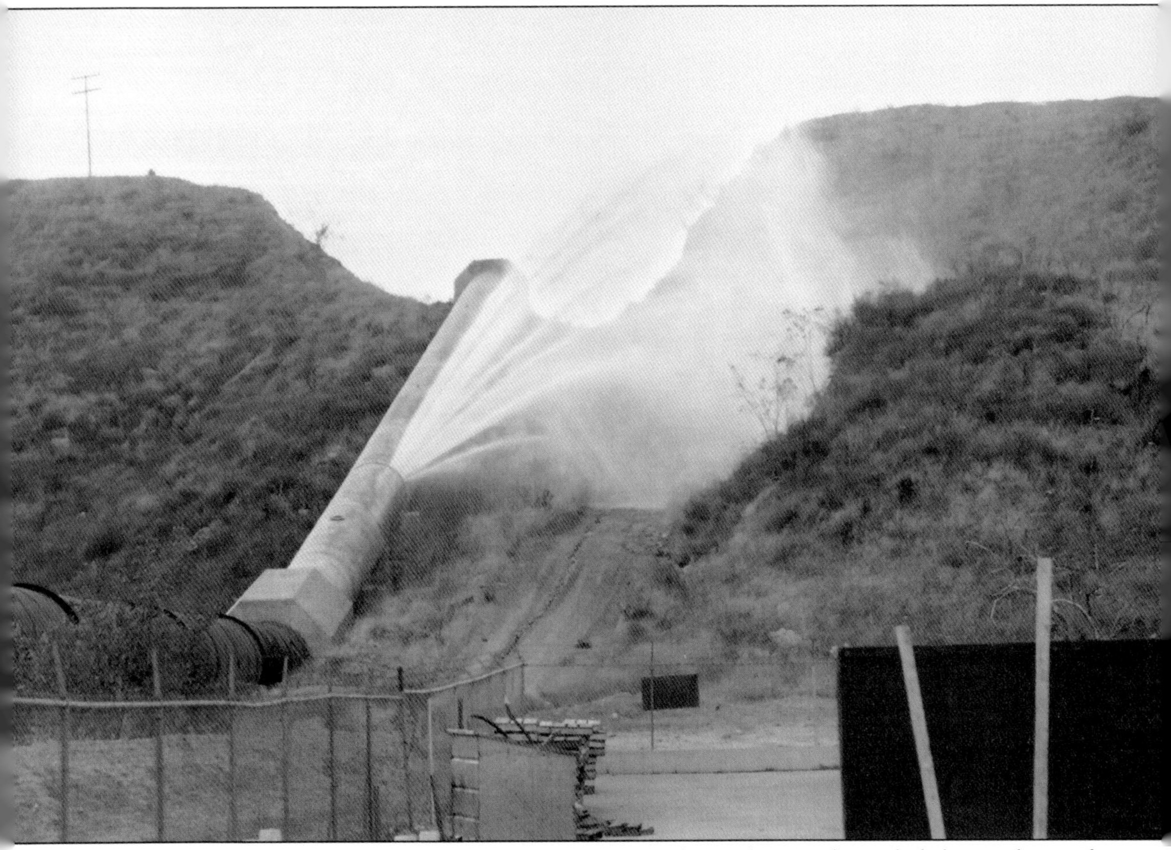

On January 17, 1994, an earthquake registering 6.7 on the Richter scale rattled the residents of the Santa Clarita Valley and Northridge, where it was centered. While the 1971 quake caused $5.3 million in damage locally, the 1994 quake caused more than $27 million in damage within the City of Santa Clarita alone. Some areas flooded as a result of burst pipes, like this one on the south side of Soledad Canyon Road, near Ruether Avenue. (Photograph by Celeste Thornhill.)

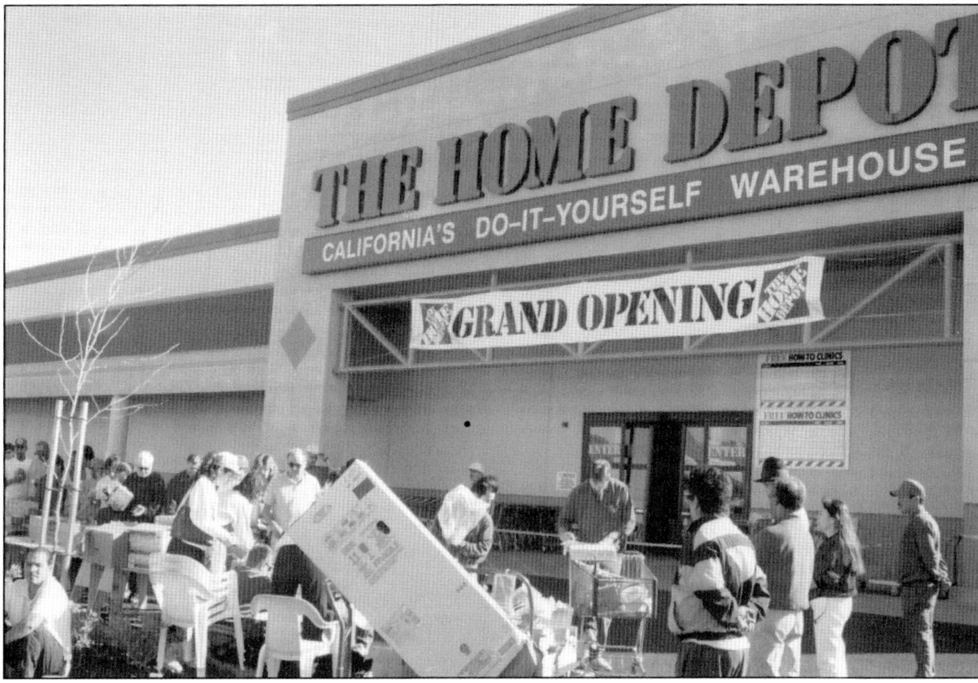

Residents needing resources after the 1994 earthquake went to The Home Depot on Soledad Canyon Road and Ruether Avenue in the part of Canyon Country sometimes called Honby. The store, which had just opened, became a distribution center for people in need. The photograph below illustrates the extreme impact the earthquake caused in local mobile home parks. This home went up in flames in the Greenbrier Mobile Estates East, located on Soledad Canyon Road on the western edge of Canyon Country. (Both photographs by Gary Thornhill.)

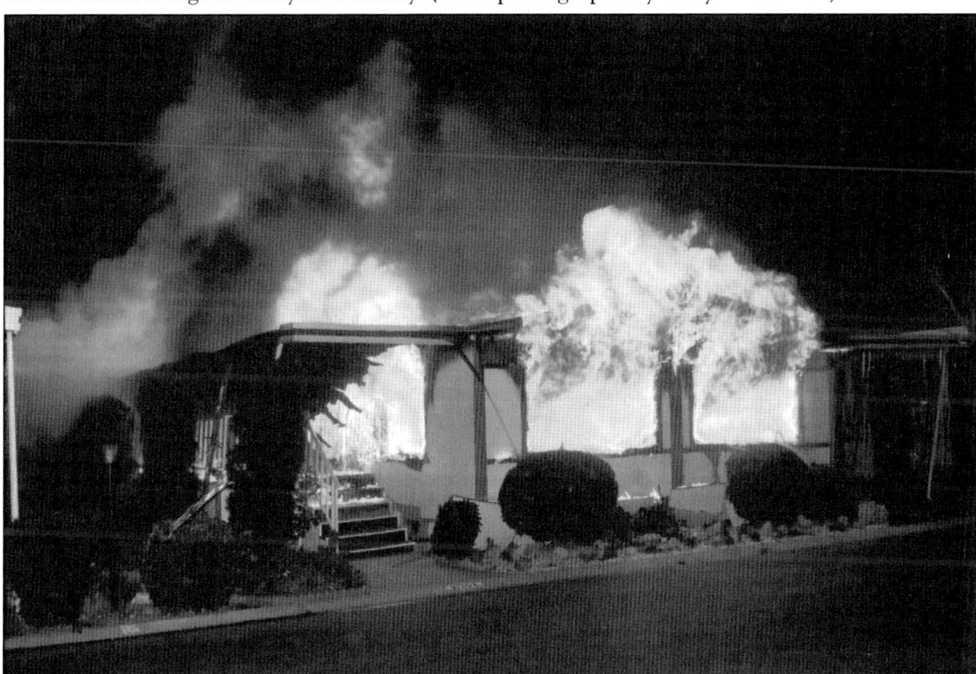

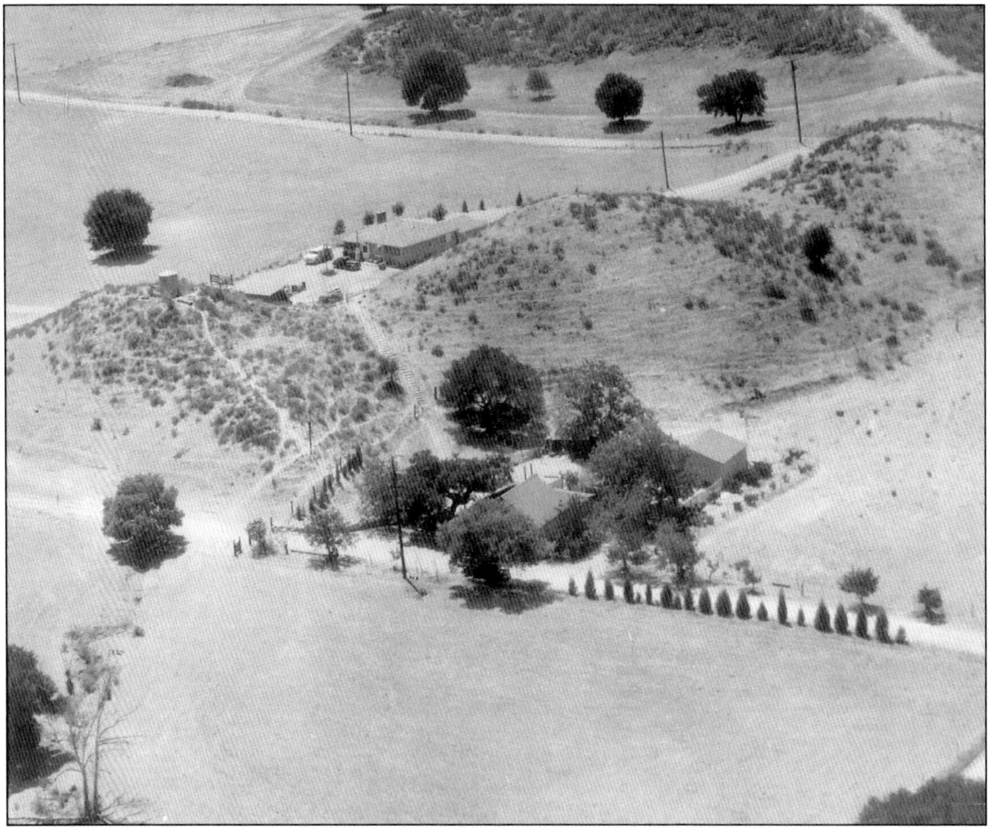

Wildfires have been an ongoing reality in Soledad Canyon. This Sand Canyon homestead belonged to the Warmuth family. In the 1930s, a fire ignited by a spark from a train spread south down the canyon. The Warmuths soaked gunnysacks and placed them on top of the wood-shingled roof, and children came home from school to stop the fire. The automatic sprinkler system at the Hewitt Chicken Ranch saved much of the canyon. (Courtesy of Mary Warmuth Sathre.)

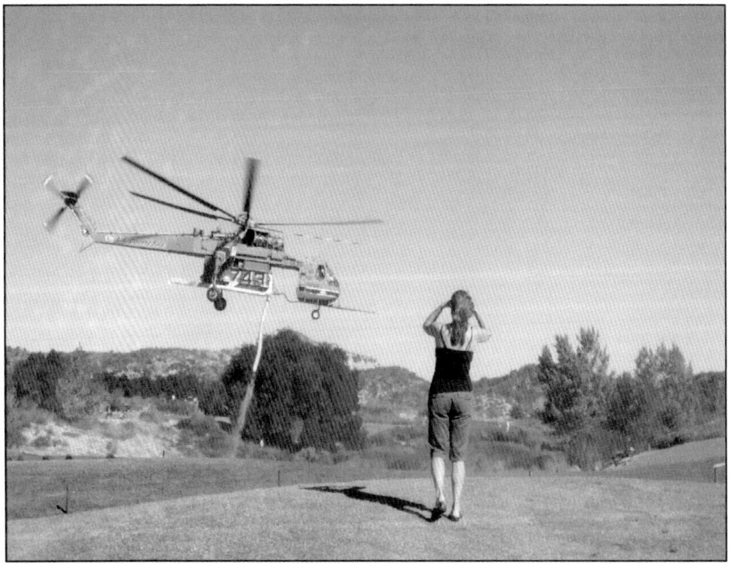

Firefighting changed a lot between then and 2007, when the helicopter shown at left drew water from a lake at Robinson Ranch Golf Club in Canyon Country. The Buckweed Fire, as it was named, burned 12,500 acres, including eight Canyon Country homes in the area of Camp Plenty Road in North Oaks. (Photograph by Rex Michael.)

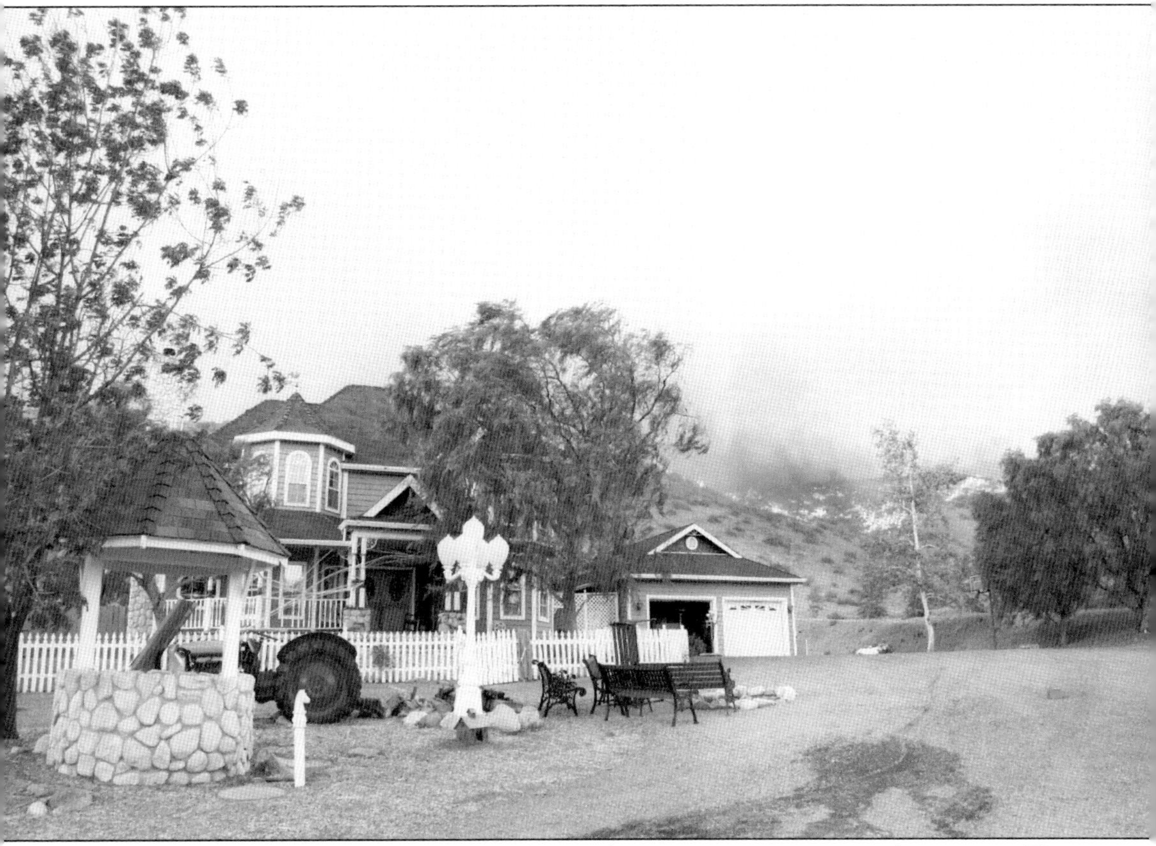

On October 21, 2007, a brushfire advanced toward a Canyon Country animal sanctuary, The Gentle Barn, on Sierra Highway near Vasquez Canyon Road. The six-acre facility, which housed over 100 large and small farm animals, was a challenge to evacuate. Cars were loaded with cats, parrots, and dogs, while a barnyard's worth of pigs, goats, sheep, chickens, horses, and cows were moved into trailers by neighbor volunteers. The remaining large animals were haltered and run down the hill. The house/office shown here was saved by firefighters, who arrived just as the fire began burning the roof. After the fire danger was over, The Gentle Barn's owners, Jay Weiner and Ellie Laks, hosted a party for firefighters. Two years later, when the "Station Fire" threatened Agua Dulce, Saugus, and Canyon Country ranches, The Gentle Barn returned the favor by providing refuge for the animals in those areas. The animal sanctuary moved into Canyon Country in 2003, choosing the area for its large horse and cow pastures, shade trees, and panoramic view of the Sierra Pelona Mountains. (Courtesy of The Gentle Barn.)

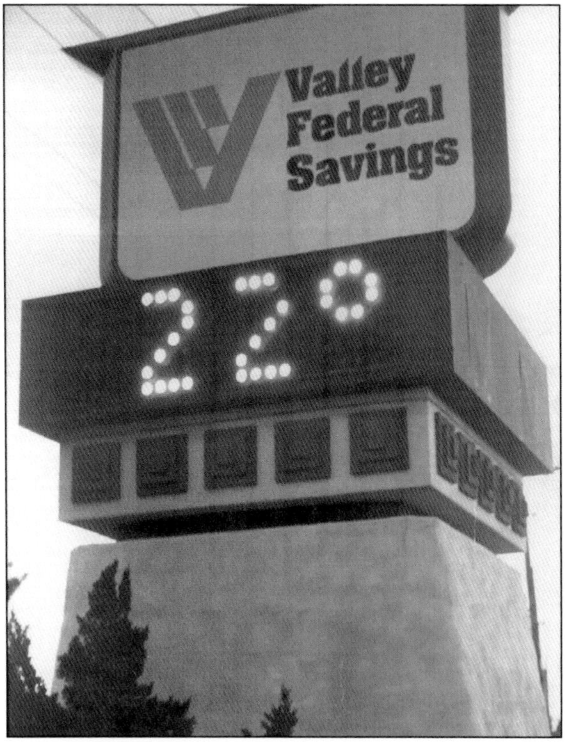

As extreme as Canyon Country temperatures can be in the summer, there are times when the Santa Clarita Valley gets a blanket of snow. These 1980s photographs offer a peek at some of those wintry experiences. In the image at left, the low temperature is registered on the digital display at Valley Federal Savings on Soledad Canyon Road. The photograph below was taken under the Golden Valley Bridge at California State Route 14 (aka the 14 Freeway). (Both photographs by Gary Thornhill.)

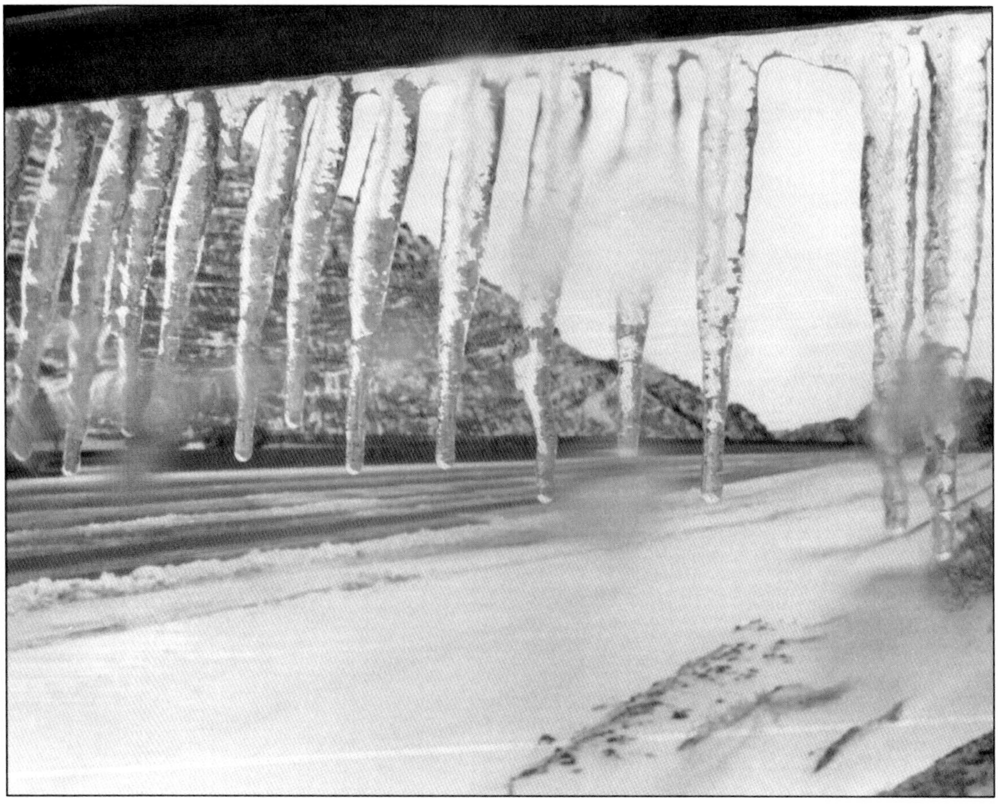

Seven

People of Progress

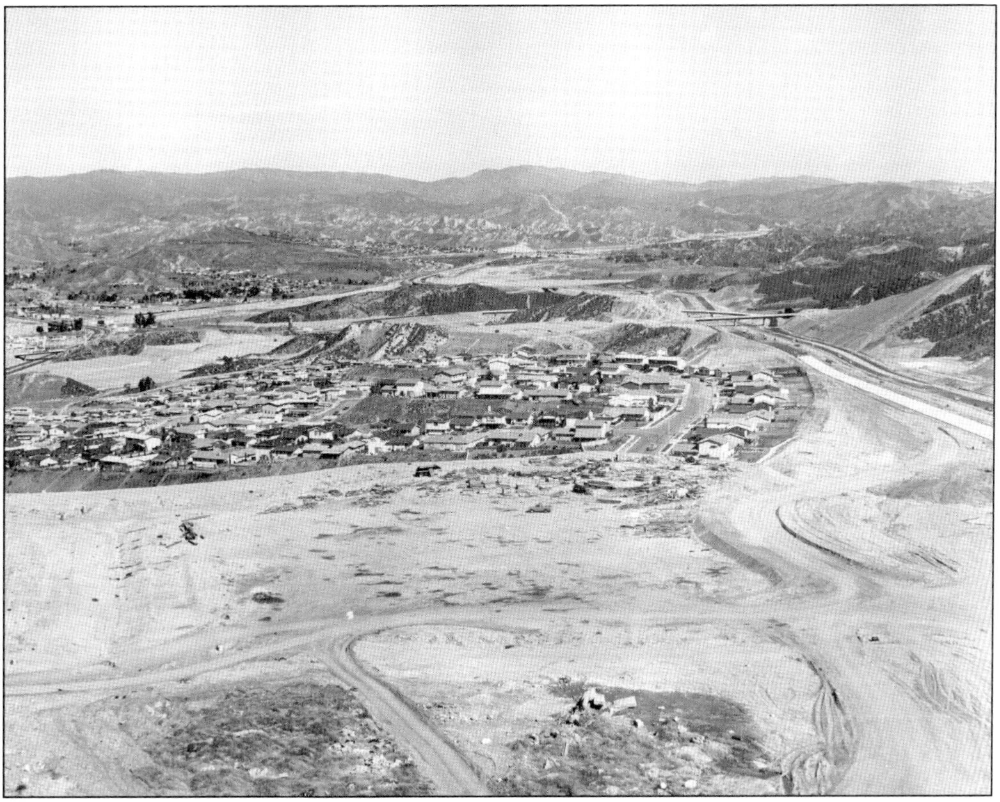

The agricultural community of Canyon Country has welcomed progress as new needs arose. In the areas of mining, railroads, and education, the region has continued to witness change. And, as in centuries before, it has been a corridor of transportation from one place to another and a destination for families seeking to put down roots. This photograph of California State Route 14 (aka the 14 Freeway) was taken in 1972 just before its completion. The thoroughfare offered a connection between Los Angeles and desert and mountain areas and facilitated transport into the Santa Clarita Valley.

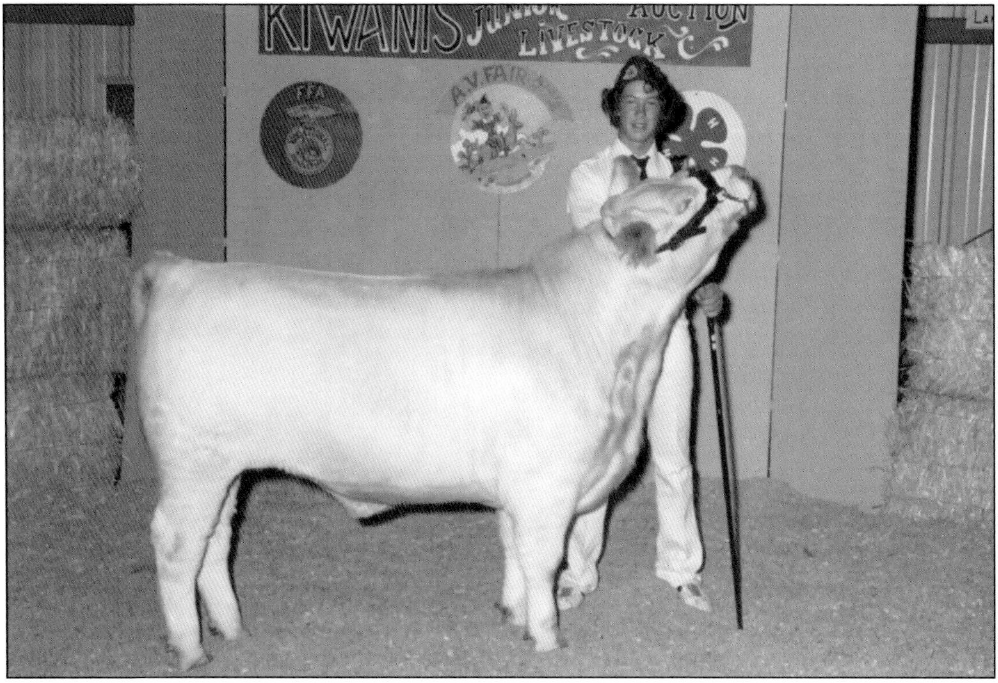

The Canyon Country Prairie Dogs was an active 4-H group in the late 20th century. Brent Parkinson, pictured above with his prize pig in 1980, was involved in a number of 4-H units raising and showing farm animals. Parkinson also raised goats, lambs, and steers. Below, a 1975 Canyon Country Little League baseball team poses at the Canyon Country Little League fields. The local club was established in 1966 just south of Soledad Canyon Road and Luther Drive. The program later moved northeast to a location that became a tract of homes called American Beauty. In the 1980s, the league moved farther north on Sierra Highway to where Canyon Country borders Agua Dulce. (Above, courtesy of Lynn Parkinson; below, courtesy of Scott Goodspeed.)

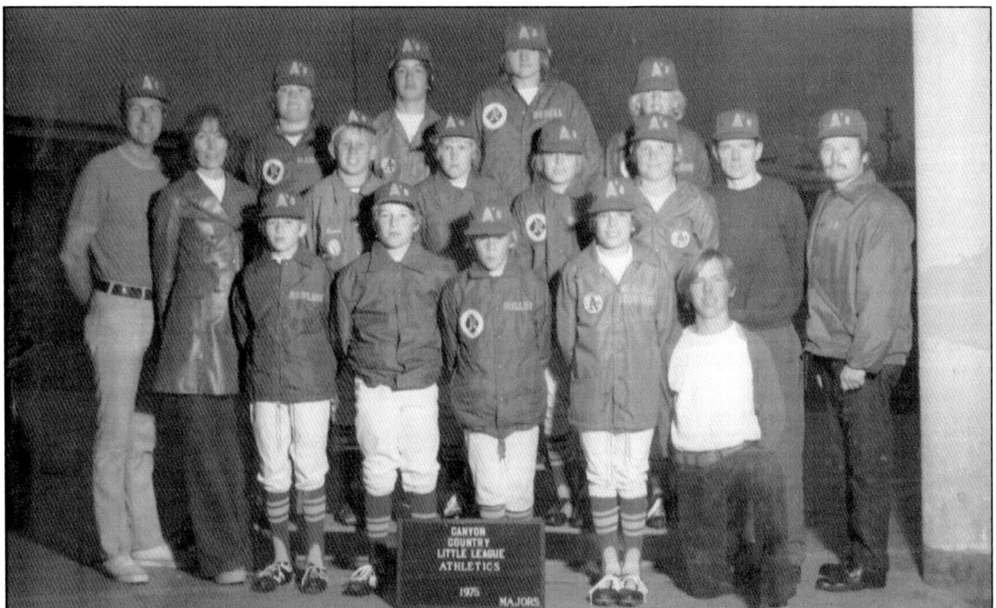

The 10-year-old Little League player at right later became an Olympic gold medalist in softball, as well as a three-time record-breaker for home runs. Crystl Bustos, who moved to Canyon Country at age three, played Canyon Country Little League baseball from ages 5 to 10, then played softball for two years. She attended Soledad Elementary School before it was closed and replaced by a movie theater complex on Soledad Canyon Road and Luther Drive. A member of the first class of Pinetree Community School, she attended Sierra Vista Junior High School and graduated from Canyon High School in 1995, where she played softball. Bustos joined the USA Softball Team (below), earning Olympic gold medals in 2000 and 2004 and finishing with a silver medal in the 2008 Olympic Games. Bustos broke the record for home runs at all three Olympic Games competitions. (Both courtesy of the Bustos family.)

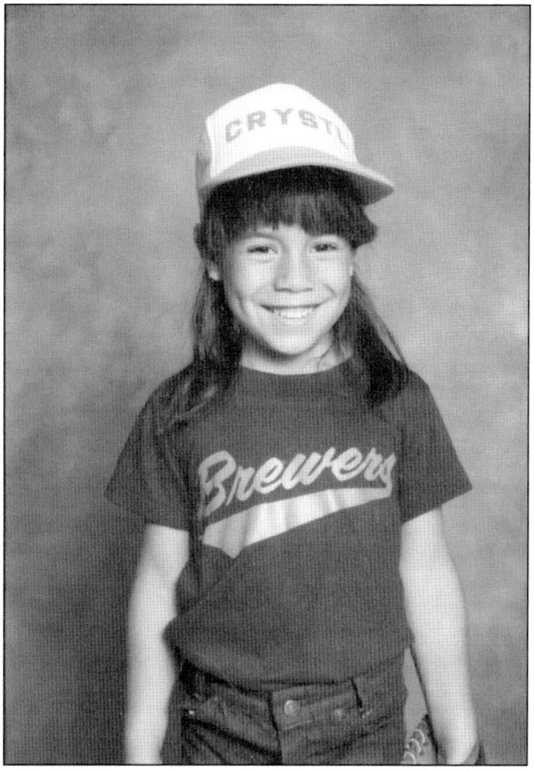

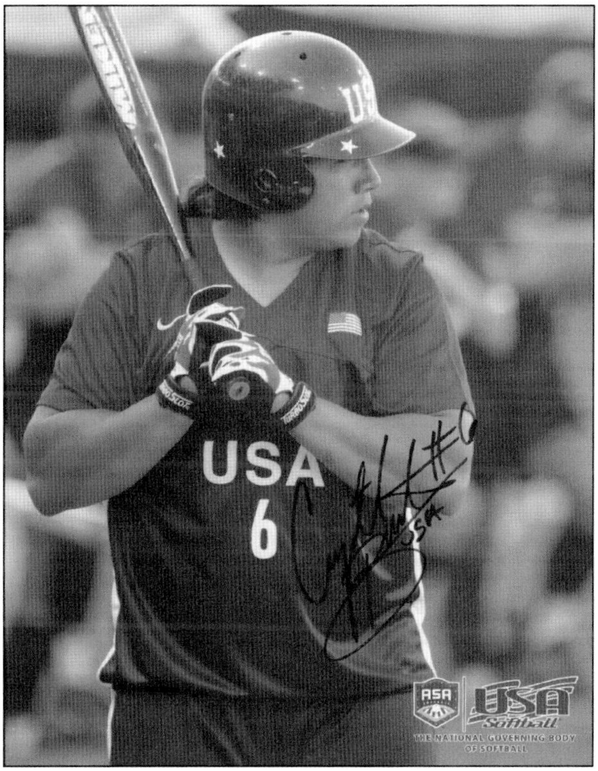

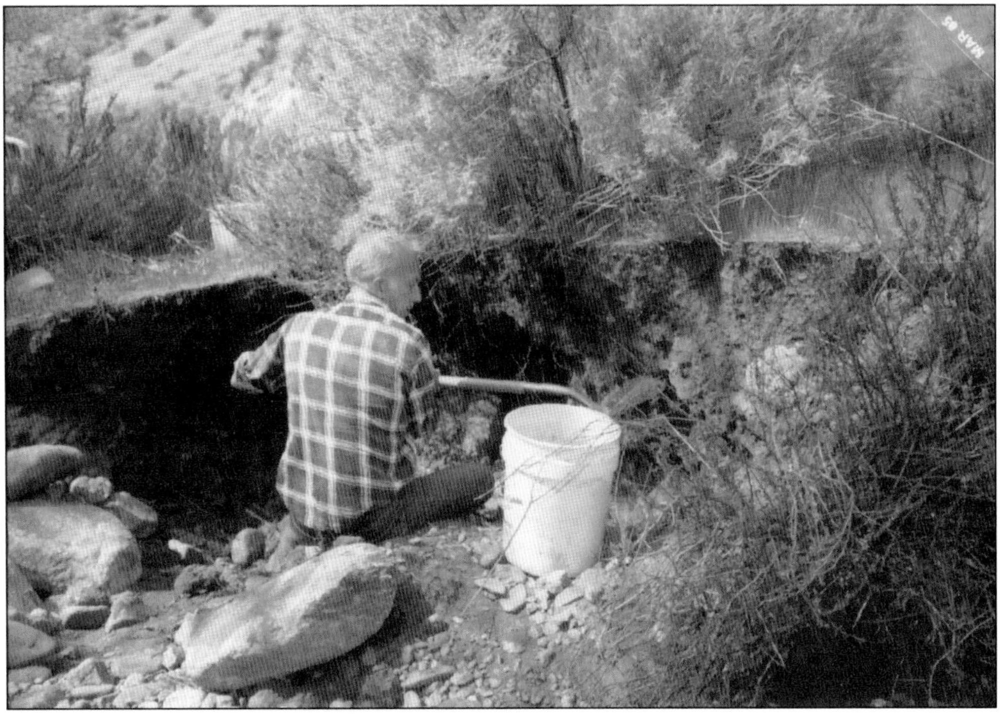

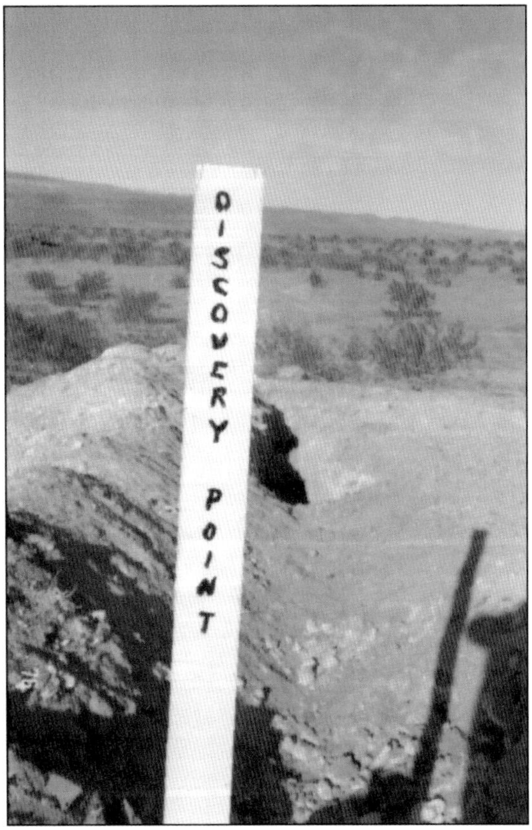

As for Canyon Country's adult population, a favorite pastime for one set of locals was well suited to the area. The Sierra Pelona Rock Club formed in 1958 with a mission to sponsor activities and promote interest and education in mineralogy, lapidary, geology, paleontology, and related subjects. Members gather for regular meetings to display and discuss their personal findings but share their passion more extensively on field trips such as the one pictured above to Texas Canyon, which is an area north of Vasquez Canyon Road where Canyon Country meets Saugus and Agua Dulce. In addition to heading out on excursions, the nonprofit group staked two claims, including a travertine onyx claim in the Mojave Desert called Discovery Point (left). (Both courtesy of Mike Moreno.)

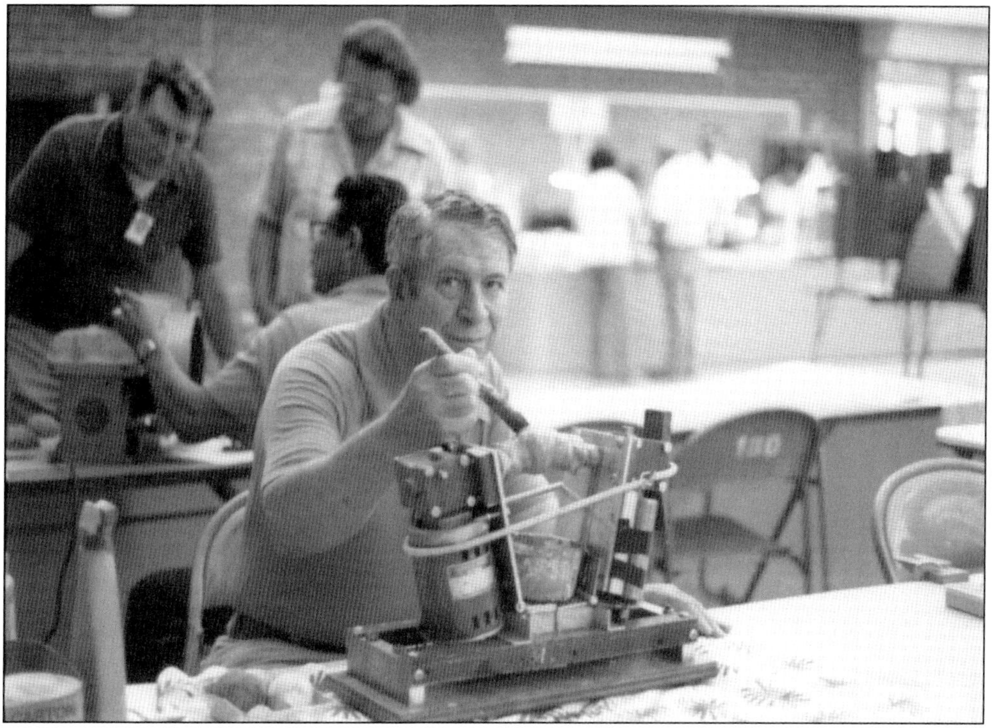

In the 1960s and 1970s, the Sierra Pelona Rock Club spent many weekends in Tick Canyon, on the eastern side of Canyon Country, before it became privately owned. Tick Canyon was known for the howlite it contained, so the club scheduled quarterly trips. After collecting rocks in their natural form, Sierra Pelona members utilized refining equipment such as the sphere-polishing machine shown in the above photograph. They would hold gem exhibitions to display the jewelry and decor they made with the pieces. The image below shows a piece of howlite from Tick Canyon that early Sierra Pelona member Mike Moreno, using his lapidary equipment, polished and crafted into "Broken Heart" following the death of his wife, Sue. The Morenos joined the Sierra Pelona Rock Club in 1961 after going rock hunting in Tick Canyon after church one Sunday and meeting some of the club's members there. Mike Moreno had worked as a delivery person for a record company, so he acquired his first lapidary equipment by trading records for it. (Both courtesy of Mike Moreno.)

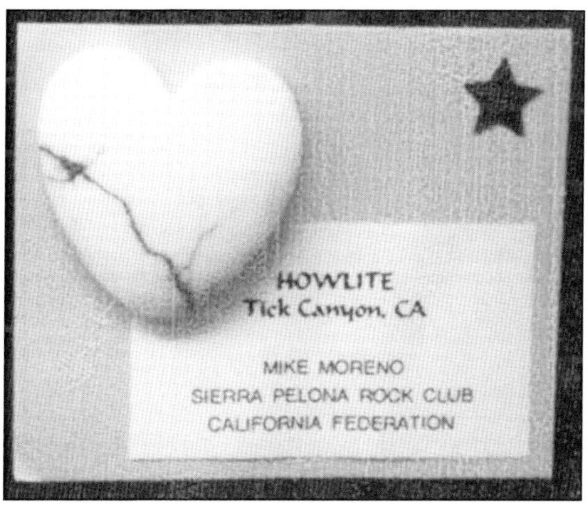

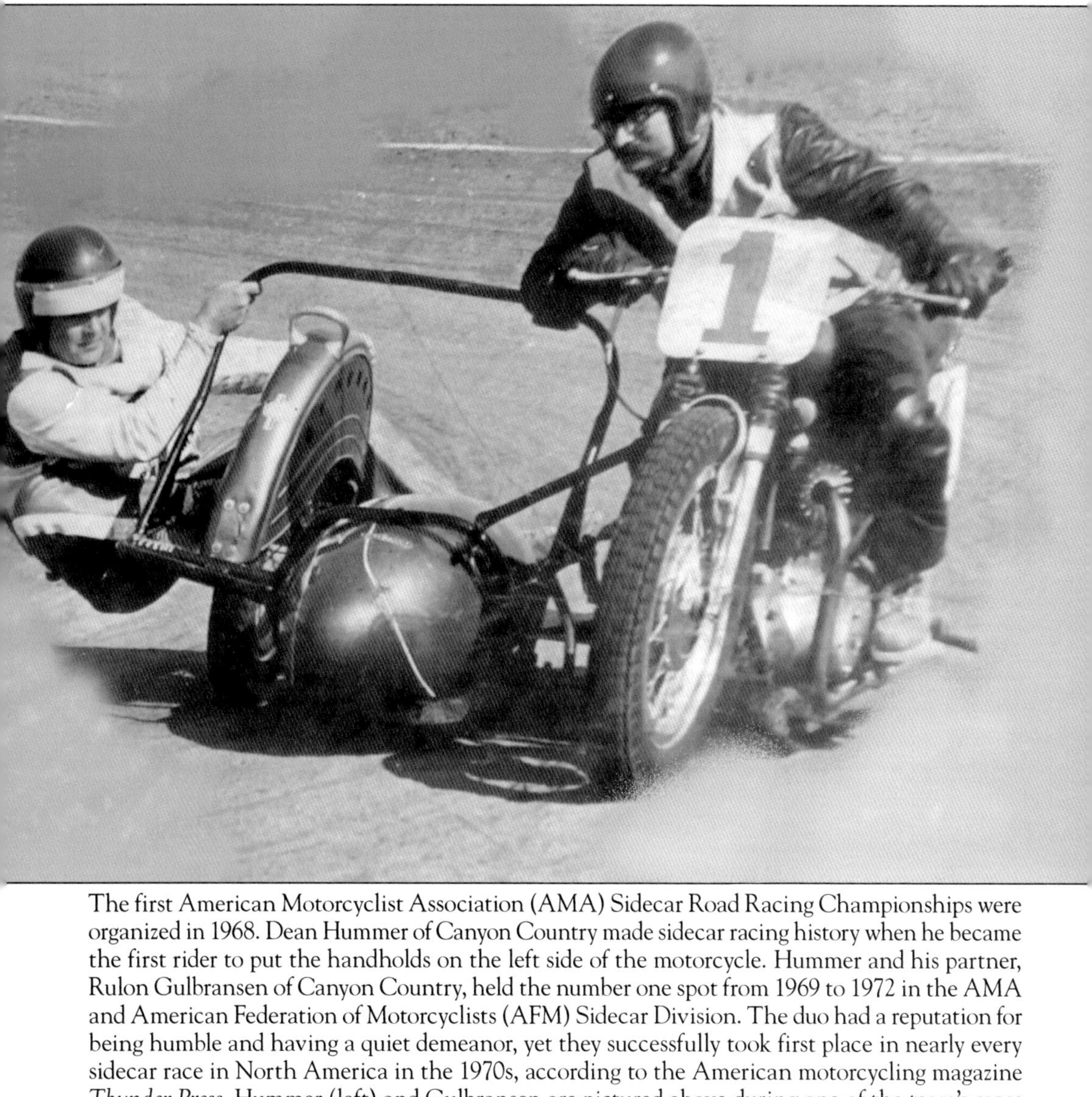

The first American Motorcyclist Association (AMA) Sidecar Road Racing Championships were organized in 1968. Dean Hummer of Canyon Country made sidecar racing history when he became the first rider to put the handholds on the left side of the motorcycle. Hummer and his partner, Rulon Gulbransen of Canyon Country, held the number one spot from 1969 to 1972 in the AMA and American Federation of Motorcyclists (AFM) Sidecar Division. The duo had a reputation for being humble and having a quiet demeanor, yet they successfully took first place in nearly every sidecar race in North America in the 1970s, according to the American motorcycling magazine *Thunder Press*. Hummer (left) and Gulbransen are pictured above during one of the team's races in 1971. (Courtesy of Alan Ferdman.)

Alan Ferdman, a North Oaks resident, became a member of the Four Aces Riding Club in 1963. Here, Ferdman is riding at Paramount Ranch Racetrack in Thousand Oaks, California. Ferdman is a longtime member and chair of the Canyon Country Advisory Committee. The committee was formed by the City of Santa Clarita in 1996 to create a stronger voice for Canyon Country and the east side of the valley. (Courtesy of Alan Ferdman.)

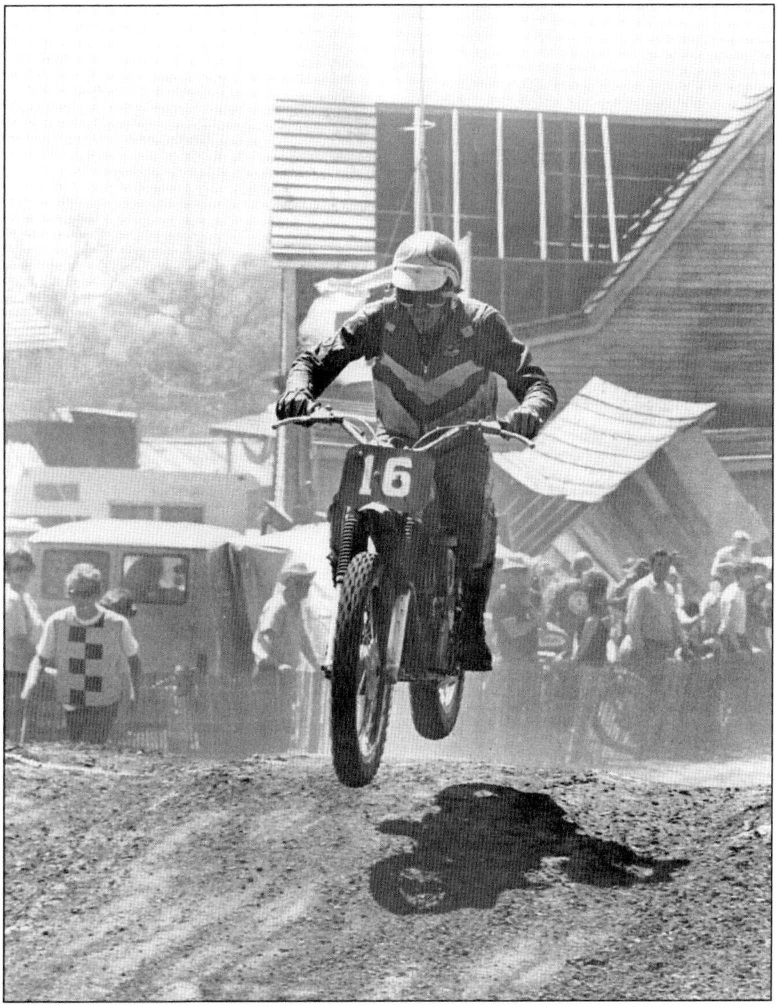

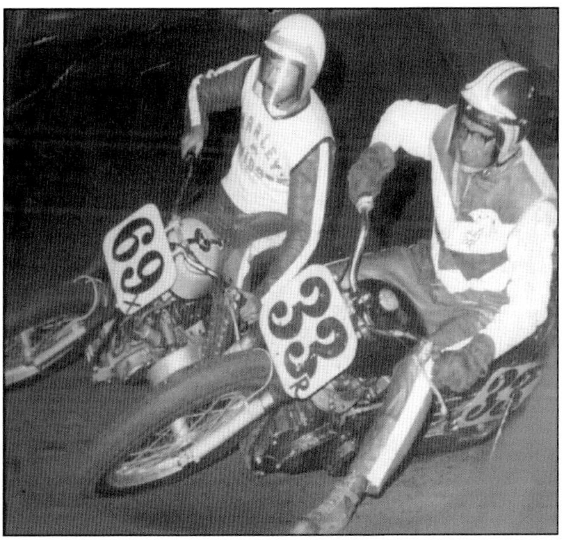

There were many motorcycle racing aficionados in Canyon Country in the 1960s and 1970s. Local men were champions in the American Motorcyclist Association circuit. Here, Ed Morris (No. 33) takes a turn at Ascot Park in Gardena. The Canyon Country resident was a member of the Four Aces Racing Club along with other motorcycle enthusiasts like Alan and Pam Ferdman, who stayed with Morris while they were getting settled in the area. The Ferdmans became politically active members of the Canyon Country community. After his sporting successes, Morris died in a car accident in November 2009. (Courtesy of Alan Ferdman.)

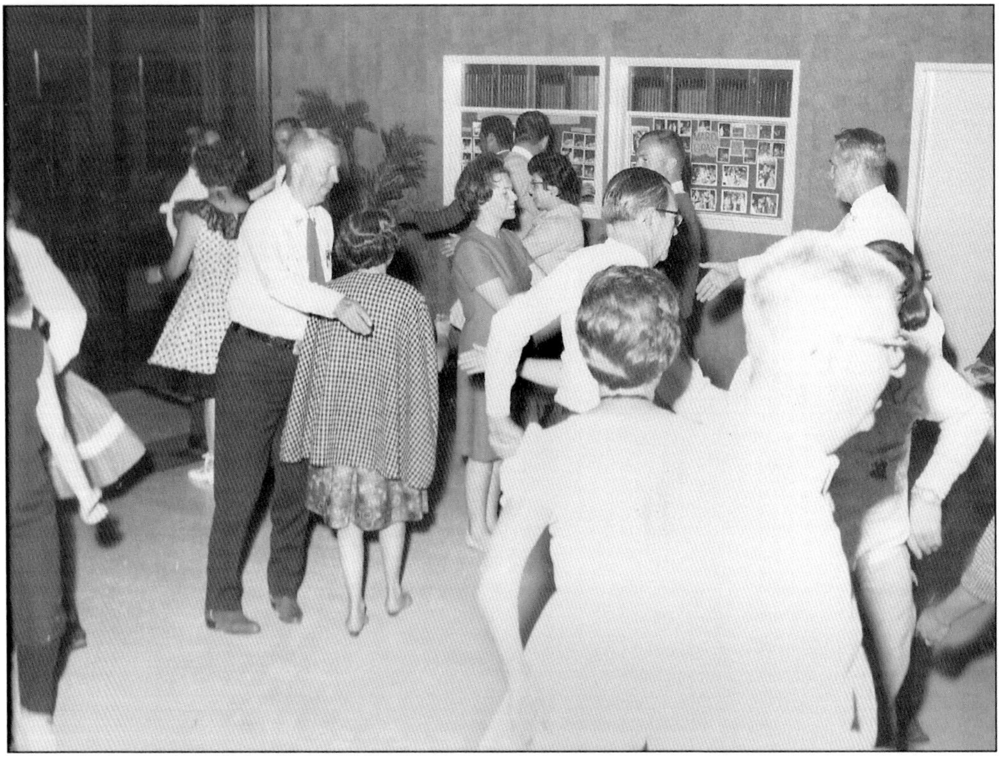

About a decade after the Sierra Pelona Rock Club came together, another Canyon Country group took shape—literally, into a square. Created by a group from the Sierra Hills housing tract in Canyon Country, the Sierra Hillbillies formed in 1967 to promote Western square dancing and round dancing. Charter members are pictured here at one of their earliest gatherings, when the group's members could only form a few squares. Throughout the decades, club members have enjoyed traveling to visit other dance groups and spending weekends camping together. (Courtesy of Robert G. Kofnovec.)

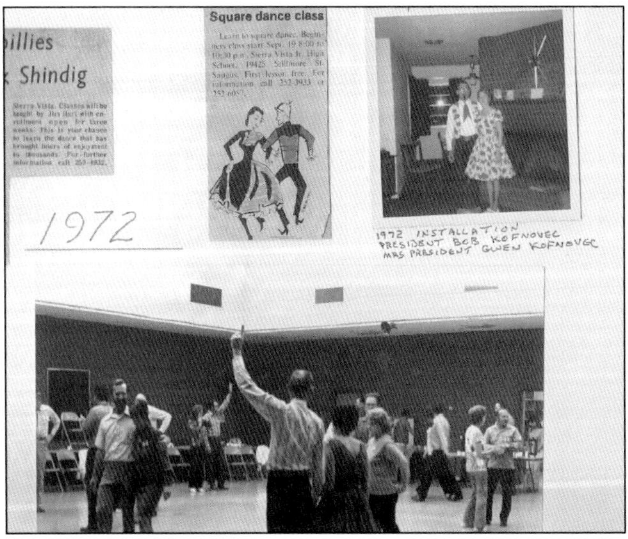

In the beginning, couples met in the multipurpose room at Sierra Vista Junior High School to provide lessons to newcomers, as shown in this 1972 image. Other groups briefly cropped up, such as the Saugus Swingers, the Friendly Twirlers, and the Sierra Vista Wheelers, but the Sierra Hillbillies have continued to thrive after four continuous decades thanks to longtime members and frequently elected officers such as Bob and Gwen Kofnovec, shown at top right. (Courtesy of Robert G. Kofnovec.)

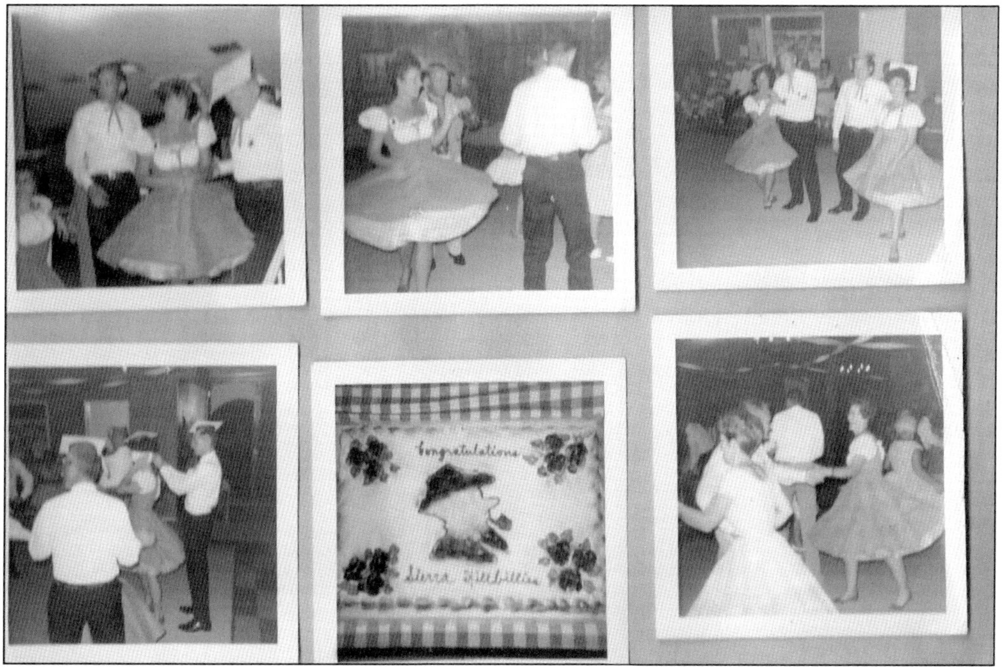

In the image above, club members wear the large square-dancing dresses and men's ensembles that were especially designed for the group. The members wearing graduation caps had just completed a series of square-dancing lessons. The photograph below was taken on January 1, 1976, when the Sierra Hillbillies participated in the Rose Parade in Pasadena, California. Club members often took the opportunity to bring their favorite style of dance into the limelight at community events, including an annual celebration of the first gold strike in Placerita Canyon. (Both courtesy of Robert G. Kofnovec.)

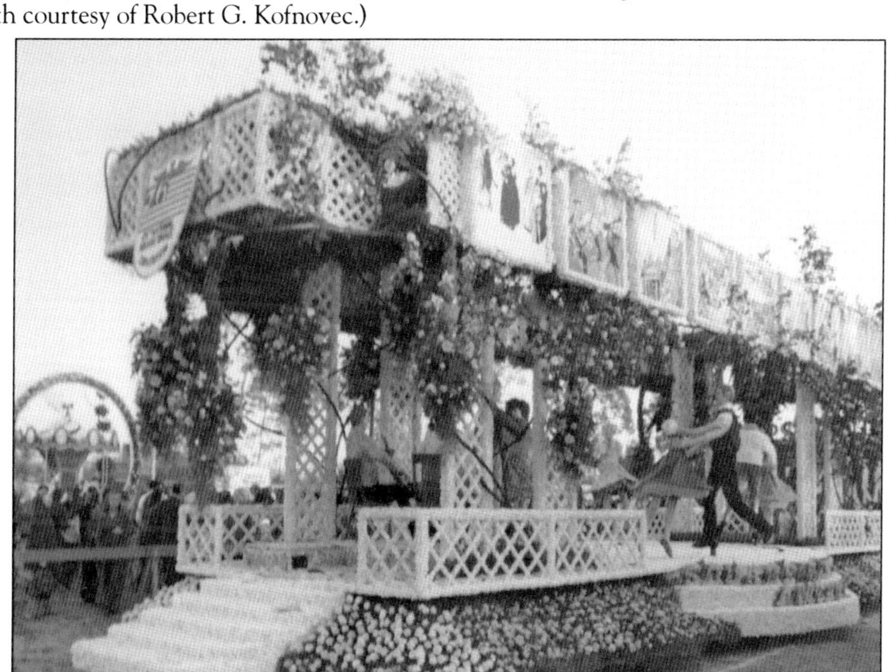

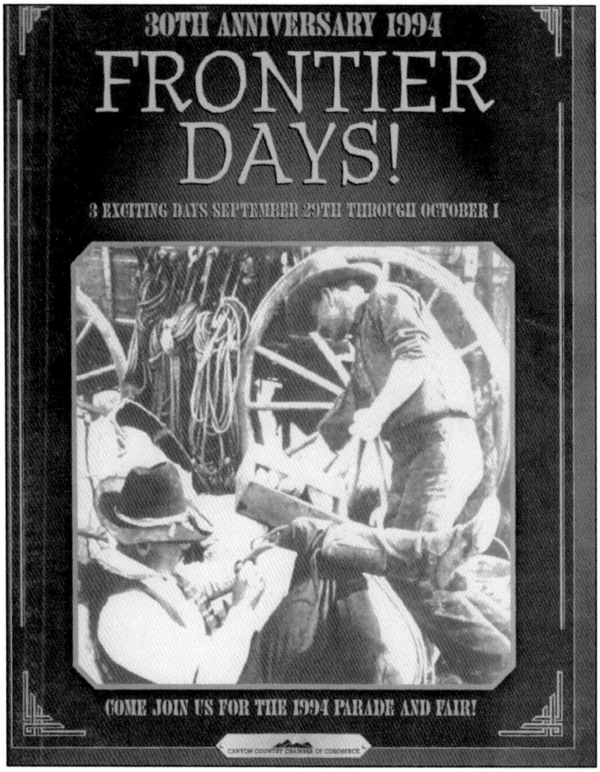

Before it was officially dubbed "Canyon Country," the eastern part of the Santa Clarita Valley had its own group of leaders called the Mint Canyon Chamber of Commerce. Organized in 1956, the group was headed by Arthur W. Evans for a few years. Evans oversaw an annual event called Frontier Days, a Western-themed festival that began in 1963 and grew in popularity over the years. Rodeo competitions were held at the Mitchell Ranch property. The Mint Canyon Chamber of Commerce—later called the Canyon Country Chamber of Commerce—sponsored Frontier Days, which was the group's major fundraiser. (Courtesy of Bob Kellar.)

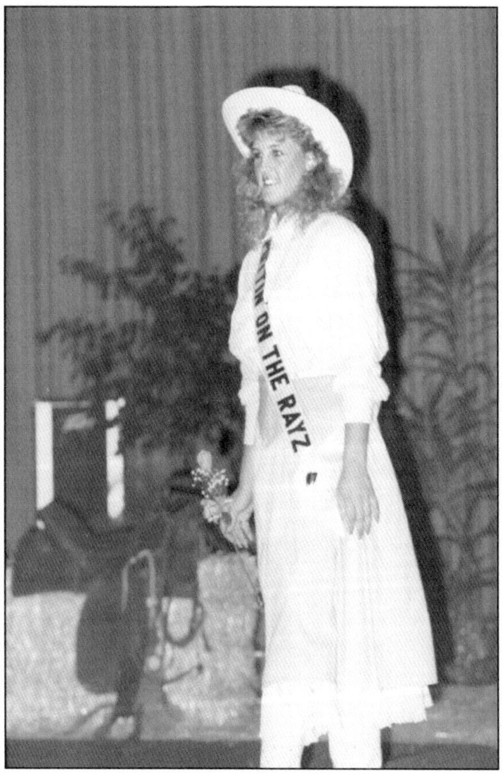

Along with a rodeo and tractor pull, Frontier Days included an annual parade and a pageant in which a Canyon Country teen was crowned "Frontier Belle." Pictured at right is 1985 candidate Liecha Wojciechowski. (Courtesy of Charmaine Wojciechowski.)

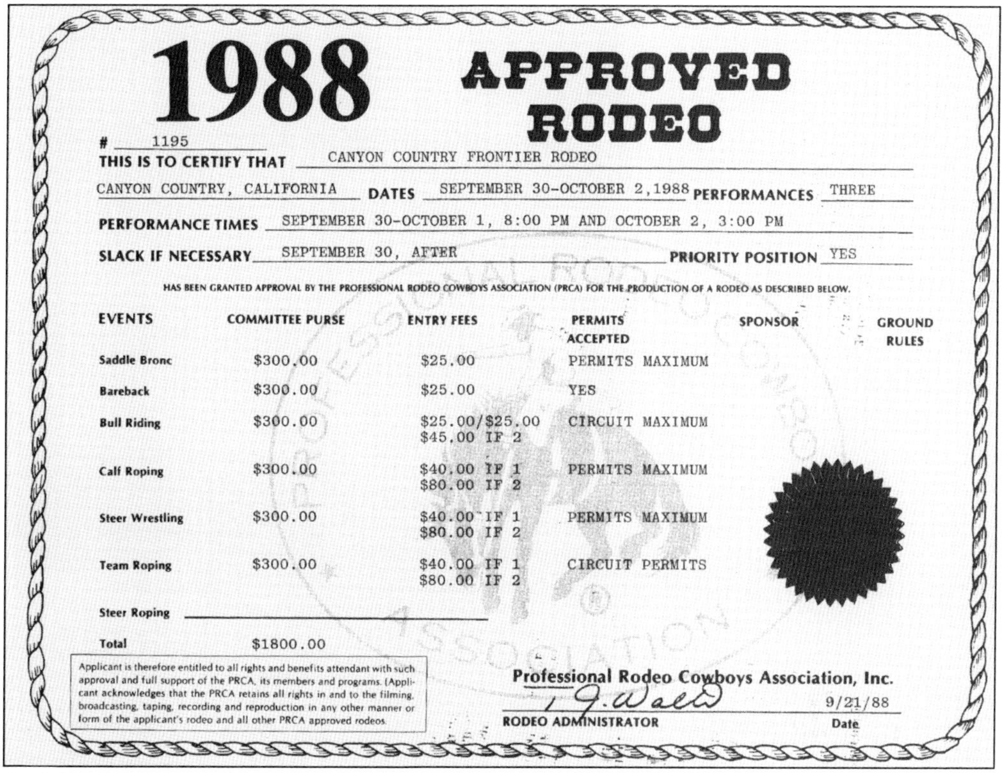

1988 APPROVED RODEO

\# 1195

THIS IS TO CERTIFY THAT CANYON COUNTRY FRONTIER RODEO

CANYON COUNTRY, CALIFORNIA DATES SEPTEMBER 30-OCTOBER 2,1988 PERFORMANCES THREE

PERFORMANCE TIMES SEPTEMBER 30-OCTOBER 1, 8:00 PM AND OCTOBER 2, 3:00 PM

SLACK IF NECESSARY SEPTEMBER 30, AFTER PRIORITY POSITION YES

HAS BEEN GRANTED APPROVAL BY THE PROFESSIONAL RODEO COWBOYS ASSOCIATION (PRCA) FOR THE PRODUCTION OF A RODEO AS DESCRIBED BELOW.

EVENTS	COMMITTEE PURSE	ENTRY FEES	PERMITS ACCEPTED	SPONSOR	GROUND RULES
Saddle Bronc	$300.00	$25.00	PERMITS MAXIMUM		
Bareback	$300.00	$25.00	YES		
Bull Riding	$300.00	$25.00/$25.00 $45.00 IF 2	CIRCUIT MAXIMUM		
Calf Roping	$300.00	$40.00 IF 1 $80.00 IF 2	PERMITS MAXIMUM		
Steer Wrestling	$300.00	$40.00 IF 1 $80.00 IF 2	PERMITS MAXIMUM		
Team Roping	$300.00	$40.00 IF 1 $80.00 IF 2	CIRCUIT PERMITS		
Steer Roping					
Total	$1800.00				

Applicant is therefore entitled to all rights and benefits attendant with such approval and full support of the PRCA, its members and programs. (Applicant acknowledges that the PRCA retains all rights in and to the filming, broadcasting, taping, recording and reproduction in any other manner or form of the applicant's rodeo and all other PRCA approved rodeos.

Professional Rodeo Cowboys Association, Inc.

T. G. Walt

RODEO ADMINISTRATOR

9/21/88

Date

In 1988, the rodeo held during the Frontier Days festival, the Canyon Country Frontier Rodeo, received accreditation by the Professional Rodeo Cowboys Association (PRCA). This made the event a sanctioned professional rodeo. The above image shows the validation from the PRCA. Pictured below is Bob Kellar, Canyon Country Chamber of Commerce president and former mayor of Santa Clarita, as he takes his turn in the pen during the Frontier Days rodeo in 1988. Less than a decade later, Frontier Days ended in 1996 after the Canyon Country Chamber of Commerce merged with the Santa Clarita Valley Chamber of Commerce in 1994. Kellar later served as a Santa Clarita city councilman and mayor. (Both courtesy of Bob Kellar.)

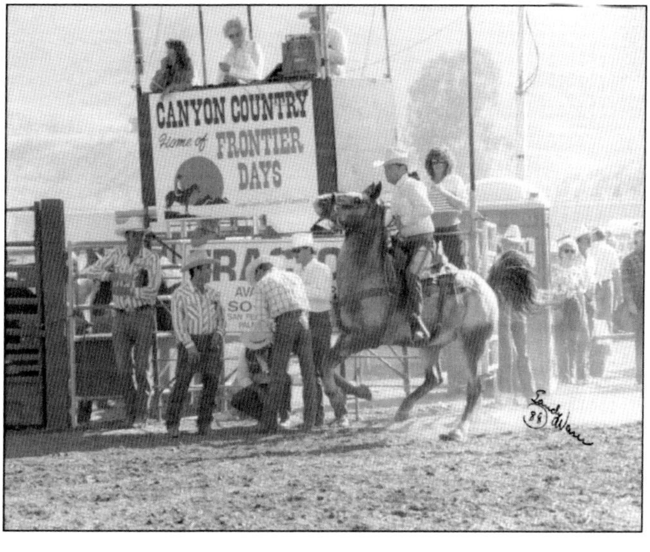

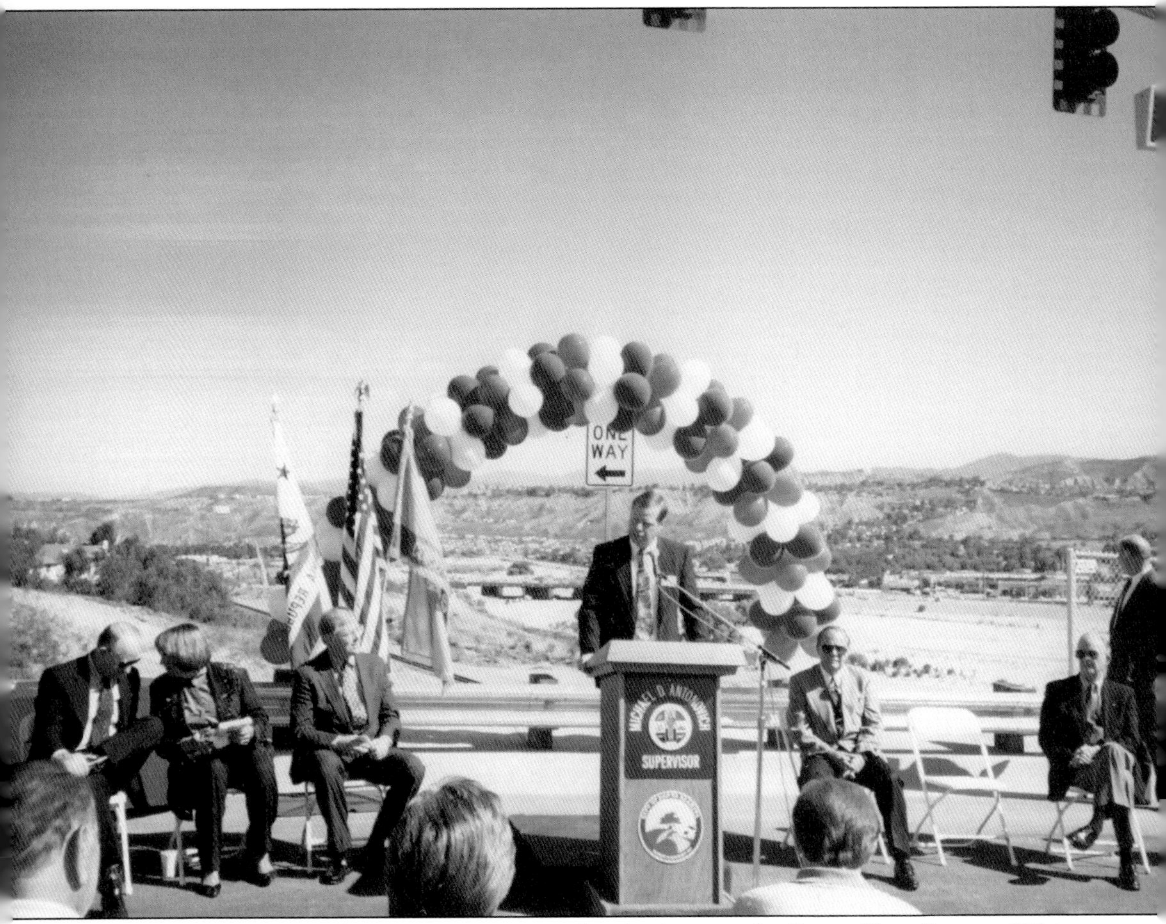

A construction project began in 1988 to provide a bridge over the Santa Clara River at Whites Canyon, just south of Soledad Canyon Road, but funds to complete the project ran out in 1990. It became a political embarrassment for Canyon Country and Santa Clarita City Council members, because the construction stalled with a bridge leading to a dirt lot and was referred to as the "Bridge to Nowhere." The ceremony shown here celebrated the opening of the notorious construction project. At the podium is Bob Kellar, who would later become mayor of the City of Santa Clarita. The bridge had been on Los Angeles County's highway plan since the 1960s and became increasingly more necessary with the building boom of the 1980s. The goal was to lessen the pressure at Canyon Country's busiest intersection at Whites Canyon and Soledad Canyon Roads. The name of the new roadway was Whites Canyon Bridge, and it opened in 1994 at a cost of $27.4 million. Within about a year, the Canyon Country Chamber of Commerce merged with the Santa Clarita Valley Chamber of Commerce after allegations of fraud by a few members of the Canyon Country group required the smaller chamber to disband. The dissolution of what was once the Mint Canyon Chamber of Commerce (then the Canyon Country Chamber of Commerce) also meant the dissolution of the Frontier Days events. (Courtesy of Bob Kellar.)

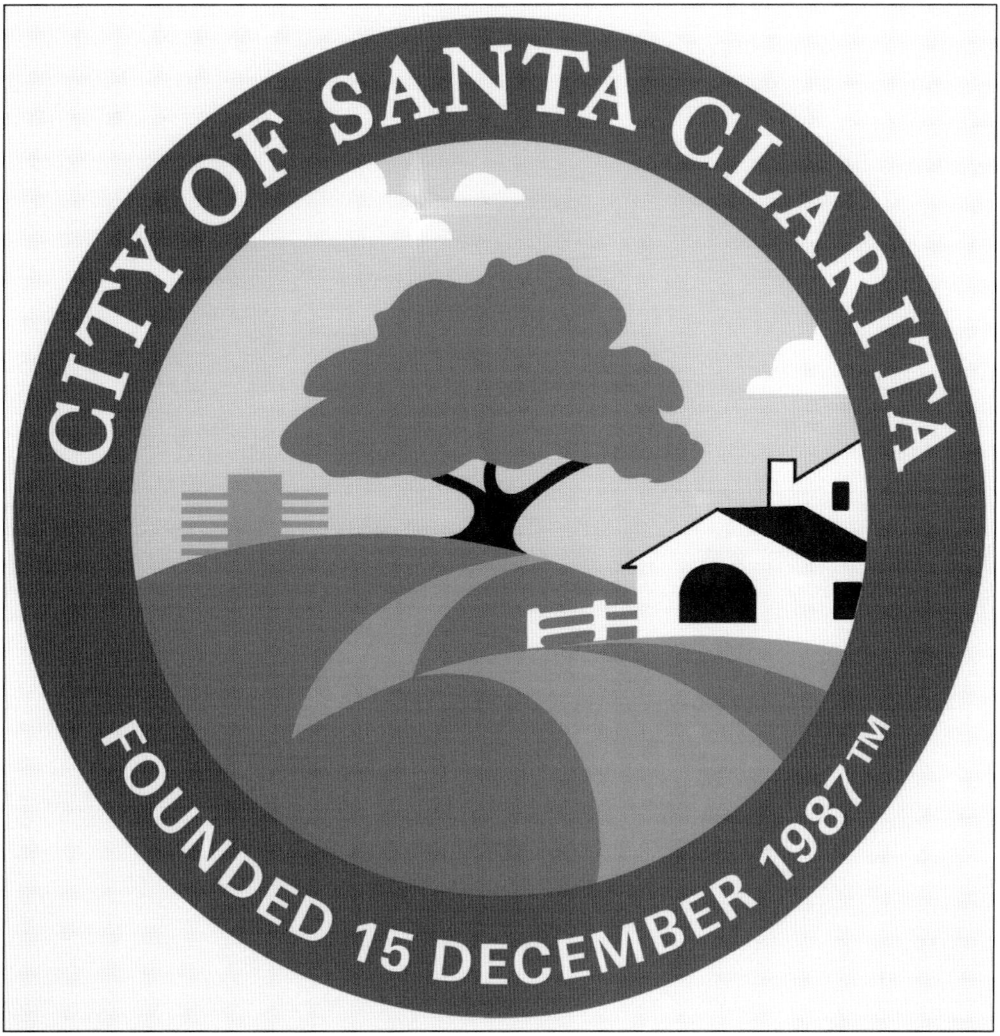

After bearing numerous titles—Honby, Soledad, Mint Canyon, Saugus—Canyon Country's nomenclature grew by one more in 1987. On December 15 of that year, most of Canyon Country became incorporated into the newly formed City of Santa Clarita. Accepted by voters on November 3, the new city included part or all of Newhall, Saugus, Valencia, and Canyon Country, totaling approximately 50 square miles. There had been previous campaigns to form a city—and one attempt to secede from Los Angeles County—but all died in the planning stages. Named for the Santa Clara River, a title given by Fr. Juan Crespi in 1769, and altered to mean "Little Santa Clara," the same name was used for the valley in which the city was situated. The new city was approximately one-quarter the size of Santa Clarita Valley. In just a few years, Santa Clarita would find and maintain its place on the FBI's list of the nation's "Safest Cities with a population of 100,000 or more." (Courtesy of Gail Ortiz on behalf of the City of Santa Clarita.)

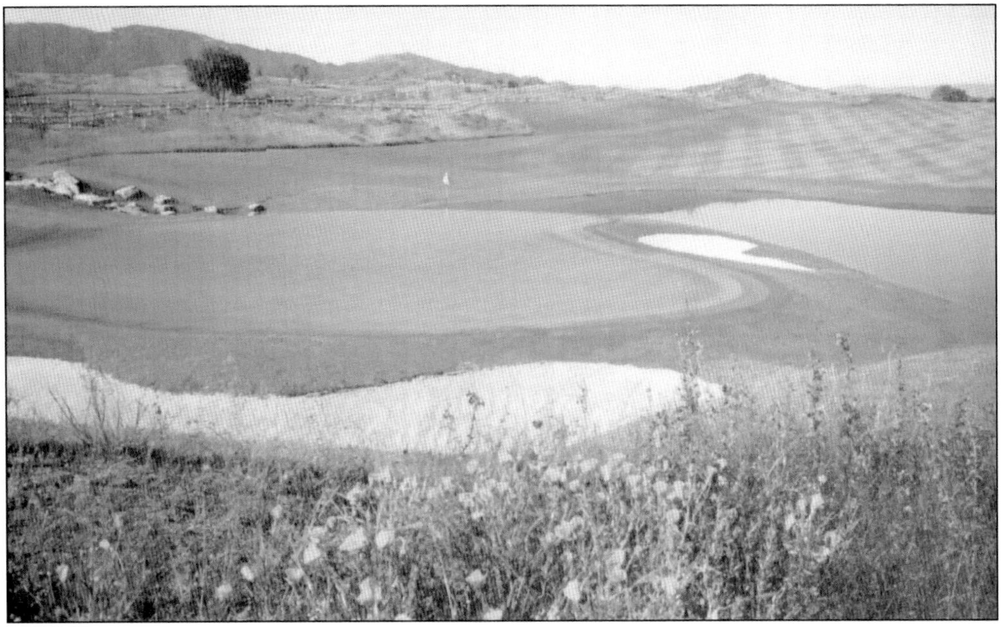

In the late 1990s, when Clement Cox opted to sell most of his acreage in Sand Canyon, the property was transformed from its 20th-century iteration as a chicken ranch to its status in the new millennium as Robinson Ranch Golf Club. Cox negotiated a sale to Ted Robinson, a golf-course owner and architect who had a part in the design of more than 160 projects around the world. Robinson, in a joint venture with his son, Ted Robinson Jr., began the first phases of the project in 1994, but the course did not open until 1999. The planned one course became two when the Robinsons saw they could successfully build both. Pictured above is the Mountain Course, and below is a hole on the Valley Course. (Both courtesy of Robinson Ranch Golf Club.)

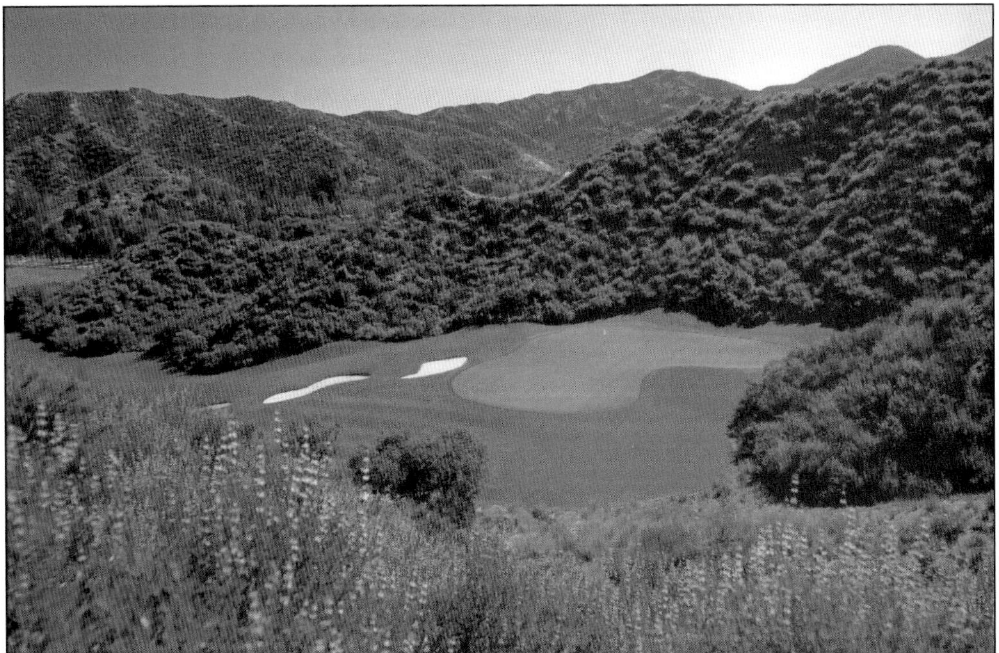

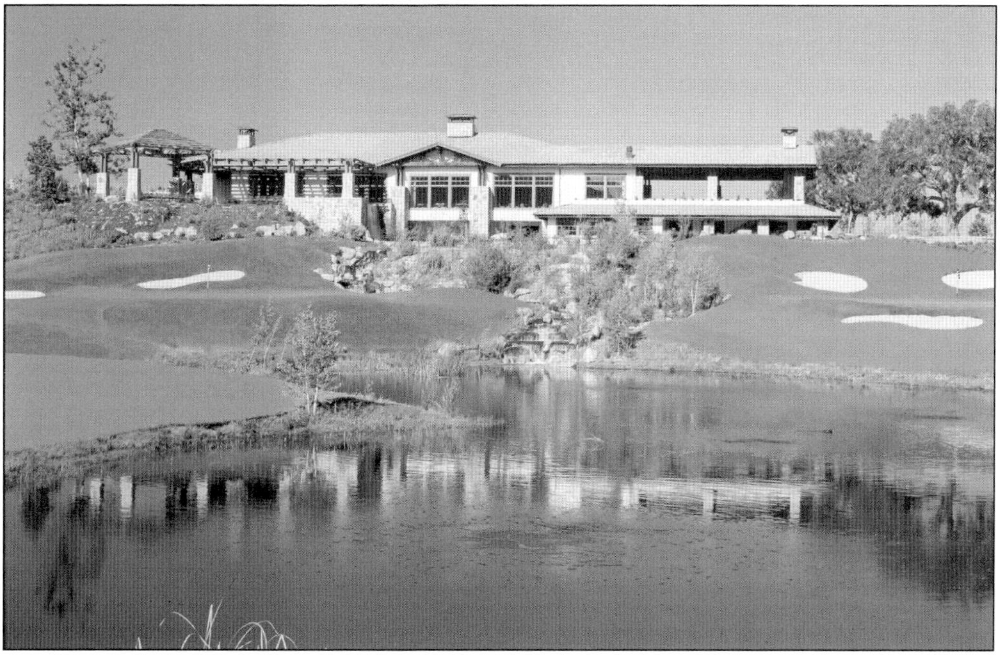

Robinson Ranch Golf Club became known for its restaurant, the Sycamore Bar & Grill, and its banquet facilities in the clubhouse (pictured). The interior's stone and wood design matched the natural outdoor landscape. Robinson Ranch was designed with water conservation in mind and designated an Audubon Cooperative Sanctuary. (Courtesy of Robinson Ranch Golf Club.)

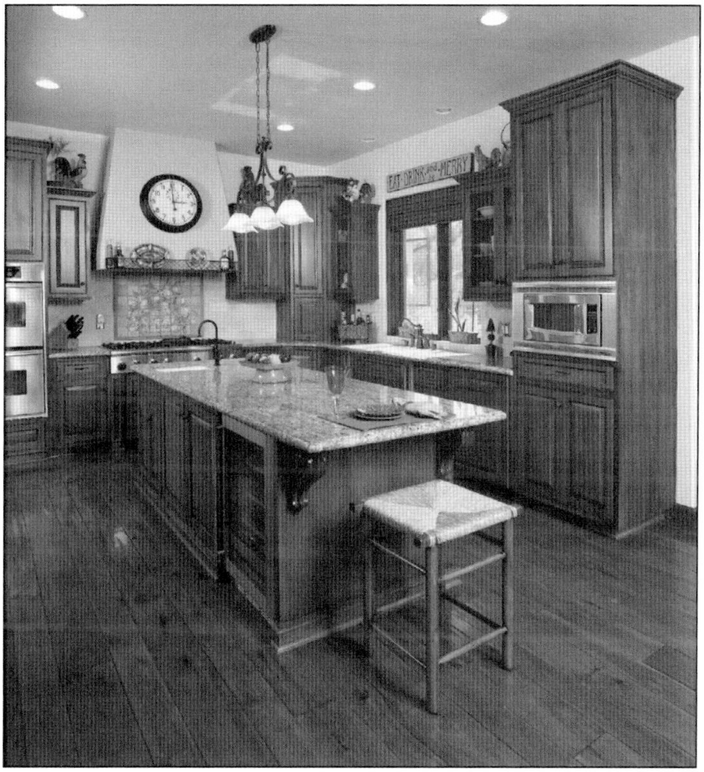

A deliberate effort was made to limit the number of homes built on the Robinson Ranch course. The Canyon Country home of Gregg and Angie Bilson, pictured at right, was on the National Kitchen and Bath Home Tour in 2009. When the Bilson's 4,500-square-foot house was custom-built by Terry Beeler in 2004, it joined approximately 70 homes inside the gates of Robinson Ranch Golf Club. (Courtesy of National Kitchen & Bath Association; photograph by John Siskin.)

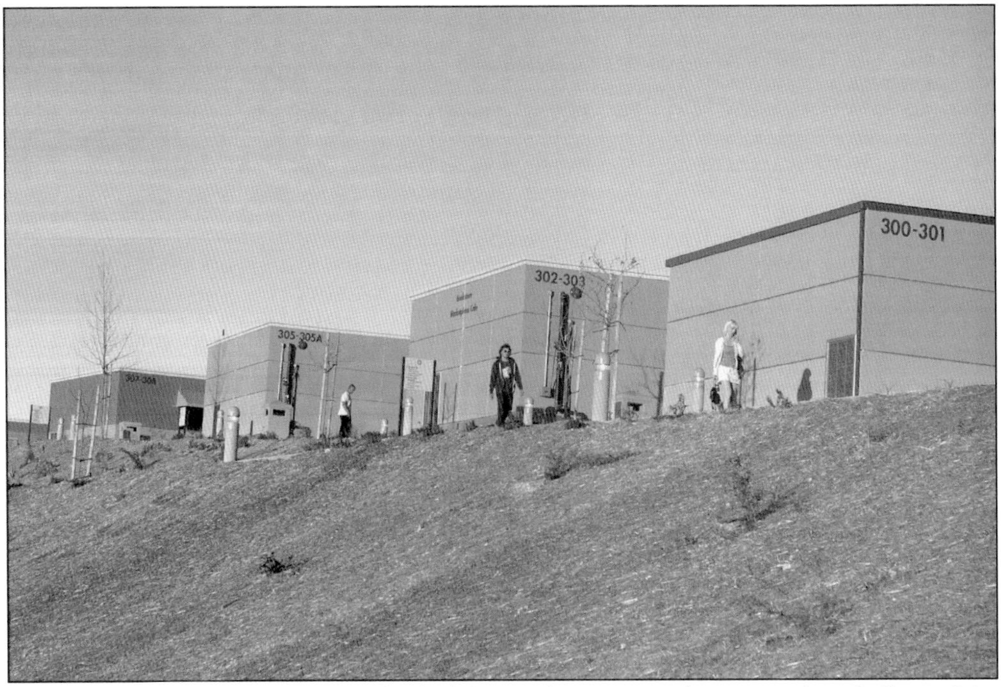

Studies had shown that about one-third of the nearly 21,300 students attending College of the Canyons resided in zip codes in and around Canyon Country. The college chose 70 acres of Canyon Country property on Sierra Highway for an expansion of the campus, and the Canyon Country Campus opened on August 27, 2007. These photographs of the school's newly constructed amphitheater (below) and a sunset shot of classrooms (above) were taken in 2007. When completed, the campus will serve 8,000 to 10,000 students. (Both courtesy of College of the Canyons.)

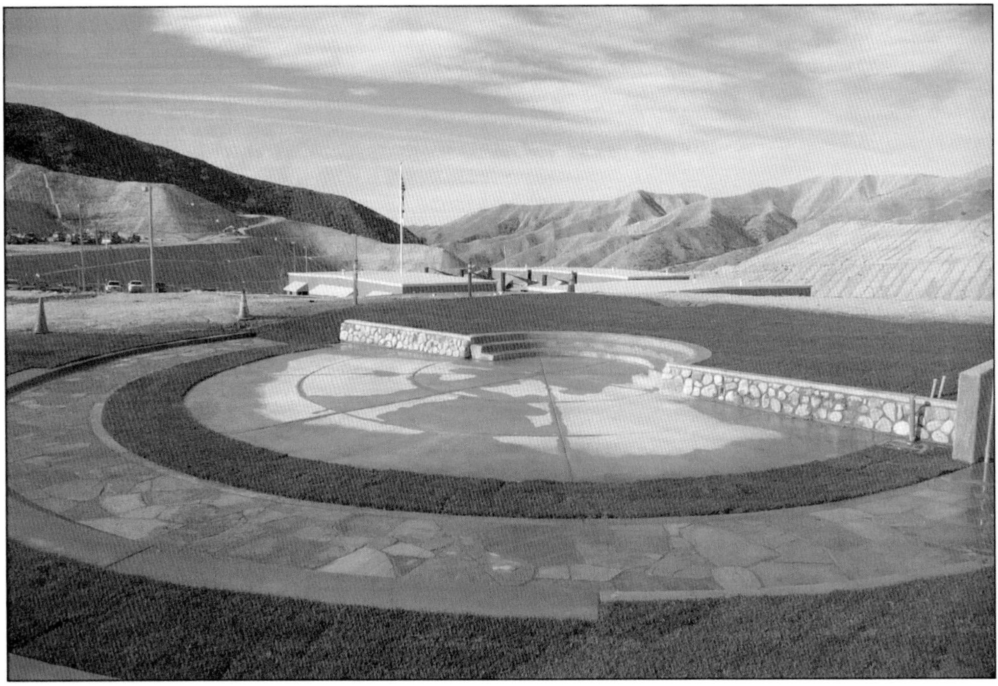

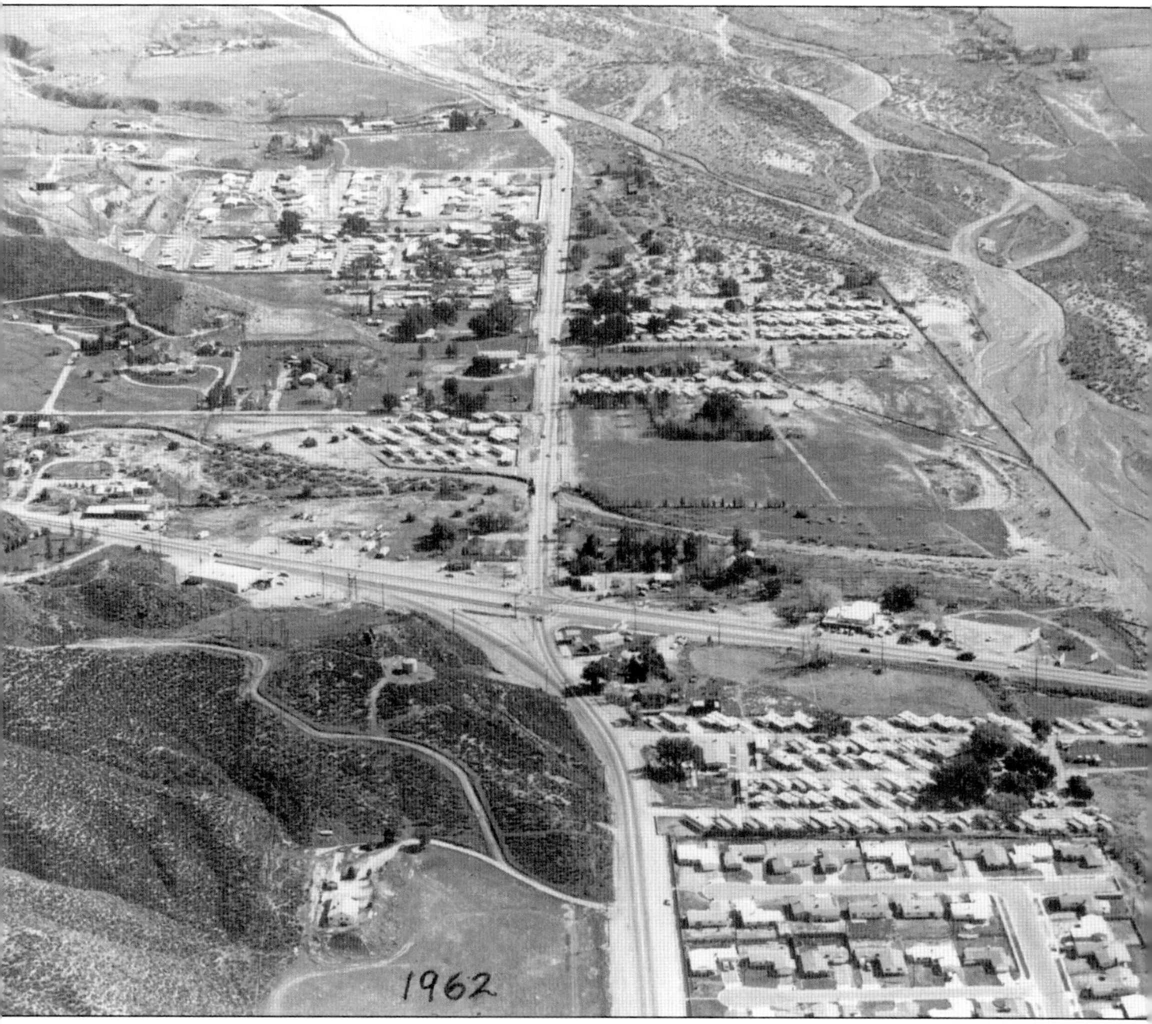

This 1962 aerial photograph of Solemint Junction offers a view of what was once Canyon Country's town center. When US Route 6 was cut short, ending in Bishop, California, instead of Long Beach, California, the merchants on Sierra Highway saw fewer motorists, and the area was no longer the town's center of commerce. Soledad Canyon Road began drawing more business traffic, and other shopping centers were planned in undeveloped areas.

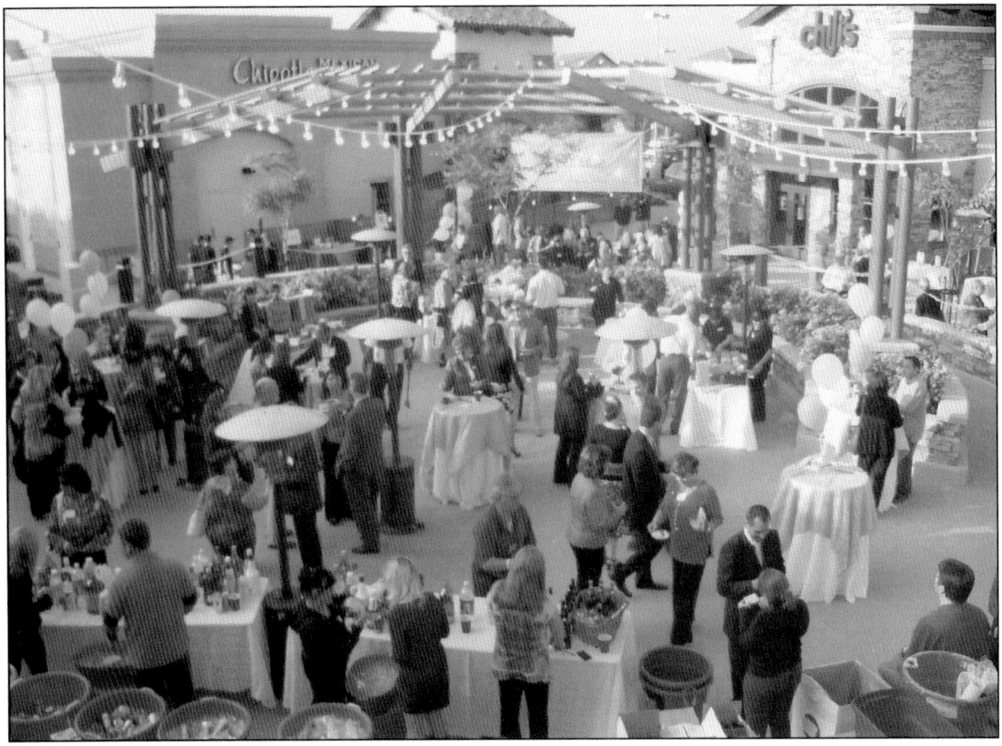

In December 2005, grading began on the Canyon Country property east of California State Route 14 (aka the 14 Freeway) between Golden Valley Road and Via Princessa. The Plaza at Golden Valley Ranch, owned by GMS Golden Valley Ranch, LLC, and managed by Terramar Retail Centers, LLC, brought a 620,000-square-foot shopping center to the area. National chain stores were located closer to Canyon Country residents than ever before. The shopping center opened in August 2008 with Lowe's (below) as one of its anchor stores. Other establishments in the center include Target, Kohl's, and several restaurants and retailers. The photograph above was taken at The Plaza at Golden Valley Ranch's 2011 grand-opening celebration, which was coordinated with the Santa Clarita Valley Chamber of Commerce. The function was held in The Plaza's amphitheater, which was built with the intention of being available for community events. (Both courtesy of Krista Lesa on behalf of Terramar Retail Centers, LLC.)

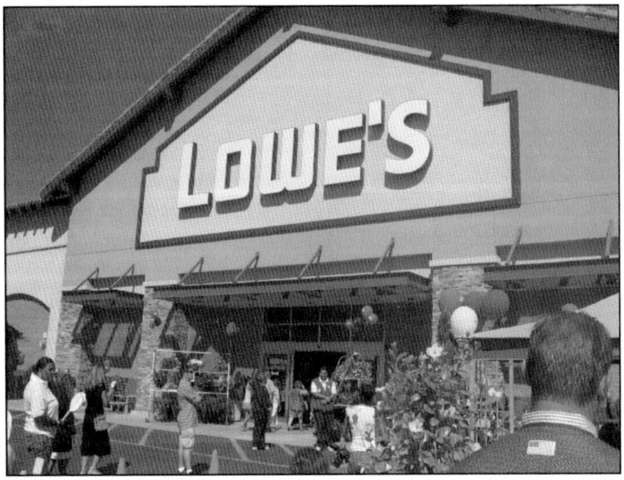

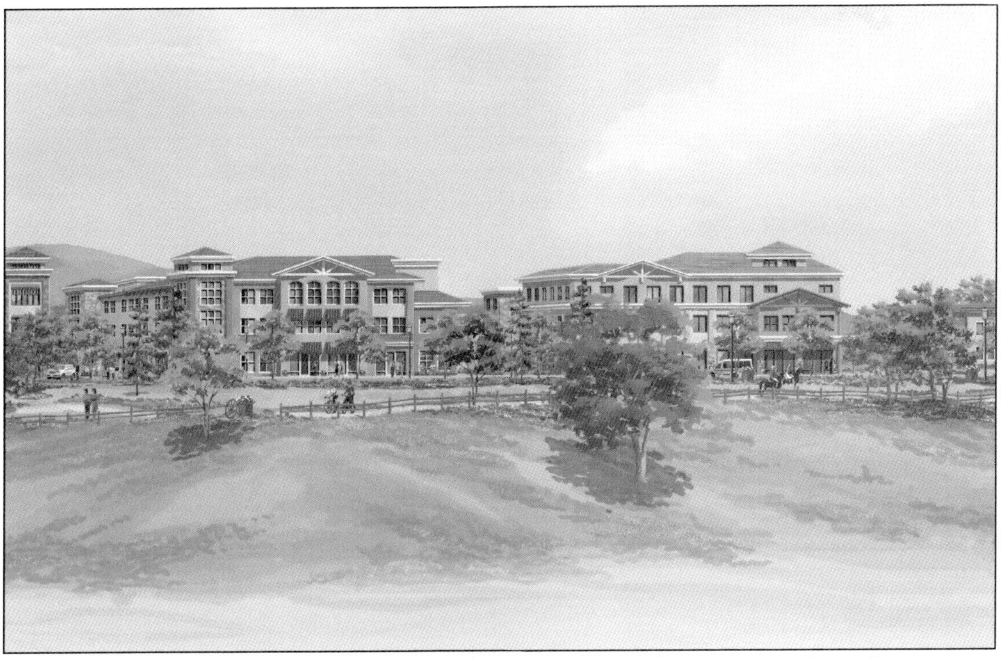

In May 2011, the City of Santa Clarita approved Vista Canyon, a planned transit-focused community aimed at creating a "town center" for Canyon Country. The community will be located on the pioneering Mitchell family's 1860s ranch property, home to the valley's first schoolhouse and close to historic Lang Station. The design links Canyon Country's history of railroads, water, gold, and cattle to its future. These renderings show the pedestrian-focused plan by JSB Development, which emphasizes transportation innovation, energy efficiency, and conservation of water and natural resources. The image above shows a portion of the Town Center, and the rendering below is a bird's-eye view of Main Street. (Both courtesy of Vista Canyon; conceptual renderings by Bill Tosetti.)

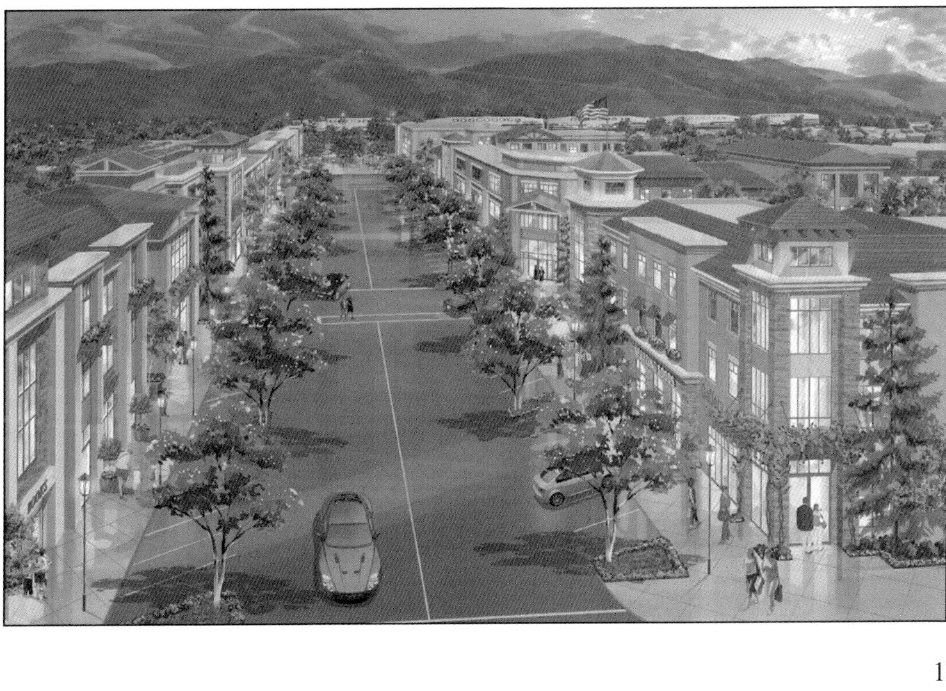

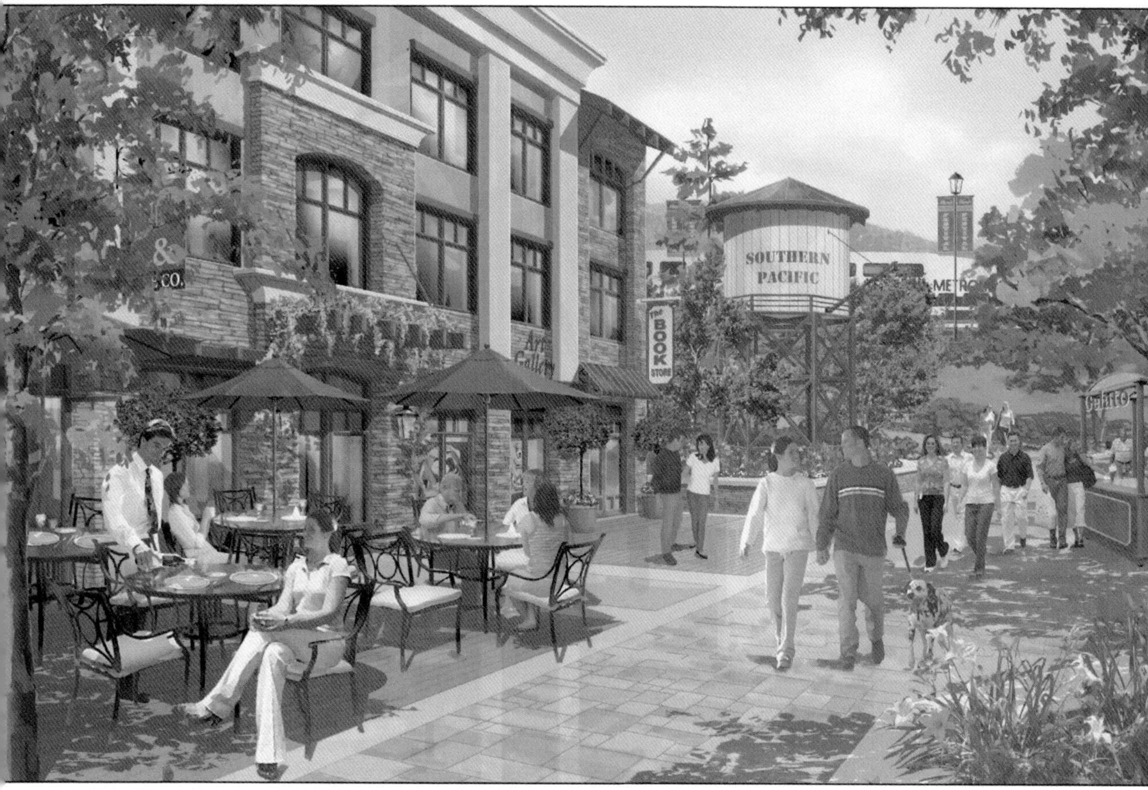

JSB Development's 185-acre plan for the town center, Vista Square, includes offices, shops, restaurants, hotels, a cinema, and homes alongside a transit center offering city bus transfers and Metrolink train stations. Residents could access a network of walkways, bike paths, and equestrian trails, plus a river education and community center. This rendering shows the community-wide system of paths and trails connecting to the town center area. Located south of Soledad Canyon Road, between Sand Canyon and Lost Canyon, the plan seeks to allow residents to enjoy living, working, shopping, and recreation in close proximity to one another. (Courtesy of Vista Canyon; conceptual rendering by Bill Tosetti.)

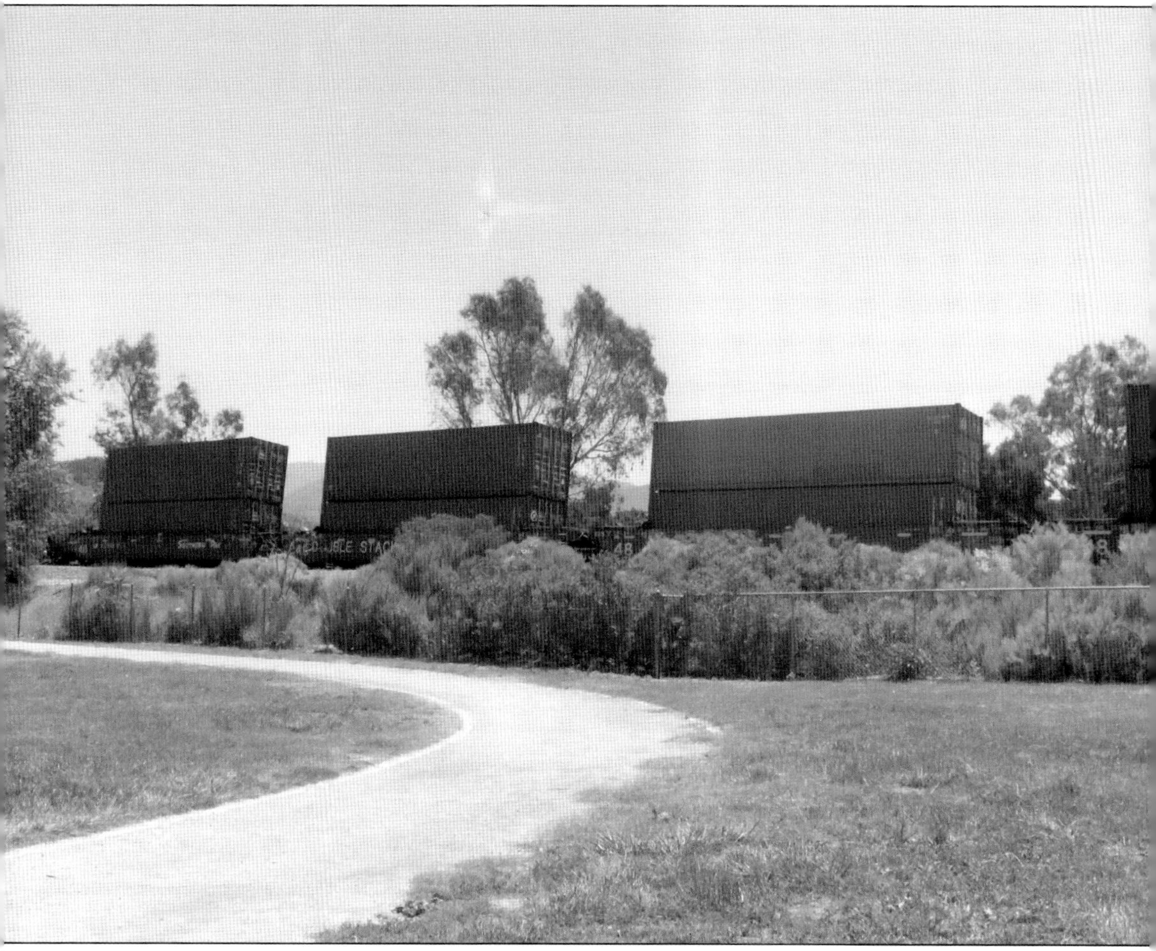

For generations of students at Sulphur Springs Community School, the sound of passing trains has been a constant. This c. 2004 photograph looks south from the Sulphur Springs schoolyard. Even after nearby Lang Station was demolished and left only with a historic marker in its place, the railroads remained in use. The trains no longer transported precious metals, but they continued serving the community for more than a century. For Soledad Canyon, the railroad not only connected two parts of the state of California, but also linked Canyon Country's past with its future. (Photograph by Martha Michael.)

Discover Thousands of Local History Books Featuring Millions of Vintage Images

Arcadia Publishing, the leading local history publisher in the United States, is committed to making history accessible and meaningful through publishing books that celebrate and preserve the heritage of America's people and places.

Find more books like this at
www.arcadiapublishing.com

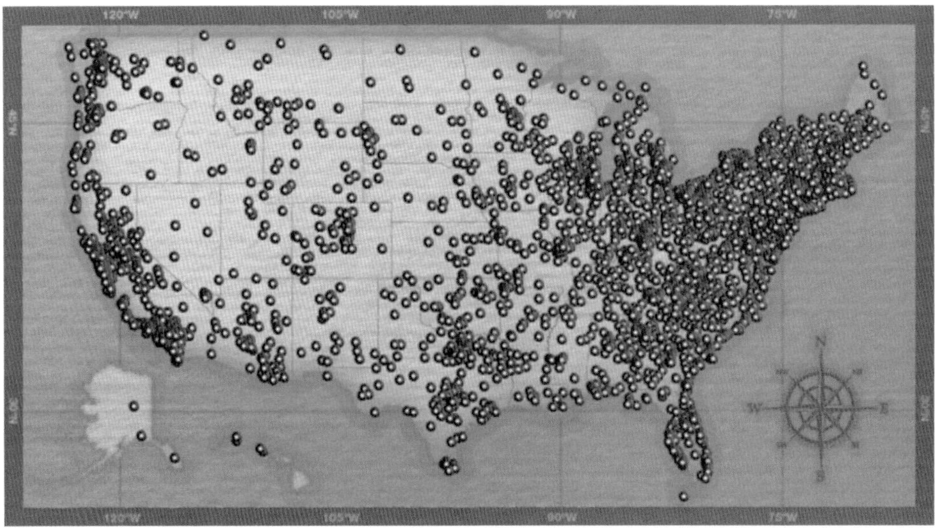

Search for your hometown history, your old stomping grounds, and even your favorite sports team.

Consistent with our mission to preserve history on a local level, this book was printed in South Carolina on American-made paper and manufactured entirely in the United States. Products carrying the accredited Forest Stewardship Council (FSC) label are printed on 100 percent FSC-certified paper.

MADE IN THE USA